Guide to Sophocles'

ANTIGONE

A Student Edition with Commentary,

Grammatical Notes, & Vocabulary

JOAN V. O'BRIEN

Southern Illinois University Press

CARBONDALE AND EDWARDSVILLE

Feffer & Simons, Inc.

LONDON AND AMSTERDAM

To Mother

Library of Congress Cataloging in Publication Data

O'Brien, Joan V
  Guide to Sophocles' Antigone.

  Guide to 7 passages from Antigone to be used with
A. C. Pearson's text of the play, with the author's
interlinear text of the Bilingual selections from
Sophocles' Antigone, or with an annotated school text.
  Bibliography: p.
  Includes index.
  1. Sophocles. Antigone. 2. Sophocles—Study and
teaching—Outlines, syllabi, etc. I. Title
PA4413.A702   882'01   77-10773
ISBN 0-8093-0779-0
ISBN 0-8093-0780-4 pbk.

CONTENTS

PREFACE

THIS *Guide to Sophocles' "Antigone"* IS AN INTRODUCTION to the vagaries of Greek tragedy and is part of an experiment in a new kind of classical text-commentary.[1] The primary audience is the student who has some rudimentary knowledge of Greek and who wants to learn to read a drama in the original. There are extensive philological, literary, historical, and cultural aids. These materials are provided only for seven passages from the play so as to encourage students to graduate as soon as possible to an annotated school edition for the rest of the play. For these passages, there are stylistic introductions to the art and thought of Sophocles, line-by-line Commentary, Grammatical Notes, and a Vocabulary. I hope the selective but in-depth analysis of these passages will deepen the students' interest in the play and provide stimulus for their subsequent reading of the entire Sophoclean corpus.

There is, too, another wider and more amorphous audience for this book. I refer to those who come to it after studying my *Bilingual Selections from Sophocles' "Antigone."*[2] *Bilingual Selections* is addressed to students who know little or no Greek but who want to study a classical play in depth; to students who want to learn some Greek while studying a great classic; to students of comparative literature; and to the general reader who may well be enticed like Lucretius' reader by the honey on the rim of the cup to drink the curative wormwood in the cup, i.e., to drink large dosages of philology in order to penetrate this great work of art.

Therefore, this *Guide* is designed to be used in one of at least two ways. In the first place, intermediate Greek students may use the Grammatical Notes and Commentary alongside the Pearson text of the play or an annotated school text.[3] They will become acquainted with the large philosophical and literary issues that the play raises, by studying the introductions and the commentaries; they will become acquainted with the pecularities of tragic diction and vocabulary through studying the Grammatical Notes and the Vocabulary. Secondly, non-Greek readers may use the same aids alongside the corresponding interlinear text of the *Bilingual Selections*. The Vocabulary is more extensive than usual for the sake of this latter audience.

My choice of passages is necessarily somewhat arbitrary, since almost every line of the text deserves equal treatment. The seven passages were chosen for comment because they readily illustrate the poet's diction, the play's ironic structure and the characters of the antagonists, Antigone and Creon. Three are character studies of the heroine (1–99, 450–70, 891–928), three of King Creon (162–214, 631–765, 1284–1353), and the seventh, the Ode on Man gives some of the playwright's deepest insights not only into the character of the heroine [4] but into Sophocles' understanding of true heroism. The 891–928 passage is also analyzed because its authenticity has been seriously challenged ever since Goethe judged it an unheroic, un-Sophoclean contradiction of the heroine's whole being. Naturally, then, it seemed appropriate to provide the tools necessary for the student to study the authenticity and appropriateness of this passage.

The Commentary tries to fulfill various needs: it points out specific examples of the playwright's technique; it provides the first extensive English commentary since Jebb's monumental work of 1891; [5] and it offers opinions of a number of different critics so that the student can gain some perspective in judging the views I offer throughout this book. Extended notes on specific stylistic or thematic problems are treated in the separate introductions to each chapter. However, since the student will use this study alongside another text of the play, no summaries of the action are provided.

Grammatical Notes are provided for those words in the Sophoclean text whose lexical first form is not readily guessed and for forms that require identification or explanation. Each note repeats the form that occurs in the text, followed by the lexical entry of the word and an identification of the form. For instance, at line 162, Creon greets the elders, calling them *andres*, "men." *Anēr* is the Greek word for "man" in its lexical form. Thus, the grammatical note at 162 gives *andres, anēr:* noun of address. Modifying adjectives are listed with their nouns, e.g., at 163, the entry is *pollōi salōi, polys salos:* dat. sing. So, the adjective *polys*, "much," modifies the noun *salos,* "surge," and the phrase is used in the dative case. Verb forms including participles and infinitives are similarly recorded with their corresponding lexical forms. The lexical form of verbs is ordinarily the first person singular of the present tense unless the verb is defective or impersonal.

Many Greek words in the Sophoclean text are elided; i.e., a final short vowel drops before another word with an initial vowel, e.g., *opōpa egō* shortens to *opōp' egō;* and when the initial vowel in the second word is aspirated, a final *pi, tau,* or *kappa* regularly assumes its aspirated form, i.e., *phi, thēta,* and *chi* respectively. Also, many words undergo "crasis," i.e., the combining of two words into one like English "don't": e.g., *kai emōn* becomes *k'amōn* (and the apostrophe in the middle of such a word indicates the presence of crasis). Whenever either elision or crasis occurs in the text, the Grammatical Notes give the uncombined or unelided form. So, for example, at lines 5–6, the notes give *est(i),* not *esth';* and *(e)mōn,* not *k'amōn;* and *opōp(a),* not *opōp'.* The complete word is given in the note to make it easier for the student to recognize the form.

The Vocabulary includes all Greek words that occur in the selections, listed according to their lexical first form. As stated above, the lexical first forms can be found in the Grammatical Notes, following the form of the word that occurs in the text. For verbs that occur in several forms the appropriate principal parts are given, e.g., *hamartanō* 2 aor. *hēmarton,* perf. *hēmartēka.* This means that all the forms of *hamartanō* that Sophocles uses in these selections are built from one of three stems, the present, the second aorist, and the perfect active. If there is only one use of a given stem, the exact form that does occur is given in parentheses after the first principal part, e.g., *diollymi (diōleto). Diōleto* is the only form in which the word occurs in the text. For nouns, the genitive is given if there is a stem change; also, the article and the gender. For adjectives, the masculine, feminine, and neuter nominatives are included. Peculiar forms that might cause difficulty and dialectical variations in spelling are included in parentheses where necessary, e.g., *hēmera (hāmera).*

The meanings are generally restricted to those appropriate to the lines cited, although, in some cases, other meanings are included as an aid in image analysis. For a fuller list of meanings the student is referred to the unabridged dictionary of Liddell-Scott-Jones (LSJ).

The lines at which most verbs, nouns, and adjectives occur in the Greek text are indicated in the Vocabulary to aid in the study of images and themes. No line numbers are included for prepositions and other words unimportant in image analysis. The line numbers are generally restricted to the selections included in the text and the images discussed in the Commentary.

There are two appendixes, one a chronological note on Sophocles' life, and the other treating his relation to the mythic material from which he created this drama.

On the matter of the spelling of Greek proper nouns, two conflicting principles come into play. On the one hand, current practice favors the restoration of Greek orthography: e.g., Dionysos instead of Dionysus. On the other hand, it seems advisable to leave familiar names in easily recognizable form. Therefore, I generally use *c* rather than *k* in names like Creon, Eurydice, and Eteocles.

Finally, the aids of this text are not meant to be ends in themselves but to serve as springboards propelling students to the standard grammars and commentaries for the treasures that lie hidden there.[6] But even from this *Guide* alone, Greek students, comparatists, and general readers willing to work with the text should find themselves able for the first time to distinguish images and themes, to observe the architectonic structure of the poet's art, and even to perceive the bewildering simplicity of the language with which the artist reaches the heights of sheer poetry.

My debts are legion. I cannot possibly acknowledge the support of family, colleagues, and friends without whom this long project would never have been completed. They know my gratitude. I wish to express gratitude here to Southern Illinois University at Carbondale for financial support; to Eugene Timpe, Chairman of Foreign Languages and Literatures, and Charles Speck, Professor of Classical Studies at Southern Illinois University, for their constant help. I owe special thanks to C. John Herington, Professor of Classics and Talcott Professor of Greek at Yale University, who provided invaluable help, although his initial proposal for a Byzantine commentary has been altered here beyond recognition; also to Mary Lefkowitz, Professor of Greek at Wellesley College, to Gregory Thalmann, instructor of Classics at Yale University, to Wilfred Major, instructor of Classical Studies at Southern Illinois University, whose close reading of the introductions and commentary removed many errors and provided new insights; to novelist Richard White, to Carroll Grimes, Chairman of Humanities at University of Pittsburgh at Johnstown, to Raymond Rainbow, Professor of English at Southern Illinois University, for helping me avoid many offenses against the English language and for their creative suggestions; to my patient undergraduate assistants, Laurie Haight and Sandra Moffitt, to Laurie for her careful preparation of the Vocabulary and to Sandie for her painstaking corrections. I take full responsibility for such errors as remain in the text; without the help of these colleagues and assistants there would be far more.

JOAN V. O'BRIEN

Carbondale, Illinois
31 May 1977

Abbreviations and Symbols

acc., accusative
act., active voice
adj., adjective
adv., adverb
An., Antigone
An., Antigone
aor., aorist
art., article
Att., Attic
ca., circa
chap., chapter
Cho., Chorus
Comm., Commentary
comparat., comparative degree
conj., conjunction
contr., contracted, contraction
Cr., Creon
dat., dative
defect., defective
demonstr., demonstrative
dep., deponent
e.g., for example
esp., especially
f., fem., feminine
ff., following
frg., fragment
freq., frequent, frequently
fut., future
gen., genitive
gen. abs., genitive absolute
Gr., Greek
Hae., Haemon
i.e., that is

imper., imperative mood
impers., impersonal
impf., imperfect
indic., indicative mood
indecl., indeclinable
indef., indefinite
inf., infinitive
interrog., interrogative
intr., intransitive
Intro., Introduction
irreg., irregular
Ism., Ismene
LSJ, Liddell-Scott-Jones, *Greek English Lexicon*
lit., literally
MS, manuscript (*pl.* MSS)
m., masc., masculine
mid., middle voice
modif., modifying
neg., negative
n., neut., neuter
nom., nominative
n., note (*pl.* nn.)
opt., optative mood
orig., originally
partic., participle
partit., partitive
pass., passive voice
pers., personal
perf., perfect
pl., plural
plpf., pluperfect
prep., preposition

pres., present

pron., pronoun

reflex., reflexive

Soph., Sophocles

s.v., *sub voce* (under the word)

sing., singular

subj., subjunctive mood

superl., superlative

trag., tragedy, tragic

trans., transitive

= equals, equivalent

> becomes

‾ macron

˘ breve

NOTE: *The works quoted in text by author's name only are listed in the Selected Bibliography.*

Guide to Sophocles'

ANTIGONE

A Student Edition

I

The Prologue

[1 - 99]

INTRODUCTION

T HE PROLOGUE to the *An.* is really act 1 of the play. Soph. plunges
the audience into the action, using the dialogue between An. and
her sister Ism. to provide his audience with the background for
understanding the drama that is to come. The heroine's first words
establish her intense love and anguish; and the following
ninety-nine lines marked with clipped, antithetically balanced
debate serve to characterize the two sisters principally through
contrast: the strong passionate woman of conviction alongside the
gentle, affectionate, but frightened girl. In this Introduction, I shall
describe Soph.'s antithetical style in the Prologue and suggest that
this distinctive style of diction delineates An.'s androgynous character and helps express the poet's deepest philosophical conviction.

As the Prologue illustrates, method is to a large extent meaning
in the art of Soph. The most striking aspect of his style here is
the extensive use of antithesis and balance. Some critics see this
as a prosaic fault,[1] finding here an example of the early Soph.—
before he achieved the heights of the *Oedipus Tyrannos.*[2] It is true
that the *An.* is the most antithetical of all Greek plays, reflecting
as it does contemporary sophistic practice. It is true, too, that the
antithetical balance seems sometimes excessive to modern taste,
and the poet's language in the iambic portions of the play (i.e.,

the Prologue and the episodes) is bewildering in its unadorned simplicity.[3] Still, the style reflects the poet's Heraclitean vision of reality. He sees truth in terms of opposites, believing, as his irony consistently illustrates, that appearances are deceptive, concealing as they do the real truth which is the reverse of the apparent. Thus, as Reinhardt pointed out (p. 104), almost every episode of this play entails a reversal by a development of the situation into its opposite: in the Prologue, the apparent sisterly unity is irreparably broken before the entrance of the Cho.; similarly, the mastery of the king so evident at the beginning of Episode 1 is shaken before the Ode on Man; these and the other separate independent reversals constitute the playwright's method of development and enact his dramatic idea. It is not until the dénouement that the audience fully recognizes, from the cumulative impact of the various confrontations and reversals, that the apparent folly of the young girl (see 95 n.) is wisdom, whereas the wise sayings of the revered king (see Intro., chap. 2) are folly (see 1347 n.). A Cho. of Soph.'s later *Oedipus Tyrannos* (1189–93) expresses the poet's antithetical vision of reality when it calls Oedipus a "paradigm of seeming": "What man, what man gains more happiness than a seeming (*dokein*), and after the seeming a turning away (*apoklīnai*)."

Nobility, too, is understood in terms of a wedding of dialectical oppositions. By virtue of An.'s defiance of the city and its king, the cityless (*apolis*) girl, utterly isolated from the citizens, becomes the one who is *hypsipolis*, "high in the city" (370). The passionate girl who speaks with the authority of an autonomous agent and performs manly deeds finally is revealed as the wonder of men, the subject of the Ode on Man (see 332 n.). Thus, the antithetical style, far from being a sophistic *tour de force,* is an appropriate vehicle both to depict character and to express the poet's philosophical conviction.

Examples of method as meaning in the Prologue include antithesis and the pointed use of duals.[4] The antithetical balance is everywhere evident. A few illustrations of duals and oxymora will demonstrate how Sophoclean grammar serves his convictions.

Greek has a dual number in addition to singular and plural, often used of two people whom the speaker considers a unit. The sisters think of themselves and of their two dead brothers as an inseparable unit (cf. 3, 13, 21–22, 50, 61–62). Therefore, until the moment when Ism. refuses to help bury her brother Polynices, the sisters speak of themselves in duals. An.'s refusal to use the dual thereafter is a grammatical reflection of the rupture between the sisters. Again, An.'s habit of speaking of her brothers in duals (21–22) is in sharp contrast to Cr.'s practice, since for him the one is the state's hero and the other a despicable traitor. The absence of duals after Ism.'s refusal to collaborate in the burial of Polynices reinforces An.'s isolation for the rest of the play.[5]

Antithesis also frequently takes the form of oxymoron, the peculiarly classical figure of speech which juxtaposes apparently contradictory qualities. The Prologue of this play presents key themes in this form. The most memorable example is *hosia panourgēsās(a)*, "playing the saintly villain" (74). It is a beautiful two-word picture of the holy criminal, holy because she is willing to play the criminal in defying the sinful but legal proclamation. The antithesis captures one of the underlying themes of the play and the essence of the heroine's grandeur. It is a grandeur that stems from the excessiveness of her character (see 332 n.)—an excessiveness that knows no compromise on matters of fundamental human rights included in the divine, unwritten law (see 450 n.). Her moral insight, *phronēma* (see 355 n.), perceives that the "criminal" act was the only true act of piety open to her. *Hosios,* "hallowed," i.e., sanctioned by divine law, is often used in opposition to *dikaios,* "just," i.e., sanctioned in the human tribunals. Soph., unlike most of his contemporaries and unlike Plato's Socrates in the *Crito,* understands that the two courts can come into conflict, a conflict which this oxymoron enhances and which the whole drama portrays. Piety for An. is reverence for the unwritten law of Zeus and Justice (450 ff.). And it is this piety that is in conflict with the human proclamation of Cr. The verb *panourgein,* (from *pan,* "all," and *ergein,* "to do a deed")[6] literally means to do all things, and it expresses that quality that An. has in common with all Soph.'s heroes: a universal daring. But the word normally had a pejorative ring and meant "to play the role of a knave who would stop at nothing."[7] Ism.'s use of *autourgos* (52 n.) for Oedipus' deed of self-blinding emphasizes the pejorative meaning here. The "deed" for Ism. is also the future deed of burial (85) that she begs

An. not to reveal. For An., however, the "deed" is the noble impiety that will be her counterproclamation (86–87) in defiant response to Cr.'s decree. This oxymoron defines the heroine's conception of piety, shows her excessive daring and simultaneously reveals her full knowledge that such daring will earn her a fatal reputation for criminality.

Hosia panourgēsās(a) is then perhaps the most impressive oxymoron in the play, but it is by no means unique (e.g., cf. 77, 924, 1167). Oxymoron comes naturally to a tragic heroine with An.'s insight into her dilemma, and it comes naturally to a tragic poet profoundly convinced that people tend to confuse appearance with reality, sin with the appearance of the sin.

Another striking element in all the dialogue portions of the *An.*—and especially in the Prologue—is the dearth of metaphorical language, particularly in reference to the heroine. This must have come as a surprise for the ancient audience as well as for the modern translator. For the diction of this play is not only more cerebral than that of any other extant Sophoclean work, but the *An.* dates from the period in which he produced the *Ajax,*[8] his most Aeschylean play in its elaborate imagery.[9] And for Aeschylus, Sophocles' older contemporary, metaphor and language are almost coextensive terms.

Now the element of language or diction in the Greek drama carries a·peculiarly heavy proportion of the meaning, a fact due in some part, at least, to the nature of the Greek theatre. The large open-air arena with its wide circular stage and vast audience necessitates broader gestures than the modern indoor theatre. Also conventions like facial masks and male actors performing female roles place severe limitations on the actors' opportunity to convey subtlety through spectacle. These factors contribute to the important role that diction played in the Greek theatre.

The imagery Soph. does employ [10] is barely suggested in the Prologue, suggested in a cerebral way through "key" words that state and repeat essential themes. The emotional vocabulary of love and hate and various words related to death and burial anticipate the principal images later connected with An., those of marriage and death. In the peripety when the messenger announces that Hae. died embracing An., an act that left his father "a breath-

4

ing corpse" (1167), these images are finally united and objectified. Still later the nautical figures converge with the marriage-death symbolism when An. and Hae. are united in the haven of death (1284). The sea symbols are more closely associated with Cr. but also apply to An. whose accursed family is a beach struck by successive waves (583 ff.).

A modern playwright would probably merge the sensuous, emotional, and intellectual from the beginning. But Soph., economic in his use of symbolism throughout the play,[11] chooses to stress the emotional and intellectual in the Prologue, leaving the sensuous almost entirely till later in the play. An.'s restrained diction together with her emotional concern provide one of the early hints that the poet is creating an androgynous hero.

The debate of the Prologue centers on *philos* and *echthros*. It is important for the modern audience to understand what these words denoted for Soph. An. tells us much about herself when, in the middle of the play (523), she cries out: "It is not my nature to join in hatred (*synechthein*) but to join in loving (*symphilein*)." What does she mean by this beautiful epigrammatic summation of her vocation?

Philos, "one's own," "dear one," "friend"; and *echthros*, "not one's own," "outsider," "enemy,"[12] have a wide range of meanings in this play. Although these are passionate, partisan words for An., they have an objective side too. Méautis fails to tell the whole story when he says An. is totally at the service of "un sentiment, l'amour,"[13] as if love for An. were only "un sentiment." *Philia*, the abstract noun from *philos*, is definitely "un sentiment" (though some scholars deny this), a sentiment to which An. is wholly devoted, but the word has another aspect. *Philos* in Homer commonly refers (or is applied) to anything of one's own. Then it broadens to denote those who are in one's family and one's circle of friends. Therefore, Polynices' claim on his sister's love was based on the strong primitive right of a member of a family as well as on her affection for her brother. By Soph.'s time, of course, the state had replaced the family as the central governing force. But the king and his niece clash over the relative rights of family and state, i.e., the rights of *philoi*, those dear to her, and the rights of the *polis*, the city-state.[14] Although isolated finally from both *polis* and

5

her surviving sister, An. emerges as the true patriot by her very defiance of the *polis* for the sake of a *philos*. The apparently *polis*-minded king, on the other hand, is in the end bereft of both *philos* and *polis*.

Thus, *philos*, "relative," "dear one," and "friend," is used by An. in its first two significations. For Cr., however, it means "friend," and a friend for him is one who places the *polis'* interests above all personal ties, whether a family or friend (187–90). Conversely, an *echthros* for An. is never an enemy of the state as it is for Cr., but it denotes for her one who is outside the family, either by birth or, in the case of Ism. (by the end of the Prologue), by her refusal to defend the rights of the family.

Therefore, when An. later (522–23) claims she was born not to join in hatred (*synechthein*) but to join in loving (*symphilein*), she is describing herself as a lover, but specifically she is bearing witness to her undying love for her brother despite his betrayal of the state.[15]

In addition to laying the foundation for the contrast between An. and Cr. through their different understanding of *philia* and *polis*, the poet also presents here in the Prologue a contrast between the "androgynous" An. and the narrowly "feminine" Ism., a contrast that will later be underlined in the Creon-Haemon Debate by a similar difference between the "androgynous" Hae. and his narrowly "masculine" father. In *Bilingual Selections*, I offer a detailed analysis of these contrasts.[16] Here I only summarize the contrast in the Prologue between the sisters.

Although Ism.'s arguments have a certain pragmatic realism about them that the Greeks considered "masculine," the audience would find her "virtuous" because she excels in the quintessentially "feminine" virtue, *peitharchia*, "obedience." (I use quotation marks throughout on "masculine" and "feminine" to indicate that these are traditional categories. I make no judgment as to which sex more often possesses "feminine" or "masculine" characteristics.) Ism. has to refuse to collaborate with her sister's care of the dead Polynices (41–43) not out of apathy (65) but because women are weak and must obey the strong (59–64). Her acceptance of this fact of life in her society leads to her reluctant conclusion: *peisomai*, "I shall obey."

The poet underlines An.'s defiance of the dictates of this conventional virtue by a striking verbal coincidence. *Peisomai* can also mean "I shall endure" (see "Vocabulary," chap. 8, under *paschō* and *peithō*). The heroine climaxes her rejection of her sister's timid obedience by exclaiming: "Let me and my folly endure this terror. *I shall* not *suffer* anything so evil as an ignoble death" (95–97). An.'s suffering *peisomai,* occupying the same position in the verse as Ism.'s earlier submissive *peisomai,* dramatizes the heroine's rejection of the traditionally "feminine" virtue.

Nevertheless, despite her disobedience, I contend that An. is "androgynous" because her character displays a wholeness that grows out of a unity of some traditional "masculine" and "feminine" qualities.[17] She exhibits "masculine" daring in "hunting for impossibilities" (92), in performing "chilling deeds" (88), acting on her own initiative (71–72) and as a result of her own decision reached in the isolation of the pre-Prologue. She has the strength, too, the iron will (cf. 474 ff.), to affirm her convictions by her own death (91). And she is quite aware that a Homeric glory will accompany that death (72, cf. 502–3). Yet these "masculine" characteristics are always linked to "feminine" traits sometimes within single phrases (74, 88, 90, 92).[18] Like Achilles or Ajax, she possesses or is possessed by a passionate excess (68, 90); but unlike the Homeric heroes, her passion is directed not to the "masculine" act of war but to the "feminine" act of love. It is her tender love for her dead *philos* that motivates her, that directs her desire for glory, her *kleos* in Homeric terms, beyond its Homeric goal of selfish personal exaltation toward an altruistic concern. Similarly, her piety (74) and her logic (74–75), although only suggested here in the Prologue, will both prove to be "feminine" in that they respond not to objective principles but to the concrete needs of her dear ones. She performs the "villanous act of piety" (74), as we have observed, not in response to abstract unwritten laws of Zeus (450 f.) but in response to laws fleshed out in her brother's corpse (456–58). Thus, for the poet, it is she rather than the seemingly *polis*-minded king Cr. that is *hypsipolis,* "high in the city," because her altruistic act, although limited to the family, presents the Athenian audience with a new ideal of *kleos,* tailored for the *polis* instead of the battlefield.

The antithetical style, then, is essential to the poet's art. The oxymora and other antitheses contribute to the contrast between

7

the sisters and between the young rebel and her uncle whose authority she defies. The antithetical method is also integral to the portrayal of the heroine whose nobility results from a weaving together (368–69) of opposites within her nature. The rest of the play and its ironic structure will also show that the antithetical style helps the poet express his philosophical conviction that the hidden truth is the reverse of the apparent.

COMMENTARY

1. *Koinon,* "common," "of common parentage," also implying "having common interests." The word is sufficiently vague to convey also their communal plight stemming from the confused relationships in the house of Oedipus. *Ismēnēs karā,* lit., "head of Ism.," is a warm term of affection (cf. *Oedipus Tyrannos* 40).

Every word in this opening line suggests endearment, e.g., the redundant *autadelphon* and the pathetic *kara* both of which remind Ism. of their close affection. An. conveys an atmosphere of unity and mutual support that will be utterly broken before the Prologue ends. From these opening remarks to her final speech in which she says she "is going to my own" (893), An. makes her whole stance on the grounds of family unity.

2–3. The awkward grammatical construction with the double question communicates An.'s anguish. She is already aware that she must die (Müller). By the *hopoin ouchi,* she apparently means that there is no ill of the house which will not be visited on the two surviving sisters. Many editors attempt to emend 2–4 but the rushing double question expresses a violence that Ism. later compares to the darkened sea before a storm (20). Only *atēs ater* (4) is inept. The "ills inherited from Oedipus" include the ancestral curse upon the house (594) and the events of Oedipus' own life—the murder of his father Laios; the marriage to his mother Jocasta; its progeny, An., Ism., Polynices, and Eteocles; and the curse upon his two sons.

The duals *nōin* . . . *zdōsain* are the first of an extraordinarily great number of duals in the Prologue (cf. 13, 21 and n., 50, 61–62, and see the Intro., this chap.). The sisters think of themselves in

8

the first half of the Prologue as an inseparable unit. An. stops using duals before Ism. does, i.e., from the moment when she realizes that her sister will not collaborate. From then on, there is a pointed use of pronouns of the first person in An.'s remarks (45, 48, 70, 71, 80, 95).

4. *Atēs ater:* this phrase is probably corrupt, although it can be traced at least to the first century b.c. The best one can do with the phrase as it stands is to make it a parenthetical remark, "leaving aside the ruin of our fortunes," but this breaks the tempestuous flow of An.'s remarks. On *atē,* see 17 n. *Atē* is the theme of the great sea ode, 583 ff.

5. *Out' aischron out' atīmon:* the fourfold *oute* culminates in this phrase. *Aischron* refers to the moral shame; *atīmon* to the lack of outward signs of honor to Polynices' body (7 ff.). On "honor," *tīmē,* see 208 n.

8. *Kērygma theinai:* the active infinitive *theinai* is proper for one who makes laws for others to keep and is not himself subject to these laws. An. is careful throughout to call Cr.'s decree a proclamation *kērygma,* not a *nomos,* "law," except ironically at 452.

Stratēgon, "general." An. pointedly uses the prosaic *stratēgos,* rather than *tyrannos.* By acknowledging that Cr. made this proclamation not as a civil ruler, *tyrannos,* but as returning victorious *stratēgos,* she puts her proposed act of burial in the worst possible light. A *stratēgos,* giving an edict to the whole people (7), would have more claim to absolute obedience than would a *tyrannos.* More important, however, An.'s choice of *stratēgos* together with *kērygma,* properly a herald's proclamation, and *steichonta* (10), properly used of military advance, suggest her militaristic characterization of her uncle-king. Still, *stratēgos* has a double focus for Soph.'s audience since *stratēgos* was the civil title Pericles held as Athens' leader.

9–10. Since their sex excludes the sisters from membership in the body politic (*pandēmōi polei,* 7), they know of the proclamation only by hearsay, a fact emphasized by the repeated refrain, "they say" (7, 23, 31). The poet constantly contrasts An.'s strength with the docility society expected of her. On woman's place in mythical Thebes and Soph.'s Athens, see Intro., this chap., and nn. on 18–19, 41, 678.

Ē . . . kaka. Jebb mistranslates *philous* here as "friends." The

9

passage means "that misfortunes proper to enemies (*or* evils proceeding from our enemies) are marching against our *philous,* loved ones (i.e., esp. Polynices)." *Philos* and *echthros* are personal, not political words for An. (see the Intro., this chap.); she uses *philos* only of members of her family (unless one gives her 572 against the MSS evidence). It is irrelevant to her that Polynices is a traitor and a political enemy of Thebes; he is a relative whom she loves, and thus he is a *philos.* Soph. later mentions that the whole Argive army was denied burial (1080–83), a fact that he suppresses here (one hardly notices the plural *tōn echthrōn,* "enemies") in order to keep the full focus on Polynices' plight. Aristotle later theorized (*Poetics* 1453b19–22) that most good tragedies depict suffering "in the context of close family relationships (*philoi*), for example, when a brother kills or intends to kill a brother."

12. *Algeinos,* "painful," i.e., causing mental anguish. Each sister has now used the word. See 64 and 468 for the instructive differences in their application of the word.

Ex hotou, "from the time when." Soph. does not give a clear chronology of the events of the preplay, but he apparently visualizes the brothers' mutual slaughter as preceding the Theban victory over the Argives (1144–48).

13–14. The double use of "two" (*duoin . . . duo*) followed by the antithetical one-two *miāi . . . diplēi* betrays Soph.'s (and contemporary Athenian) fascination with such contrasts. The compression and antithesis here is characteristic of the style of this whole play. Again (as at 3) the duals emphasize the family unit and the isolation of the two sisters (see Intro., this chap.).

16. This line and 253 point toward predawn, just after the rout of the invading Argives, as the time of the Prologue (Bradshaw, p. 203). Since *en nykti tēi nȳn* can mean both "in this last night" and "in this present night," scholars disagree as to whether the time is predawn or dawn. The conspiratorial tone of the Prologue argues for the darkness of predawn. In any case, it must be close to dawn, since the Parodos (100 ff.) hails the rising sun.

17. *Atōmenē,* "being in distress." The noun *atē* (4) to which this partic. is related is the subject of the second choral ode (582 ff.: see summary of the ode in *Bilingual Selections; atē* developed in meaning from delusion and infatuation in Homer to disaster, ruin,

guilt, and error in the dramatists). Cr. later calls the sisters "two ruins (*ata*) and revolutions" (533). See also 1345–46 n.

18–19. Normally secluded, the girls are outside the gates, a setting that suggests An.'s daring to move beyond the approved "feminine" sphere. Cf. Aristophanes' *Lysistrata* 16: "You know it is hard for women to get out." Cf. Soph.'s *Electra* 312, 517.

20. Lit., "It is plain that you are darkening with some news." *Kalchainein*, "to be purple," suggests the agitation both of the sea (that yields purple dye) and of the mind.

21. *Ou gar*, "why, of course," communicates An.'s indignation.

21–22. By using paratactical (i.e., coordinate rather than sub-ordinate) construction in *ton men protīsās, ton d' atīmasās*, An. empha-sizes that she accords her brothers the equal honor that Cr. has denied them. Knox's rendering (p. 80) conveys the brilliant use of duals in these lines: "Has not Creon, in the matter of the burial of our (*nōin*) two brothers (*nōin kasignētō*) honored the one (*ton men*) and dishonored the other (*ton d'*)?" For the sisters, the brothers are an inseparable unity (see 3 n.) but not for Cr. Cr.'s decree honoring the one brother and denying burial to the other probably would not immediately strike the Athenian audience as offensive not only because of an existent Athenian law (see 44 n.) but also because in Aeschylus' earlier *Seven against Thebes*, Eteocles, despite his violent death, achieves tragic stature and Polynices is the unseen enemy (see Appendix A). In Anouilh's *An.*, the brothers are again viewed as indistinguishable but with a difference: There they are both degenerates who die such indiscriminate deaths that their corpses are indistinguishable.

24. The text here is corrupt as the asterisks in most texts signify. Although various conjectures have been advanced, the MSS reading is as satisfactory as any. Thus I follow Pearson against Jebb in *Bilingual Selections*.

26. *Ton . . . nekyn*, lit., "the wretchedly dying corpse of Poly-nices." The participle, "dying," is transferred from Polynices, which it properly modifies, to *nekyn*, "corpse."

27. *Ekkekērўchthai*, "to have been banished by proclamation." This verb, related to the noun *kērygma* (see 8 n., 32, 34), continues the military motif.

28. The last episode of Soph.'s *Ajax* is perhaps the best com-

mentary on the importance Soph. attached to proper burial as a basic human right. See 450 and n. for An.'s belief that such burial was one of the unwritten laws of the gods.

29–30. The carrion birds here and throughout the play are a sinister reminder of the degradation that Cr. is willing to impose on his subjects. An. is identified throughout the play with "the subjugated natural world" (Segal, p. 76). See 342–43 where one of man's triumphs in the Ode on Man is the catching of birds; also at 423–25, the guard describes An. as a bitter mother bird lamenting her young—an old image (cf. Aeschylus' *Agamemnon* 49–54) put to fresh use; at 999 ff., Tiresias uses birds to convey warnings of Cr.'s excesses. See also nn. on 1291 and 1308.

Glykyn thesauron, "sweet treasure." An.'s treasured brother is a "sweet store" for birds of prey. This is one of the few times An. speaks in consciously metaphoric language (Goheen, p. 129, n. 3).

31. *Ton agathon Kreonta,* "the good Creon," spoken with obvious irony. In the language of the burgeoning sophistic movement, *agathos* was coming to mean "skilled in power-politics." See Adkins, pp. 30 ff.

32. *Legō gar ka(i) (e)me,* "yes, and for me too." An.'s repetition here conveys her incredulous indignation that Cr. should think she would obey such an order. The phrase also shows she fully understands that she will pay dearly for her piety to her brother's corpse.

34–35. *Agein . . . ouden,* lit., "not to estimate at nothing," i.e., Cr. does "not consider the matter of slight importance." *Hōs* emphasizes that this is Cr.'s viewpoint. Monetary allusions are frequent in relation to Cr., as at 296 ff. and 1036 ff. where he accuses the guard and the seer Tiresias respectively of bribery. See 1325 n. for the final tally. The tendency to judge all things in terms of their financial success received new impetus with the sophistic movement. The theme is common in Soph.'s plays (cf. *Philoctetes* 109–18 and *Electra* 1087–97). *Hos . . . drāi* is the equivalent of a dative participial phrase, "to the one transgressing in any respect (*ti*)."

36. Death by stoning was reserved for traitors and was normally performed outside the city walls. Presumably Cr. has determined to perform it before all the people to make an example of the

criminal. Stoning was the only form of punishment in which public participation was permitted. Later (775), Cr. lessens the punishment to interment with food (lit., fodder for animals) and water in order, he says, to avoid pollution; however, since Hae. has by this time told his father that the people were on An.'s side (693–95), lack of popular support may have entered into his decision. Various other motives for his reduction of the sentence have been advanced from "pedantry or cynicism" (Kitto, *Form*, p. 166) to superstitious piety.

38. *Eit(e) . . . kakē:* every Sophoclean hero expresses his adherence to his ideal in terms of nobility (Kirkwood, pp. 177 ff.). *Eugenēs* originally meant being born a noble, but for Soph.'s heroes it always indicates both noble birth and nobility of nature through action. An. asserts that Ism.'s act will prove whether she is truly noble in nature. Soph. exhibits his own peculiar blend of the aristocratic tradition (i.e., in the primacy of nature and birth) and the democratic (i.e., in his stress on deeds of nobility and in his political abhorrence of the tyrants).

39. *Talaiphron,* "poor," may imply disparagement of An.'s judgment as well as its more usual meaning of "pitiable."

40. *Lyous(a) . . . haptousa* is probably proverbial for meddling in any way. The phrase may have originated as a metaphor of weaving and, if so, may relate to the weaving image at 368. Jebb rightly rejects the suggestion that it refers to Cr.'s edict, i.e., "seeking to undo it or tighten it." At 68 Ism. characterizes An. as an excessive meddler.

41–43. The triple use of *xyn-* as prefix and preposition here reinforces An.'s offer to Ism. of full partnership in the endeavor. When Ism. responds in terms of personal danger, she, like the "weaker sister" Chrysothemis in Soph.'s later *Electra,* is more representative of accepted womanly virtue than An. or Electra is (see Intro., this chap., and 678–80 n.). However, Ism. does not make Chrysothemis' mistake of equating the dangerous with the morally wrong. Other Sophoclean women who play subordinate roles are Tekmessa in the *Ajax* and Deianeira in the *Trachiniae* 552–53 (though her subsequent actions belie her words). See 678–80 n.

43. *Xyn . . . tēide cheri,* "with my hand." Though An. does not succeed in actually giving the body full burial, she and Eurydice

both use their hands on behalf of their loved ones (see nn. on 900 and 1315); Ism. does not. The preposition *xyn* makes this a dative of accompaniment: her hand replaces Ism. as her collaborator. David Daube (pp. 5–10) claims women are more inclined to consider burial an act worthy of defiance both because they were outside the power structure and because they are naturally more in touch with birth and death than men. Daube cites Exod. 1:15 ff. where the Hebrew midwives refuse to execute Pharoah's order to kill all male newborn. Like An. they invoke a higher law ("the midwives feared God and did not do as the king of Egypt commanded"). Unlike An., however, the midwives under subsequent questioning deny their act of disobedience (Exod. 1:18).

Kouphieis, "will you aid by lifting," is one of a cluster of words in the play from the adjective *kouphos*, "light," "nimble," "airy," "tripping." The word has traditionally "feminine" associations, both positive and negative. Here, as often, it is associated with a humane act. It appears later in the compound *kouponoos*, "light-headed" or "light-hearted," "fickle," used once in a complimentary sense (342) and once negatively (617). See 342 n.

44. *Ē gar* indicates Ism.'s surprise. The absence of a caesura in the first three feet allows the astonished Ism. to pronounce *noeis thaptein* with particular deliberation. Denying Polynices burial in his native land was in accordance with Athenian statutory law (Thucydides 1. 126) though the law does not appear to have been applied for some time. Still the religious duty to bury one's relatives was considered very strong and there would be no legal defense for Cr.'s refusal for burial *outside* the city limits. However Plato (*Laws* 9. 873c) notes that the murderer of relatives shall be cast out unburied. See Intro., this chap.

45–46. The particle, *goun*, throws emphasis onto *emon*, "my," and as she says "*my* brother," An. is reminded that Polynices is equally Ism.'s brother. Thus, she adds the reproach *kai . . . theleis*. In 46, the initial stressed position of *adelphon*, "brother," prepares for her strong statement of principle about him, beginning with *ou gar dē*, "certainly not."

47. *Schetlia*, does not have its usually contemptuous ring, "wretched fool," but probably retains something of its original meaning: "able to hold out," "unflinching."

48. The emphasis falls on *tōn emōn:* "He has no right to keep me from *my own.*" Thus, her religious duty contains an element that is both deeply personal and chthonic, i.e., pertaining to the gods of the underworld, and this helps explain the difficult passage 911–28. It is important to understand the interweaving of divine and human motivation in the heroine. Kitto (*Greek Tragedy* p. 133) denies the divine dimension; Gellie (p. 47) sees a multiplicity of motives. Her motivation is far more complex than that of Jean Anouilh's *An.* Cr. reminds the latter that her brother's death was only a pretext: "Ce qui importait pour elle, c'était de refuser et de mourir" (*Nouvelles pièces noires,* p. 191).

49. *Phronēson,* "think." Ism. begins her attempt at dissuading her sister with this pregnant word, which in this play usually connotes right thinking ethically as well as intellectually (see 98 n.). Later (1023), Tiresias attempts to turn Cr. from his folly with the same *phronēson:* "Think, then, on these things, my son." Each character in the play has his or her own idea of what constitutes "right thinking" (see 176 n.). The series of long syllables in Ism.'s lines here reflects her deep pain.

50–54. Soph. here follows the version of the Oedipus story contained in the *Odyssey* (11. 275); i.e., Oedipus survives Jocasta and dies in Thebes. The *An.* shows no knowledge of the version Soph. gives in his later *Oedipus at Kolonos* in which Oedipus migrates to Kolonos and is deified there. *Epeita* (53) can mean "in the next place" and need not imply that Jocasta died after Oedipus in time (Jebb). *Apechthēs,* "utterly detested." An., of course, like Oedipus, will suffer the death of a hated outsider.

51–52. The triple use of *autos* emphasizes Oedipus' detection of his own crime and the self-inflicted nature of the punishment. The many words compounded with *autos* in this play emphasize the paradox inherent in the family curse and in personal responsibility. Soph., however, stresses the personal responsibility. *Araxās,* "having torn out his eyes," i.e., with the golden brooches fastening Jocasta's robe (see *Oedipus Tyrannos* 1268 ff.). *Autourgōi cheri,* "with self-working (i.e., working against oneself) hand." See 43 n.

53. *Diploun epos,* "double designation" for Jocasta because of her double relationship to Oedipus. Cf. *Oedipus Tyrannos* 1249 and often in that play where Oedipus points to his double horror, double

eyes, double ankles, and the double doors leading to his wife and mother.

54. "With twisted noose": cf. *Oedipus Tyrannos* 1264-66. An.'s later death, like Jocasta's, will be by hanging. Although hanging was a common method of suicide in antiquity, the physical separation from the earth and from the chthonic deities she revered (see 368 n. and 450-52 n.) accentuates An.'s isolation even in the method of death.

55. *Triton . . . dyo mian.* On the fascination with numbers displayed here, cf. 13-14.

56. *Autoktonounte,* lit., "slaying with their own hands," can mean both "killing self" and "killing relatives" (Jebb), not "by mutual brotherly slaughter." However, both context and the use of a dual participle emphasize that this murder is mutual.

58. *Monā dē,* "utterly alone." *Dē* emphasizes the *monā.*

59-60. "If in violence to the law, we transgress the decree (*psēphon,* lit., 'vote') and powers (*kratē*) of absolute authority (*tyrannōn*)." *Tyrannos* means "absolute ruler" but in mythic poetry the word is often indistinguishable from *basileus,* "king," and does not necessarily carry the imperious overtones that *monarchos* does (1163). Still, in political life, a *tyrannos* was one who usurped power usually by violent means (e.g., Pisistratus in Herodotos 1. 59), and Soph.'s Athenian audience was happy that the age of the tyrants was a thing of the past. (The whole thrust of Herodotos' history was to extol Greek freedoms and equality in contrast to the tyranny of Persia. See e.g., Herodotos 3. 80-84 where the historian's sympathies are easy to feel.) In this passage, the word *tyrannōn* "emphasizes the absolute power of Creon conferred on him by the polis in the emergency, and at the same time, by its plural form, generalizes the expression and thus lessens the suggestion that he is a 'tyrant' " (Knox, p. 63). The combined force of *kratē,* "power," sometimes "brute power"; of *kreissōn* (63) from the same stem; and of *psēphon,* properly a pebble used in an election (and thus this is an election in which only Cr. could vote), is such as to cast some doubt in the audience's mind, although not in Ism.'s, on the legitimacy of Cr.'s rule. Ism. shares Cr.'s illusion (see 666 ff., 734-36) that his *psēphon* represents the vote of the whole citizenry and An.'s proposal is therefore treasonous (*nomou biāi*).

59. *Oloumeth(a)*, "we shall die." Although Ism. is depicted as the weaker sister, her one telling argument is that her tactics would keep the family alive through the two sisters, whereas An.'s plan will destroy the family.

59–62. Ism. introduces *nomos*, "law" (59), and *physis*, "nature" (62). The play offers different views on the interrelationship of these two words, as did much contemporary literature. See Intro., chap. 4. For Ism. here, the ruler's decree is *nomos*, and human nature, especially when embodied in the "weaker sex,": has no choice but to obey it. See 175–77, and 211–14 for Cr.'s view of *nomos;* see 452 ff. for An's conviction that only Zeus can establish *nomoi* and her refusal to ennoble Cr.'s decree with the word, *nomos.*

61–62. Ism. here gives the normally accepted view of woman's role. See Intro., this chap. and 41 n.

63–64. "Next, that we are ruled by the (physically and politically) stronger (*kreissonōn*)," see 60 n. Her argument here is strictly pragmatic: obey the stronger or suffer more painful (*algiona*) calamities. For An.'s view on what constitutes pain, see 468.

65. In asking pardon of *tous hypo chthonos*, "those under the earth," i.e., presumably all her dead relatives and the gods of the underworld who constitute the "chthonic" realm, Ism. acknowledges their claim on her loyalty and her inability to defy *tois en telei*, "those in power," in Thebes. The neat grammatical balance that she accords the two groups ironically contrasts with her neglect of the rights of the one group.

67. *Peisomai*, "I shall obey." This is Ism.'s word. She will obey those in authority. Obedience is a key theme in the play: An. never does obey (219, 381, 656). Cr. later (672–76) personifies *peitharchia*, "obedience," as the civic principle, but finally he echoes Ism.'s *peisomai* (1099) when he belatedly learns obedience himself. All Sophoclean heroes grapple with obedience but they all ultimately refuse to obey (Knox, pp. 13 ff.). See 96 n. for An.'s very different *peisomai.*

68. *Perissa prassein:* "to do extreme things," "to act beyond one's sphere," "to lack moderation," "to be over-valiant." *Perissos*, lit., "outsized," comes to mean extreme, prodigious, usually with a pejorative sense. This phrase aptly characterizes An. Cr. somewhat extends its meaning later when he confines her in her prison with

the words: "Let her learn that reverence to Death is useless labor" (*ponos perissos,* 780). All Sophoclean heroes are in some way *perissos,* "immoderate," and *deinos* (see 332 ff.) and the lesser characters and the Cho. try to persuade the heroes to abandon their extreme positions. See Intro., this chap. The ending of Aeschylus' *Seven,* usually considered a post-*An.* interpolation, uses *perissos* of An., perhaps under influence of this line.

70. The adverb *hēdeōs* is best translated as the main thought: "I would take no pleasure in your collaboration." An. keeps her resolve not to accept Ism.'s help (cf. 549). Knox (p. 66) claims that An.'s dream of glory is such that she wants "no other participants to lessen her full possession of the thing for which she gives her life." An.'s later refusal to accept her sister's help tends to give substance to the Cho.'s judgment that she is harsh, obdurate (471–72), and self-willed (*autognōtos,* 875).

71. In *Bilingual Selections,* I adopt the reading of most modern editors (Campbell, Jebb, Dain), although Pearson retains the MSS reading *isth' hopoīa.* The MSS reading with a circumflex (neuter plural) would mean: "Hold such principles as you will." The other reading, *hopoiā* (feminine singular), acknowledged by the scholiast, is more forceful and appropriate to An.'s insistence on nobility *in act:* "Be such as you choose to be"—i.e., ignoble.

71–72. An.'s simple "him I shall bury" is emphatic both because of the initial position of the verb *thapsō* and because of the rare pause in the middle of the line immediately after the verb. Cf. Cr.'s later (658) *alla ktenō,* "but I shall kill (her)," and *Iliad* 1. 29, "her I shall not release." The two Sophoclean usages break the normal flow of the iambic line and add a realistic touch more common in the poet's later plays. Aeschylus *Seven* 1028 (probably spurious) *egō sphe thapsō* was perhaps influenced by this line.

72. *Kalon . . . thanein.* An.'s noble (*kalon*) act contrasts with the *hopoiā* (71) of Ism. There is no "irony of fortune" for An., since she clearly understands the consequences of her act and the nature of the noble, *to kalon* (Campbell).

73. The repetition of *philē met(a)* at the end of the line underlines the pathos of the familial attachment between brother and sister. Wyckoff mistranslates: "friend with friend." Kitto better captures the feeling of the phrase: "His love will answer mine." In An.'s

last speech (898–99) she again uses the word *philos* in anaphora, the repetition of the same word at the beginning of successive phrases. Again, in Soph.'s later *Oedipus at Kolonos,* An. uses *to philon . . . philon* (1697) to emphasize her warm relationship with her father Oedipus just before his apotheosis. The last four hundred lines of the *Oedipus at Kolonos* offer the poet an opportunity to develop the loving aspect of An. directed toward living members of her family. *Keisomai,* "I shall lie," used here of lying with Polynices and in 76 of lying with the whole family, is the usual verb for lying in death and dwelling in Hades (cf. Soph.'s *Electra* 463 and 1166 ff.). So, although the verb is also used of An.'s marriage in death (1240–41), there is no reason to take the verb as indicative of an abnormal relationship between An. and Polynices. For a view of their relationship as abnormal, now generally rejected, cf. Agard, pp. 263–65.

74. *Hosia panourgēsās(a)*: a splendid oxymoron that conveys one of the underlying paradoxes of the whole play (cf. Intro., this chap., for the usually pejorative sense of *panourgein,* "to do all things," and for *hosios* as "holy," "sanctioned by the gods"). See also, *Philoctetes* 927–28, where the disillusioned Philoctetes speaks of the most hateful tool of dire villainy, (*panourgiās. . . echthiston*). Attempts to capture the oxymoron in translation include: "pure crime" (Kitto), "this crime is holy" (Fitts-Fitzgerald), "when I have dared this crime of piety" (Wyckoff), *"saintement criminelle"* (Mazon). Oxymoron here and at 924 provides Soph. with a way of showing the inability of the ordinary man to distinguish real piety from its appearances. *Hosios,* "holy," and *eusebeia,* "piety," are used of people who honor relationships which the gods are believed to protect— i.e., 1) family relationships, 2) guest-friendships, and 3) relationships between the state and its citizens and allies. See Adkins, pp. 132–38, for a study of these words.

74–75. *Epei. . . enthade.* In comparing the relatively short time she will be with the living to the long time with the dead, An. attempts to find rational justification for her instinctual commitment. The argument is not as specious as the famous sophistry 904–20 but the purpose is the same. "The infinitely greater length of time, now and hereafter, in which she must obey the august rulers of the lower world gives them higher authority here and now and cancels her obligation to earthly government. The overwhelming sense of her present duty has pushed her into an irrational but lofty defense of it" (Linforth, p. 186).

77. *Ta . . . entīma,* "what is held in honor among the gods," i.e., the *theōn nomima,* the laws of the gods (454–55). An. juxtaposes *entīma atīmasās(a)* "be guilty of dishonoring the honored"). The sibilants at the end of this excessively rapid line punctuate An.'s indictment of Ism.'s position. Adams (p. 45) argues An.'s primary motivation here is not obedience to divine law but her *erōs* as seen in 73–76, 80–81 (but cf. 48 n.). See 90 n. on *erōs;* see 208 n. on *tīmē. Atīmia* was a legal term for the withdrawal of political rights from a citizen.

78. Ism.'s elliptical reply allows her to be evasive. Instead of completing her thought with *ta tōn theōn,* "the laws of the gods," she emphasizes her own weakness with the initial *egō.* For a somewhat similar evasion by Cr., see 667.

79. *Ephyn* connotes "I am by nature and position" and is used alongside two other key "nature" words in the play: *physis,* the noun, "nature"; and *eugenēs,* the adjective, "well-born, noble" (cf. 38 n. and "Vocabulary," chap. 8, under *phyō, physis*). Practically every word in line 79 states an essential theme: *biāi politōn drān,* "to act against the will of the citizens," *ephyn,* and *amēchanos,* "impossible," "powerless" (see 90 n.). Also, these words show how antithetical the two sisters are "by nature." An. embraces the impossible, will not be powerless, and disregards the will of the citizens.

The *politēs,* the voting members of the *polis,* constituted about 20 percent of the population in Soph.'s time. The body politic with which his audience was familiar excluded the women, the large number of *metoikoi,* resident aliens (perhaps fifty thousand), and about twice as many slaves. On An. as a *metoikos,* see the Intro. to her last speech, chap. 6.

80. *Sy men* and *egō de* are the normal contrast-words: "You for your part . . . can go on making excuses if you like but *my* next act is to bury my very own brother." The force of the *dē* in *egō de dē taphon* is "now, the next act is" and throws the emphasis onto the next word *taphon,* "tomb."

81. "To heap up a sepulchral mound." The desire that An.

expresses here to raise a tomb over the properly burned remains of her brother is not accomplished in full until Cr. so commands at 1203. Lines 255 and 429 refer to symbolic sprinklings.

82. *"Talainēs."* The word's usual meaning is "unhappy" and is normally applied to passive victims, but its original meaning, "daring," "rash," is apparent here. Ism. understands that her sister's daring is the cause of her woe.

83. *Exorthou,* "continue to direct safely." An.'s use of a nautical image here for her sister suggests that Ism. has chosen the world of Cr. in which keeping the ship of state on a straight and even course is supposedly the prime value (162 ff.).

86–87. The heroine displays an obsessive desire for full revelation of her deed. *Pollon* (= *poly*) *echthiōn,* "much more hated." *Pollon* is a strange epic form, only appearing here in Soph.'s extant works. *Echthiōn* is used here in the passive sense, the only sense known to Homer, i.e., hated, not hating. The epic tone here may be meant to suggest An.'s union with the world of Achilles, a world in which one was *echthros* if one did not do the *deeds* of a *philos.*

On the motive of An. here, Margon argues that she reveals a desire to ameliorate the family's reputation by gaining recognition as the person responsible for the burial. Such an argument seems more appropriate for Soph.'s Electra than his An.

88. Goheen (pp. 109, 154) captures the antithesis: "Hot is your heart for chilling deeds," but probably errs in suggesting that the line can also mean: "Warm is your heart for those now cold (in death)." *Psychros* is causative in meaning: "causing a cold, thrill of horror." Ism. perceives the fire and ice coexisting in her sister, but for Cr., she will only be ice (see 650).

89. *Hois . . . chrē,* "those I am morally most bound to please." *Chrē* usually has moral overtones since its original meaning was "it is necessary in accordance with the divine, moral law." Interestingly, Cr. uses *chrē* more than An. and the uses reveal his conception of morality: e.g., when he says that An. and Ism. (578) *"must* henceforth be women and not range at large (i.e., with the freedom of free wild beasts)," he probably thinks he is following a moral imperative. It is only at 1099 with his bewildered question: "What must I do?" that he finally questions his moral vision. For the Cho.'s uses of *chrē,* see 1334–35, 1349.

90. *Ei . . . g(e)*, "yes, if you *can*," i.e., if besides having the desire you also have the power (Denniston, p. 304). Both *kai* and *ge* emphasize *dynēsei*.

Amēchanōn erāis, "but you are in love with the impossible." By this phrase Ism. astutely captures the character and primary motivation of An. (Musurillo, p. 43). Critics and translators often miss this (e.g., cf. Kitto's rendering: "it is impossible)." Both *amēchanos* and *erōs* are important theme words. *Amēchanos* means 1) "without means, resources" or "at a loss as to how to act" (79); 2) in reference to things, *amēchanos* means "hard" or "impossible" (as here, 92, 175, 363). The two sisters' differing attitudes toward the impossible are instructive. While the first meaning aptly characterizes the insecure, helpless Ism. (79), An. is challenged by and in love with impossibilities (the second meaning). Cf. Intro., this chap.

Ism.'s choice of the verb for passionate desire, *erāis*, is a fitting culmination for all the *philia* words (cf. 73 n.) associated with the heroine. The association of *erōs* with An. philologically confirms the obvious fact that An.'s *philia* has a passionate aspect in addition to an objective base in family relationship (10 n.). Soph. stretches the meaning of *erōs* in this play somewhat analogously but in a different direction from that of Plato in the *Symposium*. *Erōs* is used properly of sexual desire (the desire itself, not the attainment of the desire). An., motivated by a warmly human *philia*, directs her passions toward impossible dreams. In the *Symposium* Plato, contending that the soul has its desires (206a–c), extends *erōs* to include the desire for the possession of the good. Diotima and An. both put different strains on the word, one toward pregnancy in the soul, the other toward human love in broader than physical terms. The Cho. later sings an ode on *erōs*, depicting it as a moral force (781–800). In addition to *philia* and *erōs*, a third word, *stergein*, "to love," "to feel affection for," "acquiesce," rarely has a sexual meaning. When An. finally rejects Ism. unequivocally, she declares: "I have no affection (*ou stergō*) for one who loves (*philousan*) only with words" (543). Cr.'s one use of the word exposes the servile even beast-to-master kind of affection he expects: "some citizens have been grumbling," he complains, "shaking their heads instead of properly *shouldering the yoke*, the one way of showing love for me" (*hōs stergein eme*, 292). See also 741 n. Cf. Anouilh's An.'s assault against the king: "What a king you could be if only men were animals!"

91. The force of *oukoun* is to reject Ism.'s comfort with a strong negative. *Hotan . . . sthenō,* "when my strength shall fail." The subjunctive with "an" is used in a temporal clause in future time.

Pepausomai, "I shall make an end." An. uses the rare future perfect in a middle rather than passive sense; the middle voice conveys the fact that she is in control, whereas the passive would indicate forced cessation. The line contains a veiled threat of suicide.

92. Ism. again describes An. in terms of *amēchana* (90). By saying An. "hunts after impossibilities," Ism. assigns to her sister a key image, hunting (see 344–45), and a key theme, the accomplishing of impossible feats (see 364) of Man in the Ode on Man. See Intro., this chap. At *Oedipus Tyrannos* 542 and *Electra* 1054, Oedipus and Electra each criticize others for hunting after tyranny and vanity respectively, but the characterizations are ironically applicable to themselves.

93. "If you shall speak then, you will be hated by me." An. uses what grammarians call an emotional future condition, i.e., *ei* and the future indicative instead of the more usual *ean* and subjunctive. Thus, the protasis suggests something unwanted and the conclusion conveys a threat and a final appeal to Ism.

94. *Prokeisei,* "you will be brought into a relationship with." Soph.'s choice of a compound of An.'s word, *keisomai,* "I shall lie with" my brother (73), my family (76), elucidates the contrast between the sisters' relationship with the family. By her act, Ism. will achieve a relationship of an outsider, an *echthros,* and will no longer be a member of the family, a *philos.*

95. *Me kai tēn ex emou dysboulián,* i.e., "me and the folly for which I am responsible." By joining herself to her folly in a bold zeugma, she accepts folly as her coworker replacing Ism. The phrase expresses the symbiotic relationship between An. and apparent folly, and it is in sharp contrast to the later relationship between Cr. and misery (see 1310 n.). An.'s despair and indomitable hope are both present in the personification. Cf. Soph.'s *Electra* 1311: "A long-standing hatred has solidified (like a metal) inside my soul." *Dysboulia,* "folly," is the failure to act with *euboulia,* and it recurs at

1269 (see n. on 1345). Tiresias later tells Cr. that *euboulia*, which may be translated as the art of reaching sound decisions, is mankind's greatest possession (1050; also 1098). An. appears thoughtless and foolish (see *mōros*, 469–70 n.), but she is instinctively certain that her *dysboulia* is really *euboulia*, a view that no one else except Hae. shares for two-thirds of the action. For Cr.'s view of *euboulia*, see 648 n.

96. *Pathein to deinon touto*, "to endure this dreadful wonderful fate." See the extended note on *deinos* at 332, and see 915 where she calls her burial of Polynices *deina tolmān;* i.e., a terrible daring in Cr.'s eyes, a wonderful act in her own. An., like Oedipus in the *Oedipus Tyrannos* is a *deinos anthrōpos*, both actively and passively: she dares wonderfully and terribly, and she suffers the terrible-wonderful will of the gods. In the later play, the poet emphasizes the supernatural element in the word more than he does in the *An.*

Peisomai, "I shall suffer." Earlier (67), Ism. spoke the same word in the same position in the line, but with the meaning "I shall obey." Soph. avails himself of the coincidence that the fut. of two different verbs, *paschein* "to suffer" and *peithein* "to obey," happens to have the same form.

96–97. An. is vehement in her accumulation of negatives here: lit., "I shall suffer nothing so great as to prevent me from dying gloriously." *Kalōs thanein*, "to die gloriously," echoes Ajax's statement (*Ajax* 479–80): the noble man (*ton eugenē*) must live nobly (*kalōs dzēn*) or die nobly (*ē kalōs tethnēkenai*), a conviction that is basic to Sophoclean heroism (Knox): cf. *Electra* 989, 1082.

98. *Anous*, i.e., without *nous*, "understanding." Ism. developed her idea of good sense (49–68 [cf. Cr.'s at 176]) and now concludes that her sister lacks it. Critics note the preponderance of the intellectual vocabulary like *phronēsis, nous, euboulia, phrēn* throughout this play (see Long, pp. 49–54). Since the Greeks of this period did not distinguish the intellect from the moral or volitional faculties, Soph. consistently uses intellectual words to describe moral attitudes (see Dodds, *The Greeks and the Irrational*, pp. 16–17). Ism.'s heart approves what her judgment (and/or weakness) condemns. This prepares for her later action 536 ff.

GRAMMATICAL NOTES

1. κοινὸν αὐτάδελφον . . . κάρα, κοινός, αὐτάδελφος: noun of address; Ἰσμήνης, Ἰσμήνη: gen. sing.

2. οἶσθ(α), οἶδα: perf. = pres., 2 sing.; ὅ τι, ὅστις: nom. sing. neut. (ἐστί ["is"] understood); τῶν . . . κακῶν, κακός: gen. pl. neut.

3. ὁποῖον, ὁποῖος: acc. sing. neut.; νῷν . . . ζώσαιν, ἐγώ, ζάω (pres. partic. fem.): gen. dual; τελεῖ, τελέω: pres. or fut. 3 sing.

4. οὐδέν . . . ἀλγεινόν, οὐδείς, ἀλγεινός: nom. sing. neut.; ἄτης, ἄτη: gen. sing.

5. αἰσχρόν . . . ἄτιμον . . . ὁποῖον, αἰσχρός, ἄτιμος, ὁποῖος: nom. sing. neut.; ἐστ(ί), εἰμί: pres. 3 sing.

6. σῶν . . . (ἐ)μῶν . . . κακῶν, σός, ἐμός, κακός: gen. pl. neut. (partit. gen. as supplementary predicate); ὄπωπ(α), ὁράω: poetic perf. 1 sing.

7. τί, τίς: acc. sing. neut.; τοῦτο, οὗτος: acc. sing. neut.; φασι, φημί: pres. 3 pl.; πανδήμῳ πόλει, πανδῆμος, πόλις: dat. sing.

8. θεῖναι, τίθημι: aor. act. inf.; στρατηγόν, στρατηγός: acc. sing., subject of inf. θεῖναι.

9. ἔχεις, ἔχω: pres. 2 sing.; εἰσήκουσας, εἰσακούω: aor. 2 sing.; σε, σύ: acc. sing.; λανθάνει, λανθάνω: pres. 3 sing.

10. φίλους, φίλος: acc. pl.; στείχοντα, στείχω: pres. partic. acc. pl. neut.; ἐχθρῶν, ἐχθρός: gen. pl.; κακά, κακός: acc. pl. neut.

11. ἐμοί, ἐγώ: dat. sing.; φίλων, φίλος: gen. pl.

12. ἵκετ(ο), ἱκνέομαι: 2 aor. 3 sing.; ὅτου, ὅστις: gen. sing.

13. δυοῖν ἀδελφοῖν . . . θανόντοιν, δύο, ἀδελφός, θνήσκω: (aor. partic.): gen. dual; ἐστερήθημεν, στερέω: aor. pass. 1 pl.

14. μιᾶ . . . ἡμέρᾳ, εἷς, ἡμέρα: dat. sing.; διπλῆ χερί, διπλόος, χείρ: dat. sing.

16. νυκτί, νύξ: dat. sing.; οὐδέν, οὐδείς: acc. sing. neut.

17. εὐτυχοῦσα, εὐτυχέω: pres. partic. nom. sing. f.; ἀτωμένη, ἀτάω: pres. pass. partic. nom. sing. f.

18. ἤδη, οἶδα: pluperf. (= impf.) 1 sing.; σ(ε), σύ: acc. sing.; αὐλείων πυλῶν, αὔλειος, πυλή: gen. pl.

19. τοῦδ(ε), ὅδε: gen. sing.; ἐξέπεμπον, ἐκπέμπω: impf. 1 sing., impf. used because she is thinking of her motive in summoning her sister; μόνη, μόνος: nom. sing. f.; κλύοις, κλύω: pres. opt. 2 sing.

20. δηλοῖς, δηλόω: pres. 2 sing.; καλχαίνουσ(α), καλχαίνω: pres. partic. nom. sing. f.

21. τάφου, τάφος: gen. sing.; νῷν, ἐγώ: gen. dual; τώ κασιγνήτω, ὁ κασίγνητος: acc. dual, partit. in apposition with τὸν μέν . . . τὸν δέ

22. προτίσας, ἀτιμάσας, προτίω, ἀτιμάζω: aor. partic.; ἔχει, ἔχω: pres. 3 sing. (ἀτιμάσας ἔχει = perf. tense).

23. Ἐτεοκλέα, Ἐτεοκλῆς: acc. sing.; λέγουσι, λέγω: pres. 3 pl.; δίκη . . . δικαίᾳ, δίκη, δίκαιος: dat. sing.

24. χρησθείς, χράομαι: aor. pass. partic. (but = aor. mid.); νόμῳ, νόμος: dat. sing.; χθονός, χθών: gen. sing.

25. ἔκρυψε, κρύπτω: aor. 3 sing.; ἔντιμον, ἔντιμος: acc. sing. m.; τοῖς . . . νεκροῖς, ὁ νεκρός: dat. pl.

26. τὸν . . . θανόντα, θνῃσκω: 2 aor. partic. acc. sing. m.; Πολυνείκους, Πολυνείκης: gen. sing.; νέκυν, νέκυς: acc. sing.

27. ἀστοῖσι = ἀστοῖς, ἀστός: dat. pl.; φασι(ν), φημί: pres. 3 pl.; ἐκκεκηρῦχθαι, ἐκκηρύσσω: perf. pass. inf.

28. τάφῳ, τάφος: dat. sing.; τὸ . . . καλύψαι . . . κωκῦσαι, καλύπτω, κωκύω: aor. act. inf.; τινα, τις: acc. sing. m.

29. ἐᾶν, ἐάω: pres. inf.; ἄκλαυτον, ἄταφον, ἄκλαυτος, ἄταφος: acc. sing. m.; οἰωνοῖς, οἰωνός: dat. pl.; γλυκὺν θησαυρόν, γλυκὺς θησαυρός: acc. sing.

30. εἰσορῶσι, εἰσοράω: partic. dat. pl. modif. οἰωνοῖς; χάριν, χάρις: acc. sing.; βορᾶς, βορά: gen. sing.; πρὸς χάριν βορᾶς = "to feast on at their pleasure."

31. τοιαῦτα, τοιοῦτος: acc. pl. neut.; φασι, φημί: pres. 3 pl.; ἀγαθὸν Κρέοντα, ἀγαθὸς Κρέων: acc. sing.; σοί . . . ἐμοί, σύ, ἐγώ: dat. sing.

32. (ἐ)μέ, ἐγώ: acc. sing.; κηρύξαντ(α), κηρύσσω: aor. partic. acc. sing. m.; ἔχειν, ἔχω: pres. inf. (κηρύξαντα ἔχειν = perf. inf.).

33. νεῖσθαι, νέομαι: pres. inf.; τοῖσι (= τοῖς) . . . εἰδόσιν, οἶδα: perf. partic. dat. pl.

34. προκηρύξοντα, προκηρύσσω: fut. partic. used to express purpose; ἄγειν, ἄγω: pres. inf.

35. οὐδέν, οὐδείς: acc. sing. neut.; τούτων, οὗτος: gen. pl. neut., partit. gen. with τι; δρᾷ, δράω: pres. subj. 3 sing.

36. φόνον . . . δημόλευστον, φόνος, δημόλευστος: acc. sing.; προκεῖσθαι, πρόκειμαι: pres. inf.; πόλει, πόλις: dat. sing.

37. σοι, σύ: dat. sing.; ταῦτα, οὗτος: nom. pl. neut.; δείξεις,

δείκνυμι: fut. 2 sing.

38. πέφυκας, φύω: perf. 2 sing.; ἐσθλῶν, ἐσθλός: gen. pl.; κακή, κακός: nom. sing. f.

39. τάδ(ε), ὅδε: nom. pl. neut.; τούτοις, οὗτος: dat. pl. neut.

40. λύουσ(α) . . . ἅπτουσα, λύω, ἅπτω: pres. partic. nom. sing. f.; προσθείμην, προστίθημι: aor. mid. opt. 1 sing.

41. ξυμπονήσεις . . . ξυνεργάσῃ (ξυμ, ξυν = συμ, συν), συμπονέω, συνεργάζομαι: fut. 2 sing.; σκόπει, σκοπέω: imper. 2 sing.

42. ποῖον, ποῖος: acc. sing. neut., cognate acc. with verbs in 41; γνώμης, γνώμη: gen. sing.; εἰ, εἰμί: pres. 2 sing.

43. νεκρόν, νεκρός: acc. sing.; ξύν = σύν; τῇδε . . . χερί, ὅδε, χείρ: dat. sing. (she lifts her hand as she says this); κουφιεῖς, κουφίζω: fut. 2 sing.

44. νοεῖς, νοέω: pres. 2 sing.; σφ(ε), σφεῖς: acc. sing.; ἀπόρρητον, ἀπόρρητος: acc. sing. neut. in apposition to the action of burial.

45. ἐμὸν . . . σὸν . . . ἀδελφόν, ἐμός, σός, ἀδελφός: acc. sing.; ἢν = ἐάν; θέλῃς, (ἐ)θέλω: pres. subj. 2 sing.

46. προδοῦσ(α), προδίδωμι: 2 aor. partic. nom. sing. f.; ἁλώσομαι, ἁλίσκομαι: fut. 1 sing.

47. Κρέοντος ἀντειρηκότος, Κρέων, ἀντείρω: noun and perf. partic., gen. sing. in gen. absolute

48. αὐτῷ, αὐτός: dat. sing. m.; τῶν ἐμῶν, ὁ, ἐμός: gen. pl. partit. gen. with οὐδὲν μέτα and dependent on εἴργειν; εἴργειν = ἔργειν, εἴργω or ἔργω: pres. inf.; μέτα = μέτεστι.

49. φρόνησον, φρονέω: aor. imper. 2 sing.

50. νῷν, ἐγώ: dat. dual (ethical dat.); ἀπώλετο, ἀπόλλυμι: 2 aor. mid. 3 sing.

51. αὐτοφώρων ἀμπλακημάτων, αὐτόφωρος, ἀμπλάκημα: gen. pl.; διπλᾶς ὄψεις, διπλόος, ὄψις: acc. pl.

52. ἀράξας, ἀράσσω: aor. partic.; αὐτουργῷ χερί, αὐτουργός, χείρ: dat. sing.

53. διπλοῦν ἔπος, διπλόος, ἔπος: nom. sing.

54. πλεκταῖσιν ἀρτάναισι = πλεκταῖς ἀρτάναις, πλεκτός, ἀρτάνη: dat. pl.; λωβᾶται, λωβάομαι: pres. 3 sing.; βίον, βίος: acc. sing.

55. ἀδελφώ, ἀδελφός: nom. dual; μίαν . . . ἡμέραν, εἷς, ἡμέρα: acc. sing.

56. αὐτοκτονοῦντε, αὐτοκτονέω: pres. partic. nom. dual; ταλαιπώρω, ταλαίπωρος: nom. dual; μόρον κοινόν, μόρος κοινός: acc. sing.

57. κατειργάσαντ(ο), κατεργάζομαι: aor. 3 pl. with a dual subject as often; ἀλλήλοιν χεροῖν, ἀλλήλων, χείρ: dat. dual

58. μόνα . . . νὼ λελειμμένα, μόνος, ἐγώ, λείπω (perf. pass. partic.): acc. dual; σκόπει, σκοπέω: pres. imper. 2 sing.

59. ὅσῳ, ὅσος: dat. sing.; ὀλούμεθ(α), ὄλλυμι: fut. mid. 1 pl.; νόμου, νόμος: gen. sing.; βίᾳ, βία: dat. sing.

60. ψῆφον, ψῆφος: acc. sing.; τυράννων, τύραννος: gen. pl. (generalizing plural); κράτη, κράτος: acc. pl.; παρέξιμεν, παρέξειμι: pres. 1 pl.

61. ἐννοεῖν, ἐννοέω: pres. inf.; γυναῖχε, γυνή: nom. dual

62. ἔφυμεν, φύω: 2 aor. 1 pl.; ἄνδρας, ἀνήρ: acc. pl.; μαχουμένα, μάχομαι: fut. partic. nom. dual

63. ἀρχόμεσθα = ἀρχόμεθα, ἄρχω: pres. 1 pl.; κρεισσόνων = κρειττόνων, ἀγαθός: comparat. gen. pl.

64. ἀκούειν, ἀκούω: pres. inf.; τῶνδ(ε), ὅδε: gen. pl. neut.; ἀλγίονα, ἀλγεινός: comparat. acc. sing.

65. αἰτοῦσα, αἰτέω: pres. partic.; χθονός, χθών: gen. sing.

66. ξύγγνοιαν, σύγγνοια: acc. sing.; ἴσχειν, ἴσχω: pres. inf.; βιάζομαι, βιάζω: pres. pass. 1 sing., with cognate acc.; τάδε, ὅδε: acc. pl. neut., cognate

67. τέλει, τέλος: dat. sing.; τοῖς . . . βεβῶσι, βαίνω: perf. partic. dat. pl.; πείσομαι, πείθω: fut. mid. 1 sing.

68. περισσά, περισσός: acc. pl. neut.; τὸ . . . πράσσειν = πράττειν, πράσσω: pres. inf. as noun with τό; νοῦν οὐδένα, νοῦς, οὐδείς: acc. sing. m.

69. κελεύσαιμ(ι), κελεύω: aor. opt. 1 sing.; θέλοις, ἐθέλω: pres. opt. 2 sing.

70. πράσσειν = πράττειν, πράσσω: pres. inf.; δρῴης, δράω: pres. opt. 2 sing.

71. ἴσθι, εἰμί: imper. 2 sing.; ὁποία, ὁποῖος: nom. sing. f. = such as; δοκεῖ, δοκέω: pres. 3 sing.; κεῖνον, (ἐ)κεῖνος: acc. sing. m.

72. θάψω, θάπτω: fut. 1 sing.; μοι . . . ποιούσῃ, ἐγώ, ποιέω: pres. partic. dat. sing.; θανεῖν, θνήσκω: aor. inf.

73. φίλη, φίλος: nom. sing. f.; αὐτοῦ, αὐτός: gen. sing. m.; κείσομαι, κεῖμαι: fut. 1 sing.; same form in line 76 in the same position

28

Prologue

74. ὅσια, ὅσιος: acc. pl. neut.; πανουργήσασ(α), πανουργέω: aor. partic. nom. sing. f.

75. ὅν, ὅς: acc. sing.

76. δοκεῖ, δοκέω: pres. 3 sing.

77. θεῶν, θεός: gen. pl.; τὰ . . . ἔντιμ(α), ὁ, ἔντιμος: acc. pl. neut.; ἀτιμάσασ(α), ἀτιμάζω: aor. partic. acc. pl. neut.; ἔχε, ἔχω: imper. 2 sing. (with ἀτιμάσασ [α] = perf. imper., denoting a continuing state).

78. ἄτιμα, ἄτιμος: acc. pl. neut.; ποιοῦμαι, ποιέω: pres. mid. 1 sing.

79. βίᾳ, βία: dat. sing.; πολιτῶν, πολίτης: gen. pl.; τὸ . . . δρᾶν, δράω: pres. inf.; ἔφυν, φύω: 2 aor. 1 sing.

80. τάδ(ε), ὅδε: acc. pl. neut.; προύχοι(ο), προέχω: pres. opt. mid. 2 sing.

81. χώσουσ(α), χόω: fut. partic. nom. sing. f. expressing purpose; ἀδελφῷ φιλτάτῳ, ἀδελφός, φίλος (irreg. superl.): dat. sing.; πορεύσομαι, πορεύομαι: fut. 1 sing.

82. ταλαίνης . . . σου, τάλας σύ: gen. sing. f.; ὑπερδέδοικα, ὑπερδείδω: perf. 1 sing.

83. προτάρβει . . . ἐξόρθου, προταρβέω, ἐξορθόω: imper. 2 sing.; σὸν πότμον, σός, πότμος: acc. sing.

84. προμηνύσῃς, προμηνύω: aor. subj. (= imper.) 2 sing.; μηδενί, μηδείς: dat. sing.

85. κεῦθε . . . καταύδα, κεύθω, καταυδάω: imper. 2 sing.

86. ἐχθίων, ἐχθρός (irreg. comparat.): nom. sing.; ἔσῃ, εἰμί: fut. 2 sing.

87. σιγῶσ(α), σιγάω: pres. partic. nom. sing. f.; κηρύξῃς, κηρύσσω: aor. subj. 2 sing.; τάδε, ὅδε: acc. pl. neut.

88. θερμὴν . . . καρδίαν, θερμός, καρδία: acc. sing.; ψυχροῖσι = ψυχροῖς, ψυχρός: dat. pl. neut.; ἔχεις, ἔχω: pres. 2 sing.

89. ἀρέσκουσ(α), ἀρέσκω: pres. partic. nom. sing. f.; οἷς, ὅς: dat. pl. (for sing.); ἁδεῖν, ἁνδάνω: aor. inf.

90. δυνήσῃ, δύναμαι: fut. 2 sing.; ἀμηχάνων, ἀμήχανος: gen. pl.; ἐρᾷς, ἐράω: pres. 2 sing.

91. σθένω: pres. subj. 1 sing.; πεπαύσομαι, παύω: fut. perf. (a little stronger than the simple fut.); θηρᾶν, θηράω: pres. inf.; ἀμήχανα, ἀμήχανος: neut. acc. pl.

93. λέξεις, λέγω: fut. 2 sing.; ἐχθαρῇ, ἐχθαίρω: fut. mid. (used passively) 2 sing.

94. ἐχθρά, ἐχθρός: nom. sing. f.; τῷ θανόντι, θνῄσκω: aor. partic.

dat. sing. m.; προσκείσῃ, πρόσκειμαι: fut. 2 sing.; δίκῃ, δίκη: dat. sing.

95. ἔα, ἐάω: pres. imper. 2 sing.; τήν . . . δυσβουλίαν, δυσβουλία: acc. sing.

96. παθεῖν, πάσχω: aor. inf.; πείσομαι, πάσχω: fut. 1 sing.

97. τοσοῦτον οὐδέν, τοσοῦτος, οὐδείς: acc. sing. neut.; θανεῖν, θνῄσκω: aor. inf.; μὴ οὐ is regular after a neg. main clause of prevention.

98. δοκεῖ, δοκέω: pres. 3 sing.; στεῖχε, στείχω: pres. imper. 2 sing.; ἴσθι, οἶδα: pres. imper. 2 sing.

99. ἔρχῃ, ἔρχομαι: pres. 2 sing.; φίλοις, φίλος: dat. pl.; φίλη, φίλος: nom. sing. f.

2

Creon's First Speech and the

Reply of the Chorus

[161 – 214]

INTRODUCTION

AFTER THE IRONICALLY joyful entrance of the Cho. singing and
dancing their hymn to Dionysos celebrating the king's victory over
the seven Argive invaders and especially over the dead traitor
Polynices, the king enters to give his inaugural address to the elders.
The audience immediately perceives that his priorities differ from
those of his niece: the *polis* and not *philia* is his guiding principle.
Still, in one important respect, there seems to be a family resemblance: he, like she, radiates self-confidence or perhaps arrogance.
It is difficult at first to determine which of the two qualities it
is.

We shall note here some of the ways Cr.'s style reveals the
man in this first speech and shall try to ascertain how the Athenian
audience would react to his stated principles.

There is one significant stylistic linkage between uncle and niece
and that is in their mutual penchant for the first person pronoun.
After the bond between the sisters is rent midway through the
Prologue, An. discards the duals and speaks with a predominating
egō. The style is highly irregular for a woman, let alone so young

a girl, and it gives the appearance of arrogance. The king's initial statement, on the other hand, displays appropriate piety: *theoi,* the gods, are the first subject (162). But they are only the grammatical subject, one soon realizes: the real subject is *egō* (164) and remains so throughout. Since the king's professed purpose is to lay down general norms for his rule, this emphasis on the first person requires some manipulation. He consistently manipulates the language so as to stress the fact that the remarks are his and to subordinate the fact that they are principles worthy of consideration (191, 207–10). This manipulation verges on the blasphemous at one point (184) when the grammatical structure of the sentence subordinates Zeus to him. The focus thus split between the king's principle and his ego results in a somewhat confused presentation of his rules of conduct. Yet, the initial confusion seems understandable in a new king anxious to establish his authority. The sustained pontifical tone, however, is inclined to remind the thoughtful listener of An.'s earlier insinuation about the king's autocratic bent (8).

In other respects, Cr.'s style differs sharply from that of his niece. The "long rolling sentences, the weighty rhythms, the grandiloquent use of plurals show power conscious of itself." [1] But there are other revealing aspects of his style: his addiction to sententious statements of principle, valid enough in themselves, but rigidly, even ruthlessly applied to the case of his nephew; and his pompous generalities (178, 182, 209) that put him on a level with the platitudinous guard in the next scene.[2] Such a presentation may initially dazzle the Cho. and impress the audience, but the thoughtful listener gradually perceives that the king is attempting to cover up the basic insecurities of "a weak man, used to taking second place in Thebes." [3]

His main means of concealing this insecurity is the image he projects of himself as the helmsman straightening and redirecting the ship of state. He has personally steadied the storm-tossed ship and can contain any future tempests by his straight sailing. His use of the nautical metaphor is the first sustained figure in the play and it is clear that his goal is straight and upright navigation of the state (163–90), a goal that he intends to achieve at any cost (666–67). An., we begin to realize, knew her uncle quite well when she advised Ism. to proceed on her course and keep her ship straight (83). Such counsel in effect consigned the girl to Cr.'s ship.

Although the ship of state is Cr.'s favorite figure[4] and straight sailing his goal (see "Vocabulary," chap. 8, under *orthos* and related words), the figure has a much more pregnant usage in the play as a whole. In the musings of the Cho., the sea is a constant symbol both of man's resourcefulness and of the limits of that resourcefulness (360 n.). Man's daring makes him victorious over the sea (334 ff.), but the swelling sea driven by the Thracian winds creates chaos, churning up the dark mud from the ocean floor, engulfing innocent and guilty alike (586–92). Such is the destructive power of *atē*, "disaster," as the Cho. reminds us in the foreboding rhythms of the second stasimon.[5] In addition, the youthful Hae. and the aged seer Tiresias both try in vain to warn the king that his narrow conception of navigation will be fatal: only the flexible pilot will survive (710–18; cf. 994). In the unifying image at the end of the play, the king finally cries out: "Oh, inexorable harbor of Hades, why, oh why, have you destroyed me now?" (1284–85 and n.). In the light of that final goal, the terrible irony of Cr.'s aphorism in this speech is fully revealed: "One cannot fully know the nature, spirit, and judgment of a man until he proves himself in the administration of the laws" (175–77). It is only in the light of that final goal that one perceives just how superficial the similarities between uncle and niece were: her apparent arrogance in the Prologue masks a deep conviction that her cause is just; his self confidence rests only on the tenuous strength of his power (see 348 n.).

So much for the style of the man. What about the substance of his argument? How would the Athenian audience react to Cr.'s *nomos,* his law and guiding principle, that the straight sailing of the *polis* transcends all personal consideration (178 ff.)? It was, of course, a commonplace of Athenian political thought that friendship and family love can only exist in a healthy *polis.* Indeed, Cr.'s words here find an echo in Thucydides' account of Pericles' famous Funeral Oration (Thucydides 2. 60); and the king in Euripides' *Medea* (written a decade later) almost agrees with Cr.—but with one important reservation: his children mean more to him than the state (*Medea* 329). We know, too, that Demosthenes, a century later, found this whole speech exemplary of proper official conduct since he quoted it as a corrective against Aeschines.[6]

Thus the king's principle seems theoretically sound. It is in his rigid application of the theory to the stinking corpse of his nephew that the playwright leads the audience to question the regal position. The Athenians admired the flexibility of Pericles' political performance. Cr.'s rigidity and brutality foreshadow the tactics of Pericles' successor Cleon who "had a vulgar mind, acute in a second-rate manner, without intelligence or humanity. . . . It was not his policy that was dangerous . . . it was his character. . . . In such hands any policy would go wrong."[7] A few facts from Athenian political history, its burial customs, and the poet's earlier play, the *Ajax,* will shed light on the judgment Soph. was leading the audience to make.

First of all, Soph. and his audience were breathing the clear air of free Athens at the pinnacle of her civilization after their older brothers had died at Marathon to defend the freedom of the individual against the tyranny of the invading forces of the Persian despot. At this brief moment in Athenian history, there was a dialectical tension between individual and community, with the scale tipping toward the individual. Although Pericles was to urge the Athenians to have a love affair with their city (Thucydides 2. 43. 1) and although this love demanded great sacrifice, the very basis of the love affair was the respect for the rights of the individual. Such was not the case in contemporary Sparta where Cr.'s principles and actions would have parallels in political practice.[8] Perhaps only at Athens and only during the Periclean age could the *An.* have been written. The legend that Soph. died rehearsing the *An.*[9] may, if true, reflect his tragic realization that the creative tension between *polis* and person had already gone slack in the forty intervening years.

Soph.'s own concern for the individual's religious and human right of burial was not new in 442 or 441 when he wrote this play. In the last scene of his earlier *Ajax,* Odysseus, bitter enemy of the dead Ajax, eloquently rejects the decision of the sceptered Atreidae to expose Ajax's body as "food for the sea-birds." His rebuttal to their decision has long been recognized as the best commentary on the central act of the *An.* anywhere in the Sopho-

34

clean corpus: "Do not let your violent hatred blind you to trample justice under foot. He was my most bitter enemy . . . yet you would be unjust if you dishonor him. For you would not wrong him but the laws of the gods (*tous theōn nomous*)."

The concern of Odysseus here (*Ajax* 1332 ff.) and the concern that the poet makes the audience feel throughout the *An.* is not the corpse's legal rights so much as outrage at the degrading, inhumane treatment of the dead (see 29–30, 199–206, 410–12, 697–98, 1016–22, 1039–44, 1080–83, 1198). So, although Cr., the king, had responsibilities different from those of Cr., the nearest male relative to the deceased, this first speech reveals Cr. the king impervious to the duties of Cr. the kinsman. The king's conscious repetition of the idea of "common blood," twice in a few lines (198–201) points to a fundamental irony in his position: he is both aware of Polynices' neglect of his kin and is blindly repeating Polynices' pattern. This insensitivity to human concerns, especially to blood concerns, culminates in the episode with his son whose very name denotes "Blood" (see 658 n.). But in this first speech the rejection of blood-rights is only implied. The audience would see a rigidity out of step with the concern for burial that impelled the Athenians at Marathon to bury the Persian enemy (Pausanias I. 32. 5); and they would not, to our knowledge, recall any Athenian precedent for such defamation of the traitor's corpse (the closest parallel in Hellenic records is denial of burial within Attica, in Xenophon *Hellenica* I. 7. 22).

Still, the only sign of disapproval the Cho. registers is contained in the tiny particles *pou ge,* "I suppose." With these monosyllables, they hesitantly suggest their reluctance, while acknowledging the king's *power* (*kratos*) to carry out his ruthless decree: "It is within your *power,* I suppose (*pou ge*), to legislate for us all, both living and dead" (213–14). The timid Cho. lacks the courage to say more. The untranslatable *ge* by throwing the emphasis on the word "power" is their pathetic suggestion that power does not make it right.

Thus An.'s passion and rigid adherence to her beliefs in the Prologue is followed by the authoritative address of the new king with its own principles rigidly and sententiously presented. Soon the two antagonists will meet in heated confrontation (441 ff.).

162. Calder ("Sophokles' Political Tragedy," p. 393), argues that Cr. rushes down the parodos on the spectator's left, dressed in full military armor since he is just returning from the battlefield. It seems more likely that he enters in regal attire from the central palace doors. He addresses the fifteen-member Cho. of Theban elders who constitute his council. Dramatic convention requires that the Cho. be inactive. Like most Sophoclean choruses, this one is imperceptive and cautious. But unlike most others, its members are not of the same sex as the hero of the play (cf. *Oedipus Tyrannos* or *Electra*). The difference in both age and sex between An. and the Cho. will accentuate her isolation.

Ta men dē poleos, "as for the state." This form of expression shows that the welfare of the state is the real subject of Cr.'s thought even though *theoi,* "the gods," is the grammatical subject of the sentence. The dramatic irony throughout this speech anticipates the poet's mastery of that technique in Oedipus' speeches, e.g., at *Oedipus Tyrannos* 216–75.

163–64. *Polloi . . . palin.* Cr. introduces the first sustained image in the play (167–68, 178, 189–90), that of the ship of state. See Intro., this chap. The sibilants suggest the stormy sea through which the ship has just passed.

167. *Orthou,* "was keeping upright." The nautical image, used in 163 for his own rule and here for that of Oedipus, implies continuity between the halcyon days of Oedipus' early rule (*Oedipus Tyrannos* 31–39) and Cr.'s reign. Also, since Eteocles used the ship image for his rule (Aeschylus *Seven against Thebes* 1–3, 208 ff.), a triple continuity may be suggested. See 660 n. for the prime value that Cr. attached to straightness and orderliness as virtues. Later (1206), there is grim irony in Soph.'s choice of *orthios,* "straight up" or "shrill," to describe the lament that greets Cr. as he enters An.'s tomb (1206).

167–73. Cr. refers to the Cho.'s loyalty first to Laios' son, i.e., Oedipus, and then to Oedipus' sons, Eteocles and Polynices. The thought is compressed and the mode of expression somewhat confused.

170–71. *Pros . . . hēmerān,* "by a double doom on one day."

Again (see 13–14 n.), Soph. uses numbers to express pathetic coincidence.

172. *Syn miasmati,* "with stain," or perhaps less specifically "with defilement" (Goheen, p. 114). *Miasma* is the word for the pollution caused by murder, especially the murder of a relative. The polluted person was thought to infect the whole city unless he is cleansed, banished, or killed. Cr. later contends that An. is diseased (732), but Tiresias is the first to suggest that it is Cr.'s refusal to bury Polynices that has infected the city (1023 ff., 1080–83, and 1284 n.).

174. *Genous kat(a) anchisteia,* "by being nearest of kin." As the closest male relative to the dead brothers, Cr. automatically became king, but this phrase also recalls Cr.'s neglected responsibilities as head of Polynices' household.

175–90. A century later, in a speech attacking Aeschines for his misuse of power, the orator Demosthenes quotes this whole passage with obvious approval (*On the Embassy* 246–47; cf. also his *Third Philippic* 69–70.). However, the orator was praising the speech, not the character of Cr., a fact that is corroborated by Demosthenes' alleged remark when he was about to die: "Now whenever you wish, you may play Creon's role and cast me out unburied" (Plutarch *Demosthenes* 29). Calder ("Political Tragedy," pp. 404–5) has a different assessment. He claims the ancient audience and statesmen like Pericles and Demosthenes would commend Cr. as a good statesman and condemn An. (and Socrates) as revolutionaries.

175–77. The irony of these lines is obvious, since it is precisely in the "wear and tear of practical politics," *archais te kai nomoisin entribēs,* that Cr.'s deficiencies will become apparent. *Entribēs,* lit., "rubbed." The metaphor is of a coin whose real worth will become apparent with wear (Goheen, p. 129, n. 7). Line 177 restates an old Greek proverb attributed to Bias: *Archē andra deixei,* "Rule will prove the man." Cf. Shakespeare's *Julius Caesar* 2. 1. 12.

176. *Psychēn . . . phronēma . . . gnōmēn:* these three words did not in Soph.'s time represent clearly defined, distinct spheres of the personality. The tripling adds a tone of solemnity to his statement by introducing impressive quasi-scientific distinctions. *Phronēma* (see 207) and *gnōmē* (see 640) are important theme words in the play. *Phronēma,* usually a more concrete noun than *to phronein*

or *phronēsis,* is used six times in this play and nowhere else in extant Sophoclean plays; four of the six times it is Cr.'s word, and the Cho. credits him with *phronēsis* until the dénouement. But *to phronein* in its various forms is Soph.'s special word for true perception of the good and noble, the kind of wisdom that enables one to distinguish the real from the apparent truth. Tiresias later tries to lead Cr. to true insight with this word (1023). *Gnōmē,* although sometimes used for "principle," (e.g., Thucydides 1. 140. 1), is usually limited in this play and in the *Oedipus Tyrannos* to the platitudinous and the sophistic; and as such is used by the guard and the messenger as well as Cr. and Hae. See nn. on 95, 354–55, 683–84, 904, 1347 ff.

178–91. In these lines Cr. sets down his rules (191) for distinguishing a good ruler from a bad (178–83)—cf. Plato's *Laws* 9. 856b for a similar outlook—and then he states his general and his particular intention in reference to the two dead brothers (184–91). Thus he lays the groundwork for his edict (192 ff.) by stressing the need to sacrifice personal friendship for the state.

178. *Emoi gar* should logically introduce an explanation of the previous statement but does not. Cr. is feeling his way with the elders, displaying the insecurity of a new king. On the prominence of *emoi,* see 184 n. On Cr.'s tendency to speak in general clauses ("whoever"), see 180 n.

Euthynōn polin, "guiding the city," suggests a continuation of the nautical image although *euthynōn* simply means "making straight" with no inherent implication of a ship's course.

180. *Enklēisās echei,* "has shut" (i.e., permanently): an emphatic use of the perfect tense. Some critics criticize the obscurity of Cr.'s thought here as indicative of Soph.'s early stylistic difficulties, but the confusing obscurity, the tendency to generalize and digress are part of Soph.'s conscious characterization of the insecure king (see Intro., this chap.). Cr.'s style in these respects resembles the ordinary, nonheroic characters, e.g., the guard and the messenger.

181. *Kakistos . . . dokei,* "now seems and has always seemed most base," a rhetorical phrase emphasizing *kakistos.* On the meanings of *kakos,* see 731 n.

183. *Touton,* "this man." Cr. presumes that only a *man* would defy his edict. *Oudamou,* "as nothing," "of no value." His utter

rejection of the rights of *philoi* ends in his own final realization that his own total worth is "nothing" (see 1325 n.).

184. The style in which Cr. casts his thought here characterizes him as presumptuous. He makes the main thought (*istō Zeus*, "let Zeus be my witness") parenthetic and dependent on *egō . . . siōpē-saimi*. This emphasizes *egō*, "I," and subtly relegates Zeus to a secondary role. Thus, Soph. deftly characterizes Cr. as one who unconsciously but really subordinates gods and men to himself. His presumption becomes blasphemous later (1039–44).

184–85. *Horōn aei . . . tēn atēn horōn* "seeing always . . . seeing the ruin." Here Cr. uses another grammatical twist to suggest he is on a level with Zeus. By the double use of the participle, "seeing," once modifying Zeus, once modifying "I," Cr. implies that Zeus and he share vision. It is characteristic of Cr. to base his moral determinations solely on the evidence of the senses. He has no conception of an inner vision, until perhaps 1319. Like Oedipus (e.g., *Oedipus Tyrannos* 371) he uses "seeing" for "knowing," a metaphor that is more important in Greek than in English.

186. Cr. sees madness (*atē*) instead of salvation (*sōteria*) approaching his citizens and sees himself as the "savior of the state." Cr. here, like the "savior" Oedipus (see *Oedipus Tyrannos* 48), finally proves to be the one most totally destroyed by *atē*. This line shows that for Soph. the opposite of *atē* is not health but *sōteria*, security or salvation; and the final dominance of *atē* over *sōteria* is characteristic of Sophoclean tragedy.

187–88. The irony of these lines is impressive because Cr. in effect promises to become his own enemy. The line is suggestive of the kind of irony that underlies the whole structure of *Oedipus Tyrannos*.

189 ff. The fact that Pericles some ten years later expressed the same sentiments with the same nautical metaphor in the Funeral Oration (Thucydides 2. 60. 2–3) suggests that the audience would be familiar with Cr.'s principle that the city is the savior of its citizens and that personal friendship must take second place if it endangers the state's safety. Only later in the play does it become apparent that Cr. does not speak for the state's interests (see 693 and 733–36 and n.).

190. *Poioumetha*. Cr. chooses the word regularly used for adopt-

ing children to suggest the obligation to adopt the city's friends as one's own.

191. *Toioisd(e) egō nomoisi,* "by such principles I" (see 175–77 n.). The emphatic position of "I" need not be presumptuous but his later equation of the laws of the state with his own will suggests a similar implication here.

192. *Adelpha tōnde,* "akin to these (principles)," "in full accord with them." This rare usage of the adjective *adelpha* (brotherly, akin) suggests that Cr. reserves feelings of kinship not for relatives but for his self-proclaimed principles.

194–95. These lines have an epic flavor, portraying in miniature the *aristeia,* or prowess, of Eteocles, the noble patriot. *Aristeusās* (195) and *aristois* (197) show that Cr. defines nobility in terms of military valor. His devotion to the dead is restricted to the brother who shared his own political views. He later derides An. for her unrestricted reverence to Hades (777). Finally, however, he learns one must keep the "established laws" (1113–14), i.e., those of Zeus and of Hades.

196. *Ta pant(a) aphagnisai,* i.e., to perform all the rites connected with proper burial. Jebb may be correct in preferring *ephagnisai* since *aphagnisai* usually implies purification from guilt.

197. *Erchetai katō nekrois,* "come to the dead below." Greeks traditionally poured libations into funeral urns with open bases in the belief that such offerings nourished the deceased.

198. *Xynaimon,* "brother," lit., "of common blood." See 201, 658 and n.

199. *Gēn patroiān kai theous tous engeneis,* "the land of his fathers and the gods of his race," i.e., the gods and ancestors not just of his father's house of Labdakos but those revered by the whole Cadmean people. Butterworth (p. 54) notes that Cr. here and elsewhere thinks of the brothers as sons of their father (see also 193), whereas for An., Polynices is the one born of her mother (466–67). Butterworth sees these differences of outlook as relics of the matrilineal and patrilineal outlook of an earlier age. Perhaps, but An., unlike Cr., is not exclusively "feminine" in mind-set: she invokes the gods "of our fathers" (848) and hopes for reunion with both her father and mother (898 ff.).

199–206. In his description of Polynices' act, Cr. uses emotional, epic vocabulary showing his savage hatred for the traitor. He draws attention to Polynices' "feeding on kindred blood" and his desire to enslave the Theban populace—things that establish Polynices' guilt. See 205–6 n.

201. *Haimatos . . . pasasthai*, "to feed on kindred blood," an epic phrase, and a particularly savage indictment. Cr. uses the word "blood" quite consciously twice in four lines (see *xynaimon*, 198). It is a blood relative he feels constrained to punish because that relative in turn was prepared to drink *his* relatives' blood.

202. *Tous . . . agein*, "to lead the survivors into slavery." This is the culmination of Cr.'s indictment. There is subtle irony in the accusation since Cr.'s metaphors reduce people to slaves and animals (Goheen, pp. 28–35). Cr. treats Polynices' body as if he were a slave-thing (517); Cr. accuses Hae. of being a woman's slave (756). He treats Ism. and An. as less than slaves (531–33), as females not allowed to "range abroad" (579); An. is a horse needing a bridle (477) and a field to be plowed (569); Cr.'s revised sentence against An. (775) provides her with sufficient food (*phorbēs*, lit., "fodder") to sustain animal life. Demeaning remarks about women were commonplace (cf. Aristophanes's *Lysistrata* 260–61 and 678 n.), but Cr.'s obsession with the subject was hardly commonplace. These images recoil on Cr. later when Hae. "wags" a greeting to his father (1214), spits in his father's face like an animal (1231), and when Cr. himself becomes a frightened bird (1308).

203. *Ekkekēryktai*. The impersonal use of the perfect tense conveys the absolute finality of Cr.'s decree.

205–6. Cr. here describes his decree in language quite similar to An.'s earlier (29–30) description. Yet her lines convey pathos and arouse sympathy, whereas Cr. focuses exclusively on the shame attached to the body.

207. *Toiond(e) emon phronēma*, "this is my decision on the matter." On *phronēma* as Cr.'s word, see 176 n., and as a word more descriptive of An.'s thought, see 354–55 n. In the second half of 207, the king begins generalizing again.

208. *Tīmē* can mean worship of the gods (745), intrinsic worth (76–77), rights, honor (5, 25), as well as worth or price in the political and economic senses. Cr.'s economic and political valuation (183 and 208) contrasts with that of An. and Hae.

211–14. Adams, p. 46, reads more enthusiasm into this reply of the choral leader than the text allows when he paraphrases: "Our King, right or wrong; may he always be right, but our king, right or wrong." The words *soi areskei* "please you" (211) and *enesti soi,* "it is in your power" (213), simply acknowledge Cr.'s power, but the mode of expression conveys the Cho.'s timorous disapproval. The *ge* (213) emphasizes *enesti* and together with *pou* communicates their reservation about the intrinsic worth of Cr.'s decree: "You have the power, I suppose." There is a textual difficulty in 213. I follow Jebb, Campbell, and Dain rather than Pearson's restoration of *panti tout'.* The latter reading lessens the tone of disapproval.

214. "Both for the dead and for those of us who are living." The Cho. here accepts Cr.'s contention that he has jurisdiction over the occupants of Hades' realm as well as over the citizens of his *polis.* Cr. consistently ignores Hades' autonomy: e.g., at 282–83 he finds it inconceivable that the gods have concern for Polynices' corpse. See 360 n. and 450–52 n. for An.'s reverence for Hades' rights.

GRAMMATICAL NOTES

162. ἄνδρες, ἀνήρ: noun of address; πόλεος, πόλις: gen. sing.; θεοί, θεός: nom. pl.

163. πολλῷ σάλῳ, πολὺς σάλος: dat. sing.; σείσαντες, σείω: aor. partic. nom. pl. m.; ὤρθωσαν, ὀρθόω: aor. 3 pl.

164. ὑμᾶς, σύ: acc. pl.; πομποῖσιν = πομποῖς, πομπός: dat. pl.; πάντων, πᾶς: gen. pl.

165. ἔστειλ(α), στέλλω: aor. 1 sing.; ἱκέσθαι, ἱκνέομαι: 2 aor. inf.; τοῦτο, οὗτος: acc. sing. neut.; Λαΐου, Λάϊος: gen. sing.

166. σέβοντας, σέβω: partic. acc. pl. m., modif. ὑμᾶς (164) equivalent here to a causal clause, i.e., "since you revered . . ."; similarly μένοντας (169); εἰδώς, οἶδα: perf. partic. (with pres. meaning); θρόνων, θρόνος: gen. pl.; τὰ . . . κράτη, τὸ κράτος: acc. pl.

167. ὤρθου, ὀρθόω: impf. 3 sing.

168. διώλετ(ο), διόλλυμι: 2 aor. mid. 3 sing.

169. τοὺς . . . παῖδας, ὁ παῖς: acc. pl.; μένοντας, μένω: pres. partic. acc. pl. m. (cf. 166); ἐμπέδοις φρονήμασιν, ἔμπεδος, φρόνημα: dat. pl.

170. διπλῆς μοίρας, διπλόος, μοῖρα: gen. sing.; μίαν, εἷς: acc. sing. f.

171. ἡμέραν, ἡμέρα: acc. sing.; ὤλοντο, ὄλλυμι: 2 aor. mid. 3 pl.; παίσαντες, παίω: aor. partic. nom. pl. m.

172. πληγέντες, πλήσσω: aor. pass. partic. nom. pl. m.; αὐτόχειρι . . . μιάσματι, αὐτόχειρ, μίασμα: dat. sing.

173. κράτη . . . πάντα, κράτος, πᾶς: acc. pl.; θρόνους, θρόνος: acc. pl.

174. γένους, γένος: gen. sing.; τῶν ὀλωλότων, ὄλλυμι: 2 perf. partic. gen. pl. m.

175. παντὸς ἀνδρός, πᾶς ἀνήρ: gen. sing.; ἐκμαθεῖν, ἐκμανθάνω: aor. inf.

177. ἀρχαῖς . . . νόμοισιν = νόμοις, ἀρχή, νόμος: dat. pl.; φανῇ, φαίνω: aor. pass. subj. 3 sing.

178. πᾶσαν . . . πόλιν, πᾶς, πόλις: acc. sing.; εὐθύνων, εὐθύνω: pres. partic.

179. ἀρίστων . . . βουλευμάτων, ἄριστος, βούλευμα: gen. pl.; ἅπτεται, ἅπτω: pres. mid. 3 sing.

180. φόβου του, φόβος τις: gen. sing.; ἐγκλήσας, ἐγκλήω: aor. partic. with ἔχει = perf. 3 sing. (cf. 22).

181. κάκιστος, κάκος: superl.; εἶναι, εἰμί: pres. inf.; δοκεῖ, δοκέω: pres. 3 sing.

182. μείζον(α), μέγας: comparat. acc. sing. m.; τῆς πάτρας = πατρίδος, πάτρα = πατρίς: gen. sing.

184. ἴστω, οἶδα: imper. 3 sing.; πάντ(α), πᾶς: acc. pl. neut.; ὁρῶν, ὁράω: pres. partic.

185. σιωπήσαιμι, σιωπάω: aor. opt. 1 sing.

186. στείχουσαν, στείχω: pres. partic. acc. sing. f., modif. ἄτην; ἀστοῖς, ἀστός: dat. pl.; τῆς σωτηρίας, ἡ σωτηρία: gen. sing.

187. φίλον . . . ἄνδρα . . . δυσμενῆ, φίλος ἀνὴρ δυσμενής: acc. sing.; χθονός, χθών: gen. sing.

188. θείμην, τίθημι: 2 aor. opt. mid. 1 sing.; γιγνώσκων, γιγνώσκω: pres. partic.

189. ἥδ(ε), ὅδε: nom. sing. f.; σώζουσα, σώζω: pres. partic. nom. sing. f.; ταύτης . . . ὀρθῆς, οὗτος, ὀρθός: gen. sing. f. with prep. ἐπί.

190. πλέοντες, πλέω: pres. partic. nom. pl. m.; ποιούμεθα, ποιέω: pres. mid. 1 pl.

191. τοιοῖσδ(ε) . . . νόμοισι = νόμοις, τοιόσδε νόμος: dat. pl.;

43

τήνδ(ε) . . . πόλιν, ὅδε, πόλις: acc. sing.; αὔξω = αὐξάνω: pres. 1 sing., used here to imply purpose

192. ἀδελφά, ἀδελφός: acc. pl. neut.; τῶνδε, ὅδε: gen. pl.; κηρύξας, κηρύσσω: aor. partic. with ἔχω = perf. 1 sing. (cf. 22).

193. ἀστοῖσι = ἀστοῖς, ἀστός: dat. pl.; παίδων, παῖς: gen. pl. with prep. πέρι.

194. Ἐτεοκλέα, Ἐτεοκλῆς: acc. sing.; πόλεως . . . τῆσδε, πόλις, ὅδε: gen. sing.; ὑπερμαχῶν, ὑπερμαχέω: pres. partic.

195. ὄλωλε, ὄλλυμι: perf. 3 sing.; ἀριστεύσας, ἀριστεύω: aor. partic.; δορί = δόρατι, δόρυ: dat. sing.

196. κρύψαι . . . ἀφαγνίσαι, κρύπτω, ἀφαγνίζω: aor. inf.

197. ἅ, ὅς: nom. pl. neut.; ἔρχεται, ἔρχομαι: pres. 3 sing.; ἀρίστοις νεκροῖς, ἄριστος: superl. of ἀγαθός, νεκρός: dat. pl.

198. ξύναιμον = σύναιμον, σύναιμος: acc. sing.; τοῦδε, ὅδε: gen. sing.; Πολυνείκη, Πολυνείκης: acc. sing.

199. γῆν πατρῴαν, γῆ, πατρῷος: acc. sing.; θεούς . . . ἐγγενεῖς, θεὸς ἐγγενῆς: acc. pl.

200. κατελθών, κατέρχομαι: aor. partic.; ἠθέλησε, ἐθέλω: aor. 3 sing.; πυρί, πῦρ: dat. sing.

201. πρῆσαι, πίμπρημι: aor. inf.; αἵματος κοινοῦ, αἷμα, κοινός: gen. sing.

202. πάσασθαι, πατέομαι: aor. inf.; δουλώσας, δουλόω: aor. partic.

203. πόλει τῇδ(ε), πόλις, ὅδε: dat. sing.; ἐκκεκήρυκται, ἐκκηρύσσω: perf. pass. 3 sing.

204. κτερίζειν, κτερίζω: pres. inf.; κωκῦσαι, κωκύω: aor. inf.; τινα, τις: acc. sing. m.

205. ἐᾶν, ἐάω: pres. inf.; ἄθαπτον . . . ἐδεστόν, ἄθαπτος, ἐδεστός: acc. sing. m., modif. τοῦτον (203); οἰωνῶν . . . κυνῶν, οἰωνός, κύων: gen. pl.; δέμας . . . αἰκισθέν, αἰκίζω: aor. pass. partic. acc. neut. The phrase is in appos. with "him."

206. ἰδεῖν, ὁράω: aor. inf.

207. τοιόνδ(ε) ἐμόν, τοιόσδε, ἐμός: nom. sing. neut. with emphasis on ἐμόν.

208. τιμῇ, τιμή: dat. sing.; προέξουσ(ι), προέχω: fut. 3 pl.; ἐνδίκων, ἔνδικος: gen. pl.

209. τῇδε . . . πόλει, ὅδε, πόλις: dat. sing.; θανών, θνήσκω: aor. partic.

44

210. ζῶν, ζάω: pres. partic.; τιμήσεται, τιμάω: fut. pass. 3 sing.
211. σοί, σύ: dat. sing.; ἀρέσκει, ἀρέσκω: pres. 3 sing.; ποιεῖν,
ποιέω: pres. inf.
212. δύσνουν, εὐμενῆ, δύσνους εὐμενής: acc. sing. m.; τῇδε . . .
πόλει, ὅδε, πόλις: dat. sing.
213. νόμῳ . . . παντί, νόμος πᾶς: dat. sing.; χρῆσθαι, χράομαι:
pres. inf.
214. τῶν θανόντων, θνήσκω: aor. partic. gen. pl. with πέρι;
ὁπόσοι, ὁπόσος: nom. pl. m.; ζῶμεν, ζάω: pres. 1 pl.

45

3

Ode on Man

[332 – 75]

INTRODUCTION

IT IS AGAINST A BACKGROUND not only of the king's State of the Kingdom address but also of the guard's announcement of the first burial,[1] Cr.'s angry, ill-founded accusations of bribery, and the Cho.'s suggestion of divine complicity in the burial (278, see 1345 n.) that the actors retreat and the Cho. sings the Ode on Man.

The ode hymns the glory of *anthrōpos*, mankind: "Wonders are many, and nothing is more wondrously strange than man" (332–33). Humanity's awesome, violent (see n. on *deinos*, 332) capacity to overcome its natural enemies, the sea, the earth, and the animal kingdom, forms the subject of the first strophe and antistrophe. In the second strophe, the images shift from those of external control to ones expressive of man's self-control, his capacity to create a *polis*, to overcome all obstacles except death. The final antistrophe returns to the negative element implicit in "terrible" (*deinos*) mankind. It can perform all these remarkable feats but there is no assurance that man will act in a morally upright manner (367). Yet the Cho. does hold out hope: if man weaves into the fabric of his life (368–69) two strands, devotion to human law and devotion to the justice of the gods (a phrase roughly equivalent of *agrapta nomima*, 454–55), then he will be *hypsipolis*, high in the city. But

46

cityless (*apolis*) is the man who dwells with the ignoble (370–71).

This ode is a many-faceted gem that will continue to receive fresh interpretation as it has from the time of the Byzantine scholiasts up to Heidegger and MacLeish.[2] There obviously can be no "definitive" interpretation. In the introduction to *Bilingual Selections,* by analyzing certain neglected images and themes, I have argued that critics have missed a "feminine" dimension in the ode.[3] Here I shall argue that the combined "masculine" and "feminine" elements point to An. as the *deinos anthrōpos,* the "wonder of men," and the citizen who is "high in the city." Thus, the poet, as distinct from his Cho. who provide him an ironic persona,[4] may well be criticizing the "Protagorean outlook" of his age and perhaps even the excessive "masculinity" of Periclean Athens.

The optimism of this ode is readily apparent. The Cho. gives poetic voice to the goals of Pericles and to the "Protagorean outlook." I use the phrase to signify the spirit of confidence in man, "the measure of all things," that characterized Athens in the period in which Soph. wrote the *An.* The Sophist Protagoras was in Athens briefly around this time, and this teacher of civic virtue came to be regarded as the champion of the view that man may, if he wishes, acquire the moral virtues necessary for a peaceful productive life in the *polis.*[5] The second strophe in particular expresses this optimism in the word *pantoporos,* "all-resourceful." Man can find a way out of all crises.

But in the midst of this Protagorean optimism, the poet adds a jarring note. *Pantoporos* yes, but *aporos,* without a way out of one crisis, Death. From Hades alone he can devise no escape. So, Protagorean optimism is put in the perspective of Hades. Man's resourcefulness and capacity for citizenship are weighed in the light of *das Jenseits,* that other realm out of which true justice emanates (see 361–62 n.).

In this ode, the Cho. generalizes. It makes no application of its ruminations about man's awesome capacities to either of the antagonists. There was little in Cr.'s angry words at the end of the previous episode to qualify him as the wonder of men; and certainly the soon-to-be-discovered culprit was far from their minds as they sang the glories of "masculine" prowess.[6] But the spectator can particularize by relating the themes and images of the ode to those of the whole play. The themes of wonder and of citizenship will illustrate how the poet uses the Cho. as his ironic persona.

What is the "deinotic" wonder that inspires the Cho. and how does An. exemplify this? *Deinos* is a marvelously ambiguous word (see 332 n.) that defies translation. Perhaps its nearest English equivalent is "terrible" since *deinos* implies an excess that causes awe or fear or both in the onlooker. Like "terrible," its pejorative meanings usually predominate, as when Cr. later admits that further resistance on his part is *deinon* and so is his abdication of authority (1096–97). But the word can also share the pregnant meaning of Yeats's "a terrible beauty is born." Now the initial phrase of the ode, *Polla ta deina*, with its striking reminiscence of the opening lines of Aeschylus' famous choral ode on the violence of the primitive "feminine" instinct,[7] would prepare the audience for the word to be used in its more pejorative sense: "Many things are fearful but nothing is more fearful than mankind." But the Cho.'s development of its idea soon reveals that it is thinking in a more Yeatsian vein.

The first strophic pair with its emphasis on physical prowess and culminating in Cr.'s word, *kratei* (348 n.), is more suggestive of the king's tactics than of An.'s. Man's victory in the first strophe over *theōn . . . tān hypertatān Gān*, "Earth the eldest of the gods," reinforces this suggestion because Mother Earth is that originally supreme goddess of Greek mythology (see 337–38 n.) who came to be identified with the rights of *philia*. Zeus imposed order, *kosmos*, on society when his Olympians stripped her of her former prerogatives. The Cho.'s next line, however, suggests that man's victory over Earth is pyrrhic: he may conquer her, but she remains *aphthiton, akamatān*, "imperishable and unwearied." Is there perhaps a hint that the play's champion of *philia* will in some sense also survive an analagous imposition of authority?

It is only in the second strophe that An.'s resemblance to the *deinos anthropōs* surfaces. The subject here is the talents of man which make life in a communal setting possible: *kai phthegma kai ānemoen phronēma kai astynomous orgās edidaxato*, "and he has taught himself speech and high-soaring thought and the temper required for communal existence." These are the arts in which the rebel girl paradoxically excels. Cr., like An., is concerned with *phronēma*, proper

48

ethical cognition (see 354–55), but only her "wind-swift" or, better, "high-soaring" (*ānemoen*) thought and passion (another meaning of *orgē*, see 355 n.) can help the city regain its moral compass.

Thus, she is the weaver of divine and human law that the final antistrophe hopes for. She shows that human endeavor can rise above the moral ambivalence that so often plagues it. The image of man as weaver is the only dominant image in the ode taken from the "feminine" domestic world. The bold metaphor is the poet's clearest hint that he has his androgynous heroine in mind. An.'s own uses of *deinos*, once in the Prologue (95–96 n.) and once in her last speech (915 n.), confirm the poet's view that she offers a new model for man the subjugator, thinker and weaver. The yokes and bits that equip the *deinos anthrōpos* in the first antistrophe must yield to *philia*. Yokes may have been appropriate for the Homeric hero. But for the hero of the *polis, kratos*, "power," must be tempered by *philia*.[8]

The play's emphasis on citizenship (*polis* and *politēs*, "citizen," occur some forty times in the drama) is reflected in the ode's *hypsipolis, apolis* antithesis. Clearly, by the play's ending, the king is *apolis*, without a city, in every sense of the word (see 370 n.). But no one in the play gives explicit judgment on An.'s citizenship: is she *hypsipolis*, high in the city, or *apolis*, without a city, or both?

The poet's verdict appears to be that the girl who defied the will of the citizens (79) and who insisted that one man's burial mattered more than all the state's power is paradoxically both *hypsipolis* and *apolis* (370 n.): *hypsipolis*, high in the city, because she is faithful to a higher citizenship (see 450–70) and because she is willing to be *apolis* in the first two meanings of the word (i.e., physically without a city and one who is cast out of the city); but she is perhaps also *apolis* in the third sense of the word, i.e., destructive of the city's continued existence. The poet never explicitly says so, but it does seem that the silence of all the characters on the subject of An.'s citizenship reveals his own tragic view: her own superior citizenship leads her to commit an act which, if unchallenged, would destroy positive law which is the warp and woof of the *polis*. Paradoxically, then, her "deinotic" citizenship both destroys her and provides the city with the inspiration to save itself.

Choral Rhythms: A Note

A choral ode such as the *Polla ta Deina* contains an elaborate and intricate interweaving of music, dance rhythms, and sensuous poetry. Our scant knowledge of the accompanying music and dance movements requires that we rely almost exclusively on the rhythms of the verse for insight into the sensuous beauty of the poetry. Each ode is made up of strophes and antistrophes, and the pattern of rhythms, construction, and sense established in the strophe was usually, as here, closely recalled in the corresponding antistrophe (see e.g., 354 and 365). Also, taken together, the first strophe and antistrophe of this ode form a pair that is in marked contrast to the second pair. Again, the second antistrophe, with its fear about man's moral judgment and its retreat into timidity, contradicts the tone of confidence established in the opening lines.

The modern student's difficulty in experiencing the poetry is further complicated in that the metrical system for Soph.'s poetry is altogether different from that basic to modern poetry. The meter is quantitative rather than accentual. Longs and shorts are truly longs and shorts; that is, the rhythm of the poetry is based not on accent or stress but on quantity. Long syllables take longer to say (perhaps like a musical eighth note) and short syllables are pronounced rapidly (perhaps like sixteenth notes). Perhaps at each long syllable the choral members placed their feet on the ground and at each short syllable raised a foot with only a touch of the toes. Takis Mouzenidis, Director of the National Theatre in Athens, accepts this German theory and notes that choral odes thus involve not just rhythmic recitation and song but also "bodily-realized word." [9] A dactyl (-uu), then, would perhaps be sung as an eighth note followed by two sixteenth notes and would perhaps be danced as one step and two touches of the toe.

There is in the play a formal balance called *isonomia* between the episodic, mostly iambic spoken portions and the wide-ranging sung and danced choral odes. Within the iambic discourse there is a balance maintained between An. and Cr.: Cr. dominates by virtue of his physical presence (see Intro., chap. 7), but An. dominates by the intensity of conviction and the fascination of her character. The balance, however, tips toward An. in the three central choral odes of the play: the Ode on Man, the Ode on *Atē* and the Ode on Eros. The glories of humanity, the destruction of the last root of the home of Labdakos and the moral power of Eros, these are the themes that transcend the one-dimensional world of Cr. And in the Ode on Man, with its serene confidence in the truly human, the poet provides what Albert Cook calls "a kind of long-range confidence into which Antigone's defense of the proper law between man and god may find its proper perspective among the awesomeness of man's achievement" (p. 110). Cook further perceives that the choral odes of this play, and especially the Ode on Man, give the audience a veiled and emotional prophecy of the eventual victory of *Dikē*, "justice who dwells with the gods below" (451).

In meter, the choral odes in their varied patterns match the changing emotions: they range in mode from a stern Doric to the impassioned Paeonic; in thought, the lyric is free to transcend the present situation, to explore the universal implications of the accompanying episodes.

This is not the place for a full analysis of the meters of this ode or of the other lyrical passages in the play.[10] Even from observing the metrical pattern of the first strophe, however, one can see the variety of rhythms within a few lines and the relationship between metrical patterns and thought. The glyconic (a combination of a trochee -u or spondee --, a dactyl -uu, another trochee and a final -- is Soph.'s favorite meter, capable of many variations and of subtle effects. The strophe begins with a falling rhythm (i.e., with the long coming first) of two glyconics (*pōl-lă tă deî-nă koū-dĕn ān-thrō-poū deî-nŏ-tĕ-rōn pĕ-leî*) and the central emphasis naturally falls on the repeated longs in *ānthrōpoū deînŏtĕrōn*. The second half of the strophe (377) starts with the rising rhythms of the double iambs (*pĕ-rōn hўp-ōid-mă-sĭn thĕ-ōn*, etc.), pausing on *hў-pēr-tă-tān Gān*, "Earth, the most exalted of gods." Then there is a dramatic shift to rapid, almost Homeric dactyls (-uu) in 339–40; again, the final line shifts back to the heavy *hĭppeīō*, "equine" (similar to *ānthrōpoū* above), and ends in the abrupt syncopated rhythm of the dochmaic, *gĕ-neî pŏ-leū-ōn*, "turning up the soil with his mule." Humanity and its wondrous victory over the earth is given sensuous expression by the song and dance. The emphatic pause on the exalted Earth, however, establishes a contrapuntal suggestion that deepens in the second half of the second strophe. Earth may seem to be subdued but Earth and Hades ultimately triumph. The main emphasis in this first strophe, however, obscures the counterpoint: mankind is glorious.

Commentary

332. *Deina.* The beautifully ambiguous *deinos,* twice used in two lines, is meant to characterize both mankind in general and the heroine in particular. In fact, Soph. uses *deinos* of the hero in each of his plays. The common denominators in *deinos* applicable to all Sophoclean heroes are the incapacity for moderation (Knox, p. 24) and the ironic coexistence to the point of identity of certain contraries. *Deinos,* derived from *deos,* "fear," originally meant "terrible," "dreadful," or "marvelously strong," and so Homer uses it of weapons, the glare of the foe, fire, and thunder; but as early as *Iliad* 18. 394, it means reverend or awesome (of a goddess); (the related noun *deimos* is personified in the *Iliad* 4. 440 as that terrible female force which urges on Homeric heroes); *deinos* also connotes violence and strange power: kinship has a "strange" power (Aeschylus *Prometheus Bound* 39); motherhood, too, is strangely powerful as Clytemnestra muses when she hears the "terrible" good news that hėr son, Orestes, is dead (Soph. *Electra* 767–70). The word also came to connote cleverness in extricating oneself from difficulties (Aeschylus *Prometheus Bound* 59) and was coming to describe an unscrupulous speaker in the phrase *deinos legein.* Still, unlike *sophos* (see 365 n.), *deinos* was not just beginning to degenerate in meaning with the rise of sophistic thinking; the pejorative meanings of *deinos* even in the early period usually submerged the less obvious, complimentary meanings which Soph. chooses to emphasize. Thus, Campbell errs in suggesting that *deina* here means "wonderful," since the word had paused at this point in its development from "fearful" to "clever." The ambiguities were always present in the word, but the spectators on first hearing the opening phrase would understand it to mean: "Many are the causes for alarm" (Linforth, p. 196). Almost immediately, however, with the repetition (*deina . . . deinoteron*) and with the developing theme of man's wonderful,

daring inventiveness, the audience is led to consider the wide range of possible meanings: "fearsome and marvelous, potent and strange, mighty and resourceful, wonderful but also terrifying" (Goheen, p. 53) to which one should add "heroic" and "not normal for one's sex," both of which are applicable to An. The word here also suggests a violence that is particularly feminine because of the ode's relationship to Aeschylus' *Choephoroi* 585–86 (see the introduction to *Bilingual Selections*). Müller perceives that *deinos* suggests one kind of application to the Cho. but that the deeper and contrary insight of the poet shines through for the thoughtful listener: i.e., for the Cho. the as yet unknown culprit would hardly be *deinos* in the good sense of the word, but for the poet, An. is *deinos* in the highest moral sense. In a word, it is the Sophoclean hero's heroism that constitutes his or her "deinotic" nature.

333. *K(ai) ouden anthrōpou deinoteron* (–u––––uu–). The succession of longs on the word, *ānthrōpoū,* and on the first syllable of the repeated *deîn-* establishes the central position of this phrase and thus emphasizes the Cho.'s great confidence in the *deinos anthrōpos.* The choice of the generic word for mankind, *anthrōpos,* rather than the specifically masculine *anēr* (cf. 347) which would have excluded An.'s sex (see 367 n.), signals the Cho.'s retreat from the agitated events of the preceding episode into the world of universals. For the poet as distinct from the Cho., however, the choice of the generic word also leaves open the possible application of the ode to An. The neuter *touto,* "this creature" (334), continues the generic pattern.

Pelei, "is customarily," replacing the more usual *esti,* "is," affirms the fact that the Cho. is viewing man *sub specie aeternitatis.* Cf. Parmenides frg. 8 (Diels): "The unity that is being never was, never will be, for now it is all at once as a whole." Note the series of present tenses in the ode (most past and future actions are hidden in participles or expressions like *erchetai to mellon,* 360–61). Even *edidaxato* and *xympephrastai* (356 and 364) stress the present result of past effort. Therefore, the impact of the one true future *epaxetai* (see 362 n.) is heightened.

334-35. *Poliou . . . pontou,* "over the gray sea." This alliterative, peaceful phrase (*polios* connotes serenity) contrasts with the wintry winds buffeting mankind (*cheimeriōi notōi*).

336–37. *Peribrychioisin* . . . *oidmasin* pictures Man perduring in a sea whose waves tower above his ship on both sides. Both adjective and noun connote the swollen condition of the sea.

337–38. *Theōn* . . . *Gān.* Earth is the most exalted of the divinities because she is eldest. In Hesiod's *Theogony,* Earth is the eldest god, the mother of all things including Heaven, and she is also, in the first half of the work, the chief initiator of action. Subsequently, however, her grandson Zeus limits her to an advisory role (*Theogony* 884, 891) and strips her of her former prerogatives (*Theogony* 505). So the end of the *Theogony* reveals the conquest of predominantly male divinities (the Olympians) over the earlier predominantly female divinities. In the *Theogony,* then, male gods conquer female gods. In this Sophoclean Cho., however, it is human beings conquering the eldest female god, a thrilling feat no doubt, but one that the audience would recognize as involving *hybris.*

339. *Aphthiton* . . . *apotryetai.* The oxymoron is apparent: Man wears out the unwearying Earth. See "Choral Rhythms," above, for the rhythmic effects here. The alliteration and assonance is arresting: the negatives *aphthiton* and *akamatan* "imperishable," "unwearied" suggest the unvanquished nature of Earth; *apotryetai* depicts Man at work, striving to do the impossible (see 90–92 n.). The persistent *a*-sound reinforces his persistence. Still, the Earth is not really vanquished and thus foreshadows man's ultimate defeat in his struggle against Death (361). See Müller, p. 83.

342–53. In this antistrophe, the Cho. narrows its subject from humanity, *anthrōpos,* to the male of the species, *periphradēs anēr.* The Cho. sings of his mastery over the animal kingdom in two groups, those whom he kills or ensnares in his nets (i.e., the birds, beasts, and fish) and those he enslaves for his own service (i.e., the horses and bulls). The imagery of yokes, nets, and curbs (see Goheen, pp. 26–35) that abound in these lines is in marked contrast to the imagery of the next strophe in which Man's inner control becomes the subject.

342. On *kouphonoōn,* see 43 n. The birds are free and light-hearted, i.e., before man's control. This "feminine" word suggests an association between An. (the mother bird, 424–25) and these birds, who are victims of male aggression. The Cho. uses the word pejoratively in the Ode on *Atē* when it sings of "the deceits of

fickle desires," *apata kouphonoōn erōtōn,* 617. There the "feminine" words suggest An. is the one deceived, whereas the greater deception is ultimately Cr.'s.

343. *Agrei,* "hunts down." *Agrei* is an emendation accepted by Pearson but not by Jebb for MSS *agei,* "he leads captive." If *agrei* is correct, the stem, *agr-* occurs three times in this antistrophe. The beasts are free to roam the fields (*agrioi*) until man ensnares them (cf. 349, *agraulou*). The darker side of man's skillful hunting is portrayed through the adjectives *agrion* (343), "savage"; *agraulou* (349), "wild"; and *amphilophon* (351), "around the neck," modifying the victims. The metaphors that describe Cr.'s relationships with family and subjects (see 202 n.) draw a parallel between the hunter of the ode and his victims on the one hand, and Cr. and human beings on the other (see 90 n.). The final glare of Hae. as he spits at his father in the dénouement (1231–32) is "savage" (*agrios*). The recurrence of this same word identifies Hae. with the victims of this hunter; too, it shows the results of Cr.'s dehumanization of his son, and perhaps illustrates the effect of excessive "masculinity." An.'s hunting, by contrast, identifies her with the hunted (see 92 n.).

346–47. *Speiraisi diktyoklōstois,* "in the coils of woven nets." The phrase includes both the meshes for large beasts and the nets for marine life. Man is skilled (*periphradēs*) in his clever use of varied hunting equipment. *Periphradēs,* like *pantoporos* and *hypsipolis,* the other striking four-syllabled words in corresponding positions in the next strophe and antistrophe, has varied nuances. Cook (p. 112) renders it "universal-minded"; Braun, "circumspect man"; Fitts-Fitzgerald, "All are taken, tamed in the net of his mind."

348. *Kratei.* The Cho. appropriately chooses this verb (see "Vocabulary," chap. 8, for the series of related words) for man's enslavement of animal creation since the word connotes physical force (cf. the Prologue of *Prometheus Bound* where Aeschylus calls his personification of Brute Power, *Kratos*). Cr. characteristically uses *kratos* for his power (166, 173, 738; also Ism. at 60) in preference to the more neutral *archē.* At 484–85, Cr. says of his struggle with An.: "Now I am no man—she is the man—if this conquest (*taut'* . . . *kratē*) shall rest with her."

354–65. Strophe B shifts to the arena of the mind. The Cho.

sings now of man's capacity to control himself and to live in harmony in the *polis*.

354–55. *Phthegma . . . phronēma.* These two -ma words, chosen from the new reservoir of intellectual vocabulary not yet current in ordinary speech (see Long, p. 37), announce the movement of the Cho. to cerebral concerns, but cerebral concerns lyrically expressed in lines of great musical beauty.

Ānemoen phronēma. Phronēma (or *pronein*) is frequently on Cr.'s lips (see 176, 207 n.), but is Soph.'s word, perhaps under Aeschylus' influence (see *Agamemnon* 176), for religious and ethical cognition. The adjective *ānemoen,* "wind-swift," here better translated "high-soaring," confirms this, and the latent bird-image suggests An. The ethical loftiness here is also stressed by the rhythmic similarity and assonance in *ānemoen* and *māchanoen* (the corresponding word in the antistrophe, 365), since the antistrophe addresses the dilemma of man's moral ambivalence.

355. *Astynomous orgās* connotes the feeling, disposition, or temper as well as the social impulse drawing people together into a social unity. The phrase is apolitical: *asty,* in distinction from *polis,* designates the city in its apolitical aspect; *nomos* is An.'s word for law that is in accordance with divine law in contrast to Cr.'s "mere human decree" (458–59). In using the rare *astynomos,* Soph. may be recalling Aeschylus' application of the word to the gods who guide the city (*Agamemnon.* 88). *Orgē* is a "feminine" word that usually carries pejorative connotations (e.g., "anger" at 766 and "passion" at 875), but here its original, positive meaning, "impulse," predominates. The phrase then connotes not "statecraft" (Fitts-Fitzgerald) so much as the androgynous disposition that makes true communal life possible.

356. *Edidaxato,* "he has taught himself," expresses confidence in man's own "secular" accomplishments (i.e., without the help of a Titan Prometheus or other divine aid). The middle voice expresses action done to oneself or on one's behalf. This verb is one of the two finite past tenses in the ode (see 333 n.): man has taught himself, making possible the present that is the universal time described in the rest of the ode. These verses may echo the teaching of the Sophist, Protagoras (see Intro., this chap. and 370 n.).

359. *Dysombra . . . belē. Belos,* "missile," or "arrow," is here applied to the shafts of a storm: "the pelting of the pitiless rain" (Campbell).

360. *Pantoporos; aporos:* lit., "with a way out of all difficulties; with no way (*poros*) out," i.e., "all-resourceful; without resources." The resemblance in meaning, in the juxtaposing of opposites, in word formation, in rhythmic effects and even punctuation between this phrase and its counterpart in the antistrophe, *hypsipolis; apolis,* is striking. Critics agree that these arresting oxymora are at the center of Soph.'s thought in the ode, but there is not universal agreement about the meanings of the separate phrases and about their interrelationship. Does *pantoporos* belong only to the preceding half of the strophe as the grammar suggests, or does it not relate to the second half as well: man is all-resourceful, and is without resource in nothing that will occur (*to mellon*) except for Death? Cook tries to convey the double negative: "All-coping non-coping for nothing that is to be" (p. 112). He suggests that the double negative turns out to be ominous in different ways for both Cr. and An. Again, Death marks the limiting force that thwarts technological man's advances. He who has overcome the hurdles of disease is without a way out of the ultimate struggle. The antithesis is not as sharp for the one who possesses *ānemoen phronēma.* She does in a sense transcend death in Hades' harbor (see 1284 n.). Heidegger translates the line: "Everywhere journeying, inexperienced and without issue, he comes to nothingness." His rendering ("The Ode on Man in Sophocles' *Antigone,*" in Woodard, p. 90) throws more light on Heidegger's philosophy than on the ode.

361–62. *Haida monon,* "Hades alone." The ultimate obstacle to man's progress is proclaimed with terse brevity. For Earth as a secondary obstacle, see 338–39.

Hades is the "Unseen" brother of Zeus, lord of the underworld, also called Pluto, "the rich one," i.e., the god who receives all the riches of earth. But for Soph. here, Hades is not the mythological figure; but, taken together with Zeus (126 ff., 450 ff., 605 ff, and 1040 ff.), Dikē (451), and Eros (781), Hades here and elsewhere (282–83, 773 ff., 810–16, 891–96, 1284–85) represents the rights of *das Jenseits,* the other world out of which true justice springs and in relation to which all human laws are only relative. See "Polis

57

und Hades in der *Antigone* des Sophokles," in Hans Diller, pp. 311–24, where theologian Rudolf Bultmann argues this point persuasively. An. is *hypsipolis* (370) because she acknowledges their realm and its jurisdiction over the *polis;* Cr. is *apolis* in that he tramples on the rights of the gods (745) by believing his decree and Zeus' are identical (666 ff.). Cr. sees Hades not as a power that determines human life but only as the threatening horror of death with which he can punish offenders (580–81, 777 ff.). Thus Hades destroys him (see 1284 and n.). An., on the contrary, acknowledges Hades' rights (777 ff.) and finally calls the *polis* to witness the laws for which she dies (847). She transgresses Cr.'s law because it goes beyond its sphere (449, 455 n.). When she claims she will marry Acheron (815), the terrible image of her being embraced by the grim river of pain is the superficial level of meaning. At a deeper level, the phrase suggests her wedding to true justice.

362. *Pheuxin ouk epaxetai.* The phrase is vivid: man looks all around to procure some means of escape (*pheuxin,* like its cognate, *phygās* (363) is a medical term; *epaxetai* is a military term for enlisting foreign troops in one's behalf). The fact that *epaxetai* is the only unambiguous future in the ode emphasizes the fact that Death is man's universal doom (see 333 n.). At 923, An. looks in vain for divine allies.

363–64. *Nosōn . . . xympephrastai.* Society, through mutual aid (*xym-*) has escaped (note the third image of flight in five verses) seemingly impossible (*a-māchanōn,* i.e., irremediable) diseases (see 1284 on the disease imagery). At 732, Cr. claims An. is diseased, but later Tiresias tells Cr. his folly is a disease (1051–52).

Mēchanē, "contrivance," "machine," resonates throughout this ode (see 349 and 365, also 68 n.), since the ode superficially sings of man the contriver and the accomplishments made possible by his technology. An., like the Man of the ode, is a hunter; but her weapon is not a *māchanē* (349), and her prey is not the powerless victims of the aggressive male of the first antistrophe. Her weapon is love (see 90–92 and n.), and her only prey is herself as she, like the medical world, overcomes incurable diseases but is thwarted by death. *Poros, mēchanē,* and *technē* are all Promethean words (cf. e.g., Aeschylus *Prometheus Bound* 59, 254) which were part of the

58

confident vocabulary of Periclean Athens. Cf. *Prometheus Bound* 109 ff. where Prometheus describes his feat in giving fire to mankind. He calls himself "the huntsman of the mystery, the great resource (*megas poros*), the teacher of technology (*technē*)." Although Prometheus was for playwright Aeschylus both the scientist (*sophistēs*) exemplifying man's achievement and a symbol of the ultimate inadequacy of science, the age of Pericles in which Soph. lived, somewhat like the confident age of the early 1960s, concentrated on the achievement with little thought of its inadequacy. For other contemporary texts that viewed civilization as a progressive development, see Guthrie, pp. 79–84.

365–75. Antistrophe B has been variously interpreted as "the essence of the song" (Bowra, p. 85); as indicative that man's "ultimate happiness must depend upon his piety and obedience to the gods" (Musurillo, p. 45); and as "a rather hasty attempt at relevance before the song has quite run its course" (Waldock, p. 112). Linforth, who regards the first three-fourths of the song as "a long concessive clause," observes that the audience is finally being led "to think of the danger which constantly threatens human society from man's evil propensities" (p. 199). The Cho. in this second antistrophe concentrates on the darker aspects of the word *deinos* more obviously than in the first antistrophe which radiated the confidence of the male hunter. The subject here is man's moral ambivalence.

365–66. *Sophon . . . echōn*, lit., "possessing a thing subtle beyond expectation, in his resourceful skill." *Māchanoen:* see 354 n. and 363 n. *Technē*, though often translated "art," really denotes the systematic application of knowledge so as to yield a set product. Despite the confident vocabulary, the Cho. ends on a pessimistic note (367). The emphatic first word, *sophos*, "skilled," "wise," "clever," prepares the audience to be sceptical since the word, especially when combined with *deinos*, was acquiring a depreciatory inflexion with the rise of sophistic thought (Guthrie, p. 33).

367. *Tote . . . herpei:* here the Cho. clearly articulates the fear latent in the opening phrase of the ode (*polla ta deina*). Despite the glories of man's accomplishments, there is no assurance that he will make the right moral decisions (*ep' esthlon herpei*). This thought runs counter to the optimism of Protagoras' philosophy

(see Intro., this chap.) and to the general confidence of Soph.'s age.

368–69. *Nomous . . . dikān:* there is a celebrated textual crux here. Many editors, including Jebb and Pearson, have emended the MSS reading of the participle *pareirōn,* "weaving"; but Campbell, Dain, and several recent critics rightly argue for this bold, though difficult MSS reading.

The principal objections to this reading have been that the word *pareirōn* elsewhere has been used of incidental insertion rather than of weaving into the very fabric of life and that the image is so unusual in this context. (See Goheen, p. 141, n. 3, and Musurillo, p. 44, for arguments defending this reading; Müller, p. 95, rejects it.) The image is an abrupt departure from the basic image words of the ode, but I suggest that Soph. chooses an image taken from the life of woman in conscious contrast with the other dominant male images in the ode. (See Hesiod *Works and Days* 63–64 where Athena teaches the archetypal woman, Pandora, "weaving on the very cunning loom." This is woman's work in contrast to tilling fields and raising flocks which are man's proper works.) At this pivotal point in the ode where the Cho. is laying down the basis for moral action, the poet consciously chooses an image from the domestic world. Though *pareirōn* is an alien image, the phrase *ānemoen phronēma* (see 354–55 n.) has prepared for it. The poet thus insinuates that the accomplishments of man in the ode suffer from being exclusively male (342 ff.). Also, the image is a subtle hint that the play will later reveal a woman as the truly *deinos anthrōpos.*

368. *Chthonos:* by choosing *chthōn,* "earth" (see "Vocabulary," chap. 8, s.v.), rather than *gē,* the Cho. suggests the chthonic realm in which the dead are buried as well as simply the earth which maintains the city's life (Knox, p. 112). *Chthōn* here reinforces the power of the divinity *Gē* (338 n.) to thwart man. The "feminine" element here is obvious.

369. *Theōn . . . dikān* is ambiguous (see Adams, p. 48). It can mean "that justice he has sworn by the gods to obey" or "that oathbound justice of the gods." This is the same *Dikē* that An. invokes at 451 (see n.). Not only did Cr.'s edict violate that justice of the gods, but at 304 he swore by Zeus that the perpetrator would be punished.

370. *Hypsipolis; apolis:* this pair of words balances *pantoporos; aporos* in the strophe (see 360 n.). Soph. avails himself of the ambiguity inherent in the words: *hypsipolis,* perhaps a Sophoclean coinage, can connote "high in the city is he" and "high is his city." Jebb's punctuation of a comma before *hypsipolis* is probably better than Pearson's semicolon since the *hypsipolis,* in contrast to *pantoporos* (in the strophe), refers to the man described in the preceding lines, 368–69. The man who weaves into the fabric of his life divine and human justice is *hypsipolis;* the one who rashly dwells with the ignoble is *apolis. Apolis* like *hypsipolis* is ambiguous. It can connote physically without a city (cf. Euripides *Medea* 255); one who has been cast out of the city (cf. Herodotos 7. 104 and *Oedipus at Kolonos* 1357); and one who has destroyed the city.

The Cho. here expresses its doubt about the capability of the *polis* to learn and practice the art of politics, the Protagorean *politikē technē* (see Intro., this chap.). However, it does not express its verdict on whether any citizen is *hypsipolis.*

The play reveals the poet's deeper design: not only is the seemingly *apolis* culprit (i.e., *apolis* in the first two senses of the word) finally proven to be *hypsipolis* in both its senses, but also the *polis*-minded king is finally revealed to be *apolis* in all three senses of the word. For citizenship in this ode, see Intro., this chap. The suggestion that An. is *hypsipolis* (see 361 n.) must have been quite revolutionary for Soph.'s audience which restricted citizenship to males.

371. *Xynesti:* "dwells with," or so as to convey the medical motif, "contaminates himself with" (Mazon).

373–75. The Cho. prays that the sinner *hos tade erdoi* ("who does these things") may not share its hearth or its thoughts. This Cho., which began by praising the man of daring, ends by condemning him. Müller (p. 85) takes the disputable position that the Cho. here is condemning the person who buried Polynices, and that accounts for their dismay when An. is led in. It seems rather that the condemnation is vague since the Cho. had no particular situation in mind (it had even suggested divine help in the burial of Polynices at 278). The ambiguous phrasing has the added merit of allowing the poet's own condemnation of Cr. to obtrude (Müller). The words become a prophecy against Cr. because he is rash in violating the justice of the gods (369). Here, as often in Soph.'s choral odes, the Cho. is unable to apply its great principles to concrete reality. The Cho. thus becomes an "intentional symbol of the inadequacy of everyday morality to judge the ultimate questions" (Whitman, pp. 91–92).

Tolmās charin, "because of recklessness." *Tolmē* is Cr.'s word reserved for those daring enough to transgress his laws (248, 449). See 915 where An. ironically echoes his judgment. For Soph.'s heroes, the word has the positive meaning of moral courage to act (cf. *Electra* 1051); whereas in Euripidean plays, the word almost always is used with the pejorative meaning that this Cho. gives it.

GRAMMATICAL NOTES

332. πολλὰ τὰ δεινά, πολύς, δεινός: nom. pl. neut.; οὐδέν, οὐδείς: nom. sing. neut.

333. δεινότερον, δεινός: comparat., nom. sing. neut.; πέλει, πέλω: pres. 3 sing.

334. τοῦτο, οὗτος: nom. sing. neut.; supply τὸ δεινόν

335. χειμερίῳ νότῳ: dat. sing. with χωρεῖ: i.e., man goes (driven) by wintry wind (dat. of cause).

336. χωρεῖ, χωρέω: pres. 3 sing.; περιβρυχίοισιν . . . οἴδμασιν: dat. pl. with ὑπό

337. περῶν, περάω: pres. partic.

338. τάν = τήν; ὑπερτάταν = ὑπερτάτην: superl., acc. sing. f. modifying Γᾶν = γῆν.

340. ἰλλομένων, ἴλλω: pres. partic. gen. pl.; ἔτος εἰς ἔτος: adverbial acc.: year after year. The first ἔτος is acc. of duration.

341. ἱππείῳ γένει, ἵππειος, γένος: dat. sing.; πολεύων, πολεύω: pres. partic.

342. κουφονόων . . . ὀρνίθων, κουφόνοος, ὄρνις: gen. pl.

343. ἀμφιβαλών, ἀμφιβάλλω: 2 aor. partic.; ἀγρεῖ = ἀγρεύει, ἀγρεύω: pres. 3 sing.

344. θηρῶν ἀγρίων, θὴρ ἄγριος: gen. pl.; ἔθνη, ἔθνος: acc. pl.

345. εἰναλίαν = ἐναλίαν φύσιν, ἐνάλιος, φύσις: acc. sing.

346. σπείραισι (= σπείραις) δικτυοκλώστοις, σπεῖρα, δικτυόκλωστος: dat. pl.

347. κρατεῖ, κρατέω: pres. 3 sing.

349. μαχαναῖς = μηχαναῖς, μηχανή: dat. pl.; ἀγραύλου θηρὸς ὀρεσσιβάτα = ὀρεσιβάτης, ἄγραυλος θὴρ ὀρεσιβάτης: gen. sing. after κρατεῖ.

350. λασιαύχενα . . . ἵππον, λασιαύχην ἵππος: acc. sing.

351. ὑπαξέμεν, ὑπάγω: epic inf.; ἀμφίλοφον ζυγόν, ἀμφίλοφος, ζυγόν: acc. sing.

352. οὔρειον = ὄρειον . . . ἀκμῆτα ταῦρον, ὄρειος ἀκμὴς ταῦρος: acc. sing.

354. ἀνεμόεν = ἠνεμόεν φρόνημα, ἀνεμόεις = ἠνεμόεις, φρόνημα: acc. sing.; ἀστυνόμους (> ἄστυ, town and νόμος, law); ὀργάς, ἀστυνόμος, ὀργή: acc. pl.

356. ἐδιδάξατο, διδάσκω: aor. mid. 3 sing.; man has taught *himself*.

357. ὑπαίθρεια . . . δύσομβρα . . . βέλη, ὑπαίθριος, δύσομβρος, βέλος: acc. pl. Grammatically the two adjs. modify βέλη, shafts, though in sense they describe the storm.

359. φεύγειν, φεύγω: inf., depending on ἐδιδάξατο, 356.

360. οὐδέν, οὐδείς: acc. sing. neut.; ἔρχεται, ἔρχομαι: pres. 3 sing.

361. τὸ μέλλον, μέλλω: pres. partic.; οὐδὲν . . . τὸ μέλλον (= οὐδὲν ὃ μέλλει, "nothing that is to be"); Ἅιδα μόνον, Ἅιδης, μόνος, acc., obj. of verbal idea in the noun φεῦξιν.

362. φεῦξιν, φεῦξις = φύξις: acc. sing., obj. of ἐπάξεται; ἐπάξεται, ἐπάγω: fut. mid. 3 sing., the only future in the whole ode.

363. νόσων ἀμαχάνων, νόσος, ἀμάχανος = ἀμήχανος: gen. pl.; φυγάς, φυγή: acc. pl.; ξυμπέφρασται, συμφράζομαι: perf. mid. 3 sing.

365. σοφόν τι, in apposition with τὸ μαχανόεν τέχνας; τὸ μαχανόεν τέχνας, obj. of ἔχων; ἔχων, ἔχω: pres. partic.

368. νόμους, νόμος: acc. pl.; παρείρων, παρείρω: pres. partic.; χθονός, χθών: gen. sing.

369. ἔνορκον δίκαν = δίκην, ἔνορκος, δίκη: acc. sing.

370. ὅτῳ, ὅστις: dat. sing.

372. ξύνεστι = σύνεστι, σύνειμι: pres. 3 sing.; χάριν, prep. with preceding gen. τόλμας.

374. γένοιτο, γίγνομαι: aor. opt. 3 sing.; φρονῶν, φρονέω: pres. partic.

375. τάδ(ε), ὅδε: acc. pl. neut.; ἔρδοι, ἔρδω: pres. opt. 3 sing.

4

Defense of the Unwritten Laws

[450 – 70]

INTRODUCTION

Soph. wrote this play in an age much like our own, when the traditional respect for law, so ingrained in the Hellenic psyche, was under assault especially from the new advocates of reason and from the researches of his friend, the historian Herodotos. The following age would echo with debates on *nomos*, "custom," "law," "convention"; and *physis*, "nature," "character." The poet doubtless heard such debates. And *An.* is the earliest extant play that brings such philosophical argument onto the stage.[1]

In origin, *nomos* is a deeply religious concept.[2] As early as Hesiod, it designated divine revelations through oracles, rites ordained by the gods, moral rules imposed by them, and the divine world-order. Traditionally in Athens, only the ancient laws of Solon and Draco were called *nomoi;* the ordinary decrees of the *ekklesia,* the assembly, were only *psephismata* (see 60 n.) and lacked the stature of *nomoi.* The philosopher Heraclitus (fl. 500 B.C.), who may have been a major influence on Soph.'s understanding of law, stated that all human laws are nourished by one law, the divine *nomos* (frg. 114).[3]

By mid-fifth century, however, the word *nomos* had become the rallying point for Athens' belief in the integrity of her system of law in her struggle against Persian tyranny; it stood for the particularly Athenian fusion of the ideal of order (whether conceived in

64

religious or nonreligious terms) with the practical observances of the laws of the city-state. But the fusion did not last long. The historical studies of Herodotos, showing how vastly different the laws and customs of other peoples were from those of the Hellenic world, precipitated the deterioration and relativization of the concept that became prevalent with the sophistic movement. Thus, eventually *nomos,* "law," i.e., the artificial, conventional, and sometimes false, was devalued in favor of *physis,* "nature," i.e., the natural and true.

Only the first signs of this deterioration were evident when Soph. wrote this play. For An. and presumably for Soph., there is only one *nomos* and it is in harmony with the heroine's deepest human instincts, her *physis,* her nature, which is to join in loving and not in hating, as she later (523) puts it. In the lines considered here (450–70), the heroine gives her formal defense of her act in terms of the law of Zeus.

However, this is not the first introduction of *nomos* into the play. An., Ism., and Cr. early defend their diverse positions by using *nomos* with different meanings. In the Prologue, An. urges her *nomos* (i.e., her principle) on her sister, namely that one must revere the rights of family and nature above all. Ism., however, takes *nomos* as merely synonymous with the king's decree, and so, despite her great love of family, she chooses to obey Cr.'s *nomos.* In the First Episode, while An. is putting her *nomos* into action offstage with the symbolic burial, Cr. promulgates his *nomoi,* "rules of conduct" (191), in his opening address. There, too, he shows his distrust for the custom (*nomos*) of ordinary citizens, accusing them of habitual greed in his use of *nomisma* (296), a word which means both current coin and ordinary practice. Finally, the Cho. (381–82) and Cr. (449) precipitate An.'s discourse here on the unwritten laws when each accuses her of transgressing Cr.'s "laws."

She expresses her thought in these lines with utmost simplicity. Zeus is not the author of Cr.'s decree, and no mortal can override (*hyperdramein*) the unwritten and unchanging laws of Zeus, laws of infinite age and mysterious origin (450–55). Cr. has gone beyond his sphere (see 455 n.) of influence, beyond the marker (*dikē*) of the *polis.* She uses *nomos'* derivative, *nomimon,* a word less sullied by popular devaluation and thus better able to convey the original

65

meaning of *nomos*, "tradition" or "religious custom." The phrase *agrapta nomina*, "unwritten laws," may have been a traditional one—Pericles uses it a decade later in the famous Funeral Oration—but An. uses it here in its earliest extant occurrence. Pericles gives it a secular context, but for Soph. it connotes the timelessly valid law of Zeus and of nature in distinction from positive decrees, whether oral (as in Cr.'s case) or written (as, e.g., in contemporary Athens).[4] It refers to eternal laws as distinct from the temporally and spatially limited decrees of mere men. An. is thus asserting that there is a dimension of life over which the decrees or "laws" of the *polis* and its king have no jurisdiction. Cr. has gone beyond his sphere in legislating for one who is in the domain of Hades (see nn. on 361–62 and 450 ff.).

An. fully comprehends the cost of her defiance (460): her inevitable death is a profitable exchange (note the twist of Cr.'s monetary image)[5] when compared with the sinful compromise that is its alternative. Her final remarks in the passage return to two themes of the Prologue, pain (64) and folly (95). She defines intolerable pain as the compromise involved in living by Cr.'s "law." And in a sharp thrust at the king, her triple use of *mōros/mōria*, "fool/folly," leaves no doubt about her conviction: "But if I seem to you to do foolish things now, perhaps it is a fool who convicts me of folly" (469–70).

In their desire to show the depth of An.'s religious convictions here, critics sometimes picture her as putting divine law in opposition to human law. That is not what is at stake: she sees no discrepancy between the laws of Zeus and her loyalty to humanity. She does not see herself faced with a Kierkegaardian choice between God and man. In her eyes, Cr.'s decree simply is not a *nomos* precisely because it is at variance with human decency and therefore also with Zeus' laws. In An.'s language, Cr.'s proclamation is always called a mere decree, *kērygma* (see 452 n.), not a *nomos*. Her love perceives that the burial of her brother must be in harmony with Zeus' laws. Zeus is present to her in the dishonored corpse of her brother. She comes to understand the divine not in abstract terms but through a deeply felt human experience. For An., divine law is embodied in *philia*, concern for those she loves. She reveals her instinctive faith in the ultimate oneness of Zeus' law (true *nomos*)

66

and of her loving nature (*physis*). It is this concrete religious conviction that makes her both a noble and a believable character.

Cr. answers her defense of the *agrapta nomima*, the unwritten laws, with a neatly balanced response that shows not only his ability to handle rhetorical debate in the fashion of contemporary oratory but also his utter failure to comprehend her argument. He proceeds from the general to the particular, lecturing on the just deserts awaiting iron-stiff spirits (473) and overly spirited horses (477–78), and then specifically accusing An. of insolence in her transgression (*hyperbainein*) of the established laws, *nomous . . . tous prokeimenous* (481).

He fails to hear that there may be a law transcending his decree. He sees and hears only the evidence of the senses: a female threatens to take over the man's rightful mastery (484). This leads him to the tyrannical illogic of condemning the other girl, Ism., without any evidence of her involvement. In so doing, he clearly rejects the legitimate demands of *physis,* nature, and of *philia,* family, not only by act but also by statement: "Even if she were closer in kinship than any who worship Zeus at our family altar, she and her sister (*xynaimos,* lit., 'one of common blood') shall not escape the heinous fate of death" (486–89). Cr. thus links Zeus and family and rejects both.

The debate between *nomos* and *physis* resonates throughout the play: Hae. and Tiresias both try in vain to warn the king of his misuse of *nomos* through images of the sea and disease. Cr. only hardens his position, adding to his *nomoi* the subservience of females and the unassailable position of the ruler whether he is right or wrong (659–65). The Cho. reproaches An. with the epithet *autonomos,* "follower of one's own law" (821).[6] The odes keep returning to the role of *nomos* (e.g., 368–69, 613–14). Especially notable is the Ode on Eros, where if Goheen's interpretation is correct,[7] "the great laws" (i.e., the unwritten laws) with Eros sitting alongside are in conflict with the lesser written laws (i.e., of Cr. and the *polis*). Only the androgynous hero, able to revere both Eros and the *agrapta nomima* of Zeus, faithfully fuses *nomos* and *physis*. For An., *nomos* stands for these ancient laws implanted in the human psyche by Zeus. They include basic human rights (e.g., respect for family and for burial). This *nomos* cannot be in conflict with *physis,* since its very origin is in one's natural rights, not in the rights of positive law. That this union of *physis* and *nomos* was a deep Sophoclean conviction is clear from the playwright's reassertion of it at the end of the *Oedipus at Kolonos* (1381–82).[8] He may very well owe this insight to Heraclitus,[9] but it has become the cornerstone of his religious edifice.

COMMENTARY

450–70. An. is replying here to Cr.'s indignant question (449): "Did you really dare transgress (*hyperbainein*) these laws (*nomous*)?" i.e., the laws whose majesty is vested in me (Campbell). In her answer, An. is "the prototype of the perfect citizen" (Whitman, p. 88).

450–52. These lines contain An.'s simple denial that Zeus or Justice (*Dikē*) is the source of such spurious "laws" (*nomous*). The position of "laws" at the end of the line, removed from its modifier, underlines the irony in her use of *nomos* here: she never elsewhere honors Cr.'s "decree" with the word *nomos* (see Intro., this chap., for the history of *nomos;* also see 59 n.). The Cho. later (605 ff.) addresses Zeus as the splendid, ageless god whose power none can exceed; elsewhere (*Oedipus at Kolonos* 1606), Soph. notes that Zeus is god of the chthonic realm as well as of the upper world. So Zeus and Justice do not represent two distinct realms here (i.e., Zeus the realm of Olympus and Justice the realm of Hades), even though Justice is often pictured as the personification of the rights of the dead. Instead, Zeus and Justice together represent for Soph. the realm of eternity that transcends the realm and law of the *polis* (see 361–62 n.). Thus An. is saying that the realm of eternity has not ordained laws forbidding the burial of a relative. The poet has an abiding belief in the power of Zeus and Justice, since they reappear in the curse Oedipus calls down on his son in Soph.'s last play (*Oedipus at Kolonos* 1381–81). There Justice condemns Polynices because he has broken the laws of family duty (*archaiois nomois*). (See also *Oedipus at Kolonos* 1606 and 1747 for An.'s prayer to Zeus after Oedipus' death.) *Xynoikos,* "dwelling together with." Cf. *Oedipus at Kolonos* 1382 for Justice "sitting together with" (*xyne-*

dros) Zeus; also Eros "sitting alongside" (*paredros*) the eternal laws, *tōn megalōn . . . thesmōn, An.* 796–99. There are textual and interpretive problems in this latter passage but Love seems to be pictured as sharing Zeus' power just as Justice is here.

453–55. An. here contrasts the ephemeral proclamation of a mortal with the steadfast unwritten laws of the gods. The argument here is in terms of transcendence and true law in contrast to her earlier (74–75) rationalization that she owes the dead greater reverence because she will be with them a longer time. *Asphalē,* lit., "without stumbling," denotes both "never failing to apply" and "never failing to vindicate their authority." The literal meaning of *asphalē,* "without stumbling," may also be in the poet's mind, since fate or the gods are later pictured as swooping down and crushing man (see n. on 1345–46). Kitto's use of un- in his translation of *a-grapta* and *a-sphalē,* "*un*-written and *un*changing," captures the emphatic effect of the Greek negatives. *Nomima,* the less frequently used derivative of *nomos,* perhaps better conveyed the original meaning of *nomos,* "custom." An. is evoking the power of the divinely sanctioned, ancient, and customary ordinances (cf. *Ajax* 1343). See *Oedipus Tyrannos* 865 ff. for the poet's other great statement, there in a choral ode, on these laws. Cr. finally acknowledges (1113) that one should keep the "established laws."

J. H. Finley (*Three Essays on Thucydides,* pp. 17 ff.) asserts that unwritten law is part of Soph.'s and Pericles' democratic view of man's freedom in opposition to the oligarchic view of rigid law displayed by Cr. and the Spartan oligarch, Archidamos, in Thucydides' history; Ehrenberg (pp. 22 ff.), however, correctly distinguishes between Pericles' democratic and Soph.'s theonomic view of law.

The Sophist Hippias of Elis is said to have maintained that the unwritten laws seem to stem from a higher than human lawgiver (Xenophon *Memorabilia* 4. 4. 19 ff.), and Podlecki (p. 370) suggests Soph. may have used Hippias as a source (see Introd., this chap., for possible Hericlitean influences.) In any case, Hippias does at least share Soph.'s reverence for *physis* over positive *nomos:* "but *nomos,* tyrant of mankind, violates nature (*physis*) in many ways" (Plato *Protagoras* 337d).

455. *Hyperdramein,* "to outrace" or "ride past a limit," "to go

beyond the marker (*dikē*)," in contrast to Cr.'s word *hyperbainein*, 449 and 481, properly "to transgress." See also 663 and 742–45 and the Introd., this chap. An.'s point is that human decrees are limited to the sphere of the *polis* and that Cr. is trying to ride beyond his sphere. In the Ode on *Atē*, the Cho. celebrates Zeus' power which no human trespass (*hyperbasia*) can limit (605).

456. *Aei pote*, "forever without end." The phrase conveys an idea of infinity without pointing exclusively towards the future or the past. DeRomilly (pp. 30–32) notes that the very structure of Greek tragedy shows concern for eternity through the choral songs with their meditation on eternal themes alternating with the episodes.

458. *Toutōn* and *andros* are emphatically contrasted. An. will not risk infidelity to "these laws" for the sake of "any mere man." She scorns Cr.'s hybristic attempt to supersede the gods' positive command.

459. *Phronēma*, "will' or "purpose." Since the Greeks of this period did not distinguish intellect from will, An. can easily connect Cr.'s thought with his obstinate pride. At 1261, Cr. finally realizes that "the errors of his unreasoning reason"; *phrenōn dysphronōn hamartēmata* have destroyed him. For the usual association of *phronēma* with Cr.'s belief in his own good sense, see 176 n.; see also 355 n.

462–70. In these lines, An. plays on three theme words, "pain," "gain," and "foolishness," emphasizing each by repetition. The poet thus draws attention to the different value that she gives these words from that of Cr. and Ism.

462–64. An. uses one of Cr.'s favorite words, *kerdos*, "gain" or "profit," twice in these lines, but the word carries the opposite significance for her. Whereas he judges human conduct in terms of material gain (222, 310, 326) and is convinced that the guard and Tiresias can be bought for a price (1037, 1047, 1061), *kerdos* expresses An.'s "emotional, non-rational . . . determination that willingly accepts or even seeks self-destruction, not self-advancement" (Segal, p. 66).

463. The structure of the line, with *en polloisin kakois* surrounding *hōs egō*, graphically depicts the thought.

465–68. "This series of three clauses, in which the second is opposed to the first, and the third reiterates the sense of the first is peculiarly Sophoclean" (Jebb). These lines give An.'s conception of unbearable pain, quite different from that of Ism., 63–64. It is also clear from these lines that Zeus' unwritten laws come to her in terms of and out of concern for her dead brother. She has not been thinking of these laws in the abstract–an important point to remember when comparing this passage with the controversial 904 ff. passage (see n. on 904). The lofty tone she established here degenerates in the later passage into a sophistic argument. However, the two passages are consistent in one important respect. It is in terms of the very human needs of her family that she bases her religious concern here and her sophistry there. The double burial reveals a similar intermingling of human and divine (see McCall).

469–70. An. concludes with a simple but scathing denunciation of the fool, Cr. *Mōros,* properly "dull" or "stupid," comes to denote one who is culpably ignorant. Cr., she implies, exhibits the intentional, obstinate irrationality of a closed mind. *Mōria* is the state of such obstinacy and is the opposite of *euboulia,* "good counsel," the art of making sound decisions (see 95 and 1347 n.). The line is usually translated with "folly" and "fool" to indicate An.'s triple use of the stem *mōr-,* but "folly" fails to capture the vehemence of the Greek. *Ophliskanō,* a legal term, "incur the charge of," reappears in Tiresias' final warning: "Stubbornness, you know, incurs the charge of stupidity" (1028).

The Cho.'s response to An. (471) depicts An. as a savage (lit., "raw" or "uncooked") daughter of a savage father. *Ōmos* and *hypsipolis,* "high in the city," are antithetical words. Although the Cho. calls An. *ōmos* here, the play will show she is really *hypsipolis* (370 n.). Ajax, on the other hand, is a Sophoclean hero who is truly *ōmos.* Tekmessa aptly characterizes her lover as "the great terrible man of untamed might" (*ōmokratēs, Ajax* 205).

GRAMMATICAL NOTES

450. κηρύξας, κηρύσσω: aor. partic.

451. ἡ ξύνοικος (= σύνοικος) Δίκη: nom. sing.; τῶν θεῶν, θεός: gen. pl.

452. τοιούσδ(ε) . . . νόμους, τοιόσδε νόμος: acc. pl.; ἀνθρώποισιν = ἀνθρώποις, ἄνθρωπος: dat. pl.; ὥρισεν, ὁρίζω: aor. 3 sing.

453. σθένειν, σθένω: pres. inf.; ᾠόμην, οἴομαι: impf. 1 sing.; τὰ σὰ κηρύγματ(α), σός, κήρυγμα: acc. pl.

454. ἄγραπτα . . . ἀσφαλῆ . . . νόμιμα, ἄγραπτος, ἀσφαλής, νόμιμον: acc. pl. neut.

455. δύνασθαι, δύναμαι: pres. inf.; θνητὸν ὄντ(α) (pres. partic.), εἰμί, θνητός: acc. sing. m.; ὑπερδραμεῖν, ὑπερτρέχω: 2 aor. inf.

456. γε: particle emphasizing the previous word.

457. ζῇ, ζάω: pres. 3 sing.; οἶδεν, οἶδα: perf. (= pres.) 3 sing.; ὅτου, ὅστις: gen. sing.; (ἐ)φάνη, φαίνω: 2 aor. pass. 3 sing. (neut. pl. subject takes sing. verb).

458. τούτων, οὗτος: gen. pl. referring to τὰ νόμιμα; ἔμελλον, μέλλω: impf. 1 sing.; ἀνδρὸς οὐδενός, ἀνὴρ οὐδείς: gen. sing. ἀνδρός is placed here in emphatic position.

459. δείσασ(α), δείδω: aor. partic. nom. sing. f.; ἐν, used forensically, i.e., "in the forum of the gods"; θεοῖσι = θεοῖς, θεός: dat. pl. obj. of prep.; τὴν δίκην, ἡ δίκη: acc. sing.

460. δώσειν, δίδωμι: fut. inf.; θανουμένη, θνήσκω: fut. partic.; ἐξῄδη, ἔξοιδα: plpf. = impf. 1 sing.

461. προυκήρυξας, προκηρύσσω: aor. 2 sing. in contrary to fact clause.

462. θανοῦμαι, θνήσκω: fut. 1 sing.

463. πολλοῖσιν = πολλοῖς . . . κακοῖς, πολύς, κακός: dat. pl.

464. ζῇ, ζάω: pres. 3 sing.; κατθανών, καταθνήσκω: 2 aor. partic.

465. ἔμοιγε, ἐγώ: dat. sing. with emphatic particle γε attached; τοῦδε τοῦ μόρου, ὅδε ὁ μόρος: gen. sing.; τυχεῖν, τυγχάνω: 2 aor. inf.

466. ἐμῆς μητρός, ἐμός, μήτηρ: gen. sing.

467. θανόντ(α), θνήσκω: 2 aor. partic. acc. sing. m.; ἠνσχόμην = ἠνεσχόμην, ἀνέχομαι: 2 aor. 1 sing. in contrary to fact clause; ἄθαπτον . . . νέκυν, ἄθαπτος νέκυς: acc. sing.

468. κείνοις, (ἐ)κεῖνος: dat. pl. n.; ἤλγουν, ἀλγέω: impf. 1 sing.; τοῖσδε, ὅδε: dat. pl. n.; ἀλγύνομαι, ἀλγύνω: pres. pass. 1 sing.

469. σοί, σύ: dat. sing.; μῶρα, μῶρος: acc. pl. neut.; δρῶσα, δράω: pres. partic. nom. sing. f.; τυγχάνειν, τυγχάνω: pres. partic.

470. μωρίαν, μωρία: acc. sing.

5

The Creon-Haemon Debate

[631 – 765]

INTRODUCTION

THIS SCENE IS indeed a debate, even an *agōn*, a contest or struggle for supremacy between father and son. Hae. probably does not realize that this is a contest of wills until its disastrous conclusion and surely does not want it so. But for Cr., the whole play is just such an *agōn*. His eventual downfall is so total and so pitiable because he values himself and others only in terms of power. He understands nothing of the complementarity of relationship that Hae. and An. might have achieved were it not for his own weak strength. The gentle but firm Hae. might have provided an admirable balance for the strong passion of his intense spouse. The wholeness of the androgynous An. and of the "gynecandrous" Hae.[1] escapes his comprehension. Certainly, if anyone could reach the uncomprehending king, it is his docile son. In fact, by disposition and his unique relationship as spouse of one antagonist and son of the other,[2] he is the best hope of reconciliation between these intransigent personalities. The failure of his valiant attempt is thus the turning point in the play.

Three themes of the play are central to an understanding of the struggle in this scene. They are emptiness versus isolation, piety, and obedience. The first two primarily continue Cr.'s struggle with the absent An., while the third reflects as well upon the emancipa-

73

tion of the son from his father. An examination of these themes will show how Soph. unmasks Cr. *qua* human being in this scene (Episode 1 already unmasked him *qua* king) and how the playwright thus underlines the contrasting full humanity of the absent heroine.

The words *kenos,* "empty," and *gnōmē,* "judgment," are indices of Hae.'s changing attitude toward his father. Whereas Hae.'s opening remarks contain the confident promise that he will follow his father's good counsels (*gnōmai* 635), a short hundred lines later he characterizes those judgments as empty aphorisms, *kenās gnomās* (735). *Kenos* was usually reserved for objects like houses or hands. Thus, the son's earlier fear has become reality: Cr. is as hollow as a writing tablet that is opened up and found to be devoid of contents (709 and n.). When Cr. retorts that Hae. is the empty one, devoid of wisdom (754), the spectator recognizes hollow rhetoric. But Hae. shrinks from the realization: "If you were not my father," he pleads, "I would have said you were not wise" (755). The father then irrevocably breaks the family tie not so much by calling him "the woman's chattel" (756) as by diabolically threatening to kill "the hateful thing" (760) before his son's eyes. The mild, conciliatory youth is thus forced to the realization that there is no accommodation possible with a madman (765). His last words, only slightly veiling his threat of suicide, are ironically couched in his father's vocabulary of physical sight, as though he still nurtured a residual hope of reaching the tyrant who had been his father.

So the words *kenos* and *gnōmē* reflect Hae.'s movement from faith in his father and confidence that their differences can be overcome to recognition of his father's vacuity. In the closing lines of the play, even Cr. realizes this when he calls himself a "cipher, no more than nothing" (1322). The tragedy, thus, does not annihilate a great man but simply reveals a hollow man.[3]

Another word for "empty" resonates throughout the play. It is *erēmos,* "bereft," "isolated," and it is An.'s word for the spiritual isolation that is the ironic outgrowth of her own loving act. Her decision to act on behalf of her *philos,* Polynices, results, she later realizes, in her being "bereft of loved ones" (*erēmos pros philōn*).[4] However, in this scene, Hae. applies this word to his father in one of his most effective rejoinders. When Cr. claims absolute power over the *polis,* Hae. counters: "You would be a fine monarch ruling over a desert" (i.e., an empty land, *erēmēs gēs,* 739). Hae. might have called the land *kenandros,* empty of men, as Theseus did (*Oedipus at Kolonos* 917), but his choice of An.'s word serves to contrast her isolation with his. Hers stems from the fullness of her love, Cr.'s from his emptiness.

The second theme, that of piety, is the subject of much of the debate between father and son, and keeps recurring throughout the play.[5] The theme is present from An.'s first mention of her act of holy criminality in the Prologue (74) until the last sentence of the play (1350). The issues are sharpened and defined especially in this episode and in An.'s last speech. Earlier, Cr. was obsessed with equating religion with his acts as king. In this episode, his desire for the mantle of piety surfaces again. How can he "reverence the lawless" (730) and still reverence his own kingly powers (744), he asks. Hae. tries to correct his father's error: "It is not reverence to trample on divine prerogatives" (745). The king's tyrannical response reveals his legalistic and scrupulous conception of piety:[6] he decides to reduce the death penalty for An. to a living death, providing her with enough food to relieve him of legal responsibility for her death (771–76), while still leaving her to the care of Hades, "the only god she reveres" (777). In An.'s final speech, her own painful grappling with her relation to the gods (see Intro., Chap. 6) leaves the audience to judge the winner in the contest for piety.

The third theme, that of obedience and submission to authority reveals Hae.'s growth from his opening remarks to his final choice of An.'s principle instead of blind obedience to the king. In his opening statement, his submissiveness is almost but not quite obsequious (see 635–38 n.). In *Bilingual Selections,* I consider Hae.'s sensitive but mature conduct in this scene as he progresses from qualified obedience to a necessary rejection of his father's immoral stance.[7] But here I wish to examine obedience from the king's point of view.

In an elaborate double personification of obedience and anarchy (672–76), Cr. lectures his son on the necessity for obedience as an antidote to anarchy. The two personified forces form a "frame-antithesis"[8] around the passage in which the king contends that obedience to command (*peith-archia*) preserves society, whereas lawlessness (*an-archia*) destroys its fabric. There are two examples of lawlessness that he fails to perceive: his own, since he exempts himself from the rule of law (see 667), and the state's, since its council of elders is afraid even to mention the *anarchia* of the chief executive (see 211–14). It is quite apparent therefore why he could not understand An.'s argument that obedience to an unwritten law might demand the appearance of lawlessness (450–70). The king reduces the political process to two contradictory forces, the good one identified with his own will and the evil one identified with those who would defy him. (The striking parallel between this and the "Watergate mentality" needs no comment.)

The imagery that Cr. uses in this episode is appropriately military and hierarchical. His son will succeed when posted behind his father-leader (640). Order is seen as military order (cf. *tassein*, 63, *prostassein*, 670–71, *epitassein* 664, *akosma* 660; also 677 and 730 and the notes on these lines). If all men and objects are not in proper order, *kosmos*, there is chaos. Everyone has his proper rank in Cr.'s hierarchy. First there is Cr., identical, sometimes, even superior to Zeus (657); then mature men who must never be schooled by young men (726–27); then young men; finally women, slaves, and animals all seemingly on a par. Much of Cr.'s indignation stems from disruption of this order: his son becoming a "woman's chattel," a woman daring to discourse on the meaning of law, or acting in defiance of her uncle-king, women ranging at large outside the women's quarters (578–80), a son not realizing that a woman's body is of no more value than a field bought for cultivation (569).

We have examined three of the issues in the debate between father and son. As Hae. angrily runs off stage, his departure signals his decision to stand with An. against his rigid father. In their next choral ode on Eros' invincible power, the elders probably mean to stand with the king against the apparently mindless passion of the youth. Cr.'s military and hierarchical arguments do, after all, derive from a persistent strain in Greek thought. But the poet's deeper meaning shines through: Eros is not the bewitching, playful spirit of lyric poetry but is endowed by Soph. with a new majesty in this ode. Eros is pictured as a moral force that sits enthroned as a peer alongside the eternal laws (797–99). Eros enables Hae.

to share the heinous fate of his innocent fiancée.[9] Thus, although the elders have not repudiated the king, their words in the ode unwittingly do.

COMMENTARY

632. Cr.'s first word to Hae. sets the tone since *teleiān* means both final and authoritative. There is dramatic irony in Cr.'s use of *psēphos* (lit., "pebble" used for a voting ballot in a democratic election, [see 59–60 n.]), since it will become clear that the decree does not reflect popular opinion but only his lone vote (Goheen, p. 157, n. 399).

As Cr.'s State of the Kingdom address began with his assertion of his legitimate authority over the elders, so here he leads off with words designed to recall his parental authority to the mind of his young son (the Cho. in 627 introduced Hae. as the youngest of Cr.'s children). The two episodes are similar too in ending with emotional outbursts that betray respectively the insecurity of Cr. as king (Episode 1) and the failure of Cr. as father (this episode). The episode with Tiresias will reveal his failure in revering the gods.

633. *Lyssainōn:* Cr. earlier (492) applied this rare word to the "raving" Ism. when she appeared to be under An.'s influence. The choice of this vehement "feminine" word, usually restricted to the Furies or raging dogs, prepares for Cr.'s later argument that his son is a woman's slave.

634. *Pantachei,* "by any and all means," intimates what he later (671) avers: Cr. expects his son's reverence and obedience no matter what the father does.

635. *Sos eimi* expresses Hae.'s confident filial piety. Polynices makes a similar confession in *Oedipus at Kolonos* 1323. Hae. is only saying here what would be expected of any Greek son. (See Aeschylus *Suppliants* 707–9, Pindar *Pythian* 6. 23–27, Plato *Laws* 4. 717d; also, two metopes on the north side of the Parthenon, under construction about the time Soph. produced the *An.* depicted scenes of filial piety.) Bowra is probably correct in observing (p. 74) that when Hae. later left in a rage he was "by conventional standards deeply in the wrong."

Sy . . . echōn. Cr. misses the beautiful ambiguity of this phrase. It can connote "if" or "when" or "since you guide me well." Hae. is thus able both to mollify his father and maintain his own integrity. *Sou . . . hēgoumenou* (638) contains a similar equivocation.

635-36. *Kai. . . aporthois.* Hae. uses his father's favorite nautical image (see 163 n.), lit., "having good judgments (*gnōmās*), you guide me in a straight course." For the meanings of *gnōmē*, see 176 n.; for the significant change in its meaning for Hae. by the end of this episode, see Intro., this chap.

637-38. *Meizdōn,* "more important," "greater in value," can almost serve as a one-word index of Cr.'s value system. Hae. here is trying valiantly to uphold that system. The king earlier (183) laid down the principle that the welfare of the state is of greater value than a *philos,* a relative or friend; in this episode (652), he will aver that there is no greater wound than a false friend like An. and that there is no greater evil than disobedience (672); Hae. then will counter that sons have no greater glory than their father's good name (704). Finally, however, the son will reject his father's value system with another comparative, *hēsso,* "inferior," an antonym of *meizdōn:* "You will never find me yielding to dishonor" (747). See 1350-51 n.

638. *Sou . . . hēgoumenou* gives Hae. another way of signifying that there are limits to his loyalty to his father's will. The phrase can mean either "if" or "when you guide well."

639-80. Long, p. 156, and Webster, pp. 148-49, both analyze this speech. First, there is a general statement about the advantages of obedience and the dangers of disobedience (639-46); then (646-47) Cr. contrasts the troubles begotten by disobedience with the joys it brings to one's enemies; next (648-72) he applies these principles to Hae. and to the plight of An.; he concludes (672-80) with a personification of Obedience and Anarchy, drawing both specific and general conclusions from this personification.

In this speech, Cr. makes two identifications which he abandons by the end of the episode: first, that his power is identical with the city's power and second, that his judgment is identical with the city's law (Reinhardt, p. 94). When he learns the city's opposition to his will, he then dares to stand alone against the city in interring An. (773 ff.). Thus, by the end of the episode the audience perceives in retrospect that Cr.'s proclaimed principles (639–46) were empty sophistic rhetoric. This speech of Cr. presents an oligarchic and tyrannical view of law and government whereas Hae.'s reply is an argument for the democratic law of reason and participation.

639. Cr. says Hae. is morally obliged (see 89 n. on *chrē*) to an absolute filial obedience.

640. *Opisthen hestanai* introduces a military metaphor of a soldier posted behind his leader. Cr. thus sets the tone he will maintain during the whole scene (see 670–71 and n.). In Soph. *Ajax* 1249, Agamemnon, a figure sharing some traits with Cr. in this play, uses the inversion of ranks as a symbol of anarchy.

643–44. Here Cr. voices the normal Greek outlook toward friends and enemies. It was not a Greek virtue to be kind to one's enemies; furthermore, the fear of providing one's enemies with an opportunity to mock one (647) was predominant in Greek ethical thought from Theognis 1033 onward (cf. Soph. *Ajax* 367).

648. Cr.'s contemptuous tone here in the face of the obvious strength of a member of the "weaker sex" (see 678 n.) betrays his insecurity. It is in this episode that Cr.'s conception of *phrenes*, "reason," "sense"; and *euboulia*, "the art of making sound decisions," becomes clear. An. and Ism. showed their differing basis for reaching judgments in the Prologue (see 95 n., also 469–70 n.). Here Cr. gives his criteria for making sound judgments; these are remarkably close to those Plato's Protagoras will espouse (Protagoras 318e–319a): "The student at my school will learn nothing but what he came for: the art of arriving at sound decisions (*euboulia*) on matters public and private—how to make a financial success of his family affairs, and how to become most influential in public affairs." For Cr.'s final admission of *dysboulia*, the opposite of *euboulia*, see 1347 n.

650. *Psychron parankalisma touto*, "this thing becomes a cold embrace." Cf. 88. There are several Sophoclean devices employed here to express Cr.'s contempt: the contemptuous neuter pronoun *touto*, the oxymoron "frigid darling," the use of an abstract noun for a concrete. In the dénouement, Hae. will in fact choose An.'s cold embrace (1221–22). Cf. Euripides' very different *psychrān . . .*

79

terpsin "cold joy," for Admetus' melodramatic contemplation of a cold statue that he would take into his bed in place of his beloved wife (Euripides *Alcestis* 353).

653. "No! Loathe (*ptysās*, lit., 'spit out') this girl. Cast her out as your foe!" The messenger's later account of Hae.'s death shows that Cr.'s command will be fulfilled in a manner quite different from his intention. Hae. himself will become an outcast and with animal ferocity will spit in his fathers face (*ptysās prosōpōi*, 1232) just before he embraces An. in death. With the later repetition of the exact grammatical form of the verb *ptysās*, Soph. uses the messenger to convey Hae.'s final answer to his father's command here.

654. This line is ambiguous. Either "leave her for someone down there to marry" or "let her find a husband below." Normally the verb *nympheuein* is restricted to the passive voice when applied to women, i.e., they are given in marriage. An active use may imply grudging acknowledgment of An.'s "masculine" strength.

656–57. The double repetition of "city," *polis*, beginning one line and ending the next, suggests that Cr. continues to view his prosecution of his niece as an act of great patriotism.

658–59. *Alla ktenō*, lit., "but I shall kill." The abrupt pause after this phrase, unusual in the middle of a line, dramatizes the determination of his decision. *Ephymneitō Dia xynaimon* is a strong, blasphemous expression. The present imperative, *ephymneitō*, used for continuous action, has the force: "Let her go on praying." With the phrase *Dia xynaimon*, "Zeus of kindred blood," Cr. is consciously rejecting blood claims and the religious claims of Zeus (see 198 n.). At 486–88, he began this process of rejection when he refused mercy to An. and her "blood sister" even when they worshipped at Zeus' altar. Now he completes the rejection, choosing to acknowledge only the claims of the *polis* (656–57). In the Ode on Love (794), the Cho. blames Hae. for valuing love over the claims of a *xynaimos*. Commentators more sympathetic to Cr. would deny blasphemy here. For them, Cr. here either (a) is rejecting not validity of blood ties but Polynices' right to be considered a relative or (b) is asserting that the interests of the *polis* override transcendent religious claims. If (b) is the case, Cr. is short-sighted rather than blasphemous.

660. *Akosma,* "disorder" or "insubordination." *Akosmos* is the negative adjective from *kosmos,* "order," a word often applied to political or military order (see 677 and 730), but in a woman's world applied to the order of beauty, ornament. In this scene, we grasp Cr.'s conception of order; at 901, we see An.'s, when she applies *kosmein* to the honoring and dressing of her brother's body for burial.

661-62. Cr.'s tendency to trite aphorisms is again apparent (see 178 n. and the Intro., chap. 2).

663-67. Pearson placed these lines after 671 on the grounds that *touton ton andra* referred to the man described 666 ff. But Jebb effectively argues against the transposition from their MSS position on the grounds that Cr. is making the point that an obedient citizen who learns to obey in all things would, if required, be the best ruler. Dain-Mazon concur.

663. *Hyperbās,* "overstepping," appropriate for civil law; whereas *hyperdramein,* "override," "transgress," introduces the element of *hybris* against divine law (455).

664. *Epitassein* "to impose commands," proper for the act of a master on a slave. For Cr. there are only two possibilities: either the ruler imposes commands or there is anarchy.

666-67. Cr. draws practical conclusions from his principles. Like the Spartan King Archidamos in Thucydides' *History* 1. 84. 3 (see 453 n.), Cr. insists on rigorous discipline and unquestioning obedience to one man, but Thucydides allows the Spartan king a much more plausible defense of authoritarian rule in terms of obedience to laws, not just to one man. Cf. *Oedipus Tyrannos* 625-30 for Oedipus' view that the king must be obeyed whether right or wrong.

Literally translated, these lines say: "It is necessary to obey him in little things and just things and their opposites." What Cr. really demands is obedience whether he is just or unjust. However, he disguises his meaning by substituting *t'anantia,* "the opposites," instead of *t'adika,* "unjust." Since the phrase "in matters just and unjust" was apparently axiomatic (cf. Solon 41 in Edmonds 1:154 and Aeschylus, *Choephoroi* 78), the Athenian audience would see through the disguise. Cf. Eliot Janeway's observation that the roots of Watergate were planted in the assumption implicit in such cases as the Japanese-American confinements "that the government is always right—even when it violates the Constitution."

668. *Touton . . . ton andra,* "this man," i.e., the man who thus obeys.

670–71. Cr. uses both military and storm imagery here. Hae. must not abandon his position as comrade on the flank (*parastatēs*); *prostetagmenon* is related to *tassein* (see 634 n., 639–40).

672–76. Cr. personifies two abstractions, *an-archia,* "no rule," "lawlessness," "a lack of leadership," as the destroyer of cities; and *peith-archia,* "obedience to rule," as the savior of cities (see Intros., chap. 1 and this chap.) For a similar belief in the saving nature of obedience, see Aeschylus *Seven against Thebes* 224–25. Cr.'s simplistic dichotomy between these two opposing forces, one good, the other bad, is a far cry from the vision of Athena in the *Eumenides* where she established a court of the Areopagus so that neither lawlessness nor tyranny (*to mēt' anarchon mēt' despotoumenon,* Aeschylus *Eumenides* 696) may prevail. There the god maintains a delicate balance between these two forces in the cosmos (*Eumenides* 526 ff.). But here, in effect, Cr. abrogates to himself the entire "masculine" role of commanding and consigns the rest of the *polis* to "feminine" obedience. Cr. and An. bring two principles of obedience into collision: 1) the principle of absolute military obedience which Cr. transfers to familial relationships, 2) the principle of obedience to a higher law. See Soph. *Philoctetes* 1247 ff. for a similar clash.

673–74. Cr. uses the rhetorical device anaphora, i.e., the repetition of the initial word *hēde,* in successive clauses for emphasis. *Anastatous,* properly, "driven from one's home," pictures cities as driven into exile by *anarchia.*

676. *Ta polla somat(a)* does not mean "the greater part" but "the many bodies," i.e., all persons who live in obedience to authority. The poet uses *sōizdei,* "preserves," to chart the changes of direction in Cr.: first (189), it was the country that "keeps us safe"; here, it is obedience; but finally, he admits one should end one's life preserving the "established laws" (1113), i.e., the unwritten laws of Zeus (see 453–55 n.).

677. *Tois kosmoumenois.* See n. on *akosma,* 660.

678–80. The agitated repetition of the particle *an* reveals Cr.'s horror at being considered inferior to An. The line is particularly ironic, since he finally is defeated not by one woman but two, An. and Eurydice (see 1315 n.). Cr.'s obsession with this thought reveals his deep-seated insecurity, although the thought of such inferiority would be a disgrace for any Athenian male. (Cf. Pericles' celebrated view that women are best off when they have no reputation among men either for good or evil [Thucydides 2. 45. 2]; Aeschylus *Seven against Thebes* 200–201, 230–32; also, Aristophanes *Lysistrata* 450–51: "No! never shall women conquer us!") Still, apparently, woman was not to be maltreated (cf. Aristophanes *Clouds* 1443 ff.) or reduced to the level of slavery as Cr. presumed. Cr.'s disregard for the sanctity of the family bonds would also disturb the audience. The evidence of vase paintings, for instance, attests to the tender affection accorded to woman in her subordinate, severely limited, and patronized position as wife, mother, and housekeeper. There is conflicting critical opinion as to whether tragic women like An. and Electra can be taken as evidence of high esteem for normal Athenian women. Kitto, Gomme, and others think yes; Lacey, Pomeroy, and others disagree. See Pomeroy, pp. 127–57, where she gives full bibliography on the subject and notes that scholars who argue for woman's high position tend to limit themselves to the evidence of tragedy and believe the tragic women were modeled on contemporary culture. Those who cite comedy and oratory incline more to view women as oppressed, subjected to husbands fifteen years their seniors, purposely kept uneducated, and living in secluded dark women's quarters. See nn. on 18–19 and 41–43, and Intro., chap. 1. Sociologist Philip E. Slater, *The Glory of Hera* (Boston: Beacon Press, 1968), may be right in his analysis of the gynephobia and male insecurity that grew out of the male-dominated, often homosexual society of fifth century Athens. He contends that the society produced "a self-repeating cycle of sex antagonism and narcissism" (p. 70). Women deprived of satisfactory marital relationships exerted excessive influence over sons; the sons in turn tended to become insecure and to fear "any female who was a whole woman" (p. 66).

679. *Ekpesein* "to be displaced," i.e., to lose one's throne or rule.

681. The choral leader speaking for the Cho. continues the sycophancy and thoughtless obedience that usually characterizes this Cho. (see 211–14, 724–25 n.) in its nonchoral pronouncements.

683–723. This speech of Hae.'s balances Cr.'s previous speech (639–80). It begins with a general proposition on good sense and ends with a general reflection (721). In the body of the speech, Hae. applies the general proposition to An.'s situation and discusses wisdom, reputation, piety and flexibility (the elaborate simile on the tractable man balances Cr.'s personification of Anarchy and Obedience). His concluding remarks apply his reflections to his father. As Cr.'s speech revealed the blindness of an insecure authoritarian father, Hae.'s reveals the blindness of an idealistic youth who thinks he has the ability to instruct his father and to convince him to mend his ways (see Reinhardt, pp. 94–96). There are striking similarities in form and content between this speech of Hae. and the speech of Artabanos to his nephew, King Xerxes in Herodotos 7. 10.

683–84. Hae. begins with a complimentary allusion to his father's concern for wisdom or good sense, but tactfully suggests that the divine origin of wisdom prohibits the blind filial obedience which Cr. demanded (640). Cr.'s obsession with understanding, *phronein,* and wisdom, *eu phronein,* climaxes in this episode. See Hae.'s remarks: 707, 710–11, 719, 723, 753–55; Cr.'s sarcastic retort 726–27 and 754; and Tiresias at 1051, 1090, 1098; from 1261–69 on, the theme recoils on Cr. (see n. on 1347 ff.). The theme is basic also to the fabric of *Oedipus Tyrannos* where *phronein* is used especially of Oedipus' ability to keep his wits about him and where *eu phronein* signifies his final wisdom to perceive the truly good.

685. Hae. refrains from specifying "in what respect" (*hopōs*). Cr. errs, but *hopōs* gives the first indication that Hae. knows his father's ship deviates from its straight course. *Orthōs* is meant to remind Cr. of his goal of straight sailing (675).

686. Hae. shrinks from telling his father his error by switching from a statement of fact, ("I would not be able to") to a prayer, ("may I not be capable of saying," i.e., "may I not bring myself to say").

687. *Chaterōs,* "elsewhere". I follow Pearson's reading here. If one retains the MSS reading *chaterōi* (dative singular) as Jebb and Mazon do, the sentence would mean: "some good thought might come to another person also."

688. Jebb and Dain follow another reading of the text: *pephyka.*

In that case, the line would mean: "It is my natural office to watch out on your behalf." The reading of Pearson seems right in that it contains the double meaning "you are not in a position to observe" and "you are not qualified to observe" (Müller, p. 166).

Proskopein, "to observe." In these next few lines, Hae. accommodates himself to his father's predisposition to evidence of the senses by using many sense words.

690. *To. . . son omma deinon.* The word order places the emphasis on *your* dread expression. Hae. reports the fears of common citizens (*dēmotēi*) as if they were speaking their minds. There may be a verse missing after 690.

691. *Logois toioutois,* lit., probably "because of such words," i.e., "when such words are spoken" (Jebb).

692. *Hypo skotou,* "in the darkness," i.e., "out of the glare of your eye." See 700 n.

693. *Odyretai,* "laments." An. earlier (504-5, 509) claimed she had the people's support, but this is the first clear indication that Cr. is not, in fact, representing popular opinion about the state's best interests as he claimed (178 ff.). Kitto (*Form,* p. 125) observes that Shakespeare would have elaborated this one line of Hae.'s into a whole scene. This episode thus reveals the voice of the people spoken by the young Hae., as a later episode (988 ff.) reveals the voice of the gods spoken by the aged seer Tiresias.

694-95. The three superlatives together with the emphatic position of *pasōn gynaikōn,* "of *all* women," are indicative of the emotional attachment of the people and Hae. to An. Hae.'s praise of An. from 694-99 is both warm and full.

Eukleestatōn, lit., "of superlative fame," i.e., "most heroic" (see 703 n.). *To kleos* was the Homeric word for the good fame of the heroes.

Phthinei, "wastes away." This verb is usually reserved for the natural waning of time or of the moon, and so its use here emphasizes the unnatural wastefulness of An.'s untimely death.

696. *Autadelphon.* See 1 n.

696-97. Hae. repeats almost verbatim his father's words announcing the decree (205-6). Critics have questioned the consistency of Hae.'s remarks here, since An. was not in fact able to prevent birds from mangling Polynices' body. Obviously, the symbolic burial sufficed for Hae. as it did for An.

699. The phrase "worthy of golden honor" combines a monetary and light image. An.'s brilliance and worth show how Hae.'s conception of gain differs from Cr.'s (see 701–4 and n.).

700. *Toiād(e)* . . . *phatis*, "such dark rumor," i.e., dangerous for Cr. Hae. uses more color words and light imagery than anyone else in the play. An. from 694–704 is described with light images; and it is Hae.'s hope to dispel the dark rumor currently associated with his father.

703–4. *Ti* . . . *meizdon:* "For what is a greater cause of glory (*agalma*) for children than the good fame (*eukleiās*) of a prosperous father." Hae. has just told his father that at present it is An. who has the *eukleia* (695 and n.). *Eukleia* and *agalma* are heroic words which naturally complement each other. The sentence "brings together briefly two distinct ideas, which are later to be found indistinguishable, Creon's standing as king and the 'criminal' actions of Antigone" (Long, p. 153). The continued vitality of *eukleia* as an inspiration to noble action can be seen in the fact that Pericles advised the families of the fallen Athenian soldiers to be cheered by their *eukleia* (Thucydides 2. 44. 4). But Pericles' *eukleia,* unlike Cr.'s, was rooted in honor (*to tīmāsthai*), not in gain (*to kerdainein*).

705. *Mē* . . . *phorei:* "Do not carry just one disposition (*ēthos*) in yourself" (Cf. Theognis 213 ff.). Cr.'s stubborn self-will is also characteristic of An. The Cho. earlier (471–72) called An. the unbending (*ōmos*) offspring of an unbending father, one who did not know how to bend (*eikein*) in adversity. Both Cr. and An. are confident of possessing the intelligence and soul (*psychēn,* 708) that others lack. Knox (p. 70 ff.) points to this conviction as basic to the "heroic temper," a temper which Cr. does not really possess, for at 770 he changes his mind on two major points, granting a reprieve to Ism. and lessening An.'s sentence. He also reneges on the rules of statecraft he set down in his first speech (see 734 n.). "There is a calculating and fearful head behind that heroic mask" (Knox, p. 73).

709. *Houtoi.* . . *kenoi:* "Such people when unfolded (like a letter) at once appear to be empty." Hae. uses a strange metaphor here that will turn out to be peculiarly prophetic of his father's life (Knox, p. 178, n. 18). He speaks of a folded writing tablet which

one opens only to find that it is devoid of all content. In the dénouement, Cr. finally sees and acknowledges that his life adds up to a cipher (1325). On the pervasiveness of the emptiness theme, see the Intro., this chap. Cf. also Euripides *Hippolytos* 985.

711. *To . . . agan.* The metaphor *teinein agan,* "stretching a bow or string too tight," naturally leads into the following extended simile. Both figures have to do with rigidity. Lines 711-17, among the most figurative in the play, serve to contrast Hae.'s more imaginative style with the more direct and uncompromising approach of An.

712. *Rheithroisi cheimarrois,* "rivers swollen by storms." Hae. deftly uses his father's storm image (670) against him. This Homeric figure (*Iliad* 4. 452) of the bending of trees in winter streams has a close parallel in the "Debate on Constitutions" (Herodotos 3. 80). There, a Persian noble, Megabyzos, argues that oligarchy is superior to democracy, because the untaught democratic rabble rushes wildly into state affairs with the fury of a swollen winter stream (*cheimarrōi potamî ikelos*). The democratic Hae. echoes Megabyzos, but for Hae., it is the *tyrannos,* not the *dēmos,* "the populace," that is in danger of displaying headless impetuosity.

713-18. *Hypeikei,* "give way" (cf. *hypeike,* 716 and *eike,* 718). Hae. uses metaphor, fable, and simile to describe the overrigid, the taut that must loosen or break. First the overstretched lyre (711), then the fable, perhaps from Aesop's fable of the oak and reed (Babrius 36) which Athenian boys like Hae. would have learned in school, and finally the extended simile of the sailor capsizing because he refuses to shorten sail. The piling up of images here, all based on *teinein,* "stretching" (714, 716), climaxes Hae.'s desperate attempt to convince his father to retreat. And while the arguments share superficial similarities with Cr.'s against the stubborn An. (473-78), the tone and purpose is different. Cr. brutally insisted that the most unyielding are most easily broken, whereas Hae. seeks to bring about some flexibility in his father before it is too late (718, 723).

715-17. Hae. returns again (see 685) to his father's nautical conception of statecraft (163 ff.). The emphatically placed *hyptiois* (716) suggests the moment of capsizing. *Enkratē* (715), "holding fast," here used of the sheet that controls the course of the ship, is the word with which Cr. alluded to An. (474) as the stiffest iron that snaps in the fire.

718. Hae. the first warner of Cr., climaxes his argument here: "Do yield! and let your anger relent." Lit.: "allow a change from (*or* to) your anger." Later (1029), Tiresias, the second "warner," climaxes his warning with: "Yield to the claim of the dead" (*eike tōi thanonti*). I adopt the reading of Campbell (*Paralipomena Sophoclea,* p. 28) and of Dain who follow one MS against Jebb, Pearson, and several later MSS. Long (p. 87) effectively answers the main objections to this reading (the weakness of *kai,* "also"). The asyndeton (lack of connective) after "yield" dramatically emphasizes the three images of overrigidity in the preceding lines. He is not saying "Yield from your wrath" *eike thymou* (Jebb and Pearson's reading) but simply and absolutely: "yield—cease from your wrath." The *kai* then is best taken as a postponed connective for the two imperatives (*hyperbaton*). Furthermore, the dative form, *thymōi,* is more natural after the verb of giving.

721. On the theme of emptiness, see 709 n.

720–23. "The real stress is on the last line" (Campbell). Still, the *ei d'oun* is both elliptical and implies a negative: "But if in fact the case is otherwise" (Denniston, pp. 464–66).

723. *Tōn legontōn eu,* "those speaking well," i.e., the wise (see 683–84).

724–25. Critics complain of the fatuity of this Cho. However, Soph. consciously chooses the Cho. through its leader's remarks in the dialogue portions (as distinct from the choral odes) to express the fatuous observations of ordinary public opinion. This is a consistent feature of Sophoclean tragedy.

726. The climax of the learning wisdom theme for Cr. (See nn. on 1347 and 95). *Dē* and *kai* both accentuate Cr.'s indignation as does the fact that Cr. directs the remark not to Hae. but to the Cho. Kitto (*Greek Tragedy,* p. 169) notes this is a habit of Soph.'s characters when too angry to answer directly (*Electra* 612, *Oedipus Tyrannos* 429, 618).

729. *Ta erga.* Hae. means "the facts of the case." Cr. chooses to understand Hae. to mean "my deeds."

730–61. The rest of this scene is cast in stichomythia, dialogue in alternate lines. The form is particularly effective in scenes like

88

this where speaker B gives an ironic, or sarcastic twist to a word or thought just expressed by speaker A. Shakespeare makes similar uses of stichomythia. In Greek, however, the device is more natural and is not limited to such scenes of sharp antithesis and sarcastic repetition. In this scene, Cr. reintroduces the theme of piety (see 74 and Intro., chap. 1, and 924 n. for An.'s final statement on *eusebeia*). The king remains so secure in his belief that his act is a pious one that he is impervious to his son's argument that he is trampling on the gods' prerogatives (see 745 and 777). Armed with his piety but pressured by Hae., Cr. moves toward a "doctrine of power" (Goheen, p. 91).

731. "I would not urge (*keleusaimi*) you to revere traitors (*kakous*)." Cf. An.'s use of *keleusaimi* (69) for a measure of the difference between the gentle Hae. and his stubborn, passionate fiancée: "I would not urge you—nor would I welcome you as a coworker." *Kakos* can mean worthless, traitorous, cowardly, criminal, or sick. Cr.'s response (731) chooses to twist his son's remark about evil, traitorous men into a reference to disease.

732. *Epeilēptai.* Cr. continues the military language. Disease "has attacked" here. See 1284 where it is finally apparent that Cr., not An., is diseased.

734. *Hēmīn ha(e)me* juxtaposes the royal plural *hēmīn* and the singular *eme.* Lit.: "Will the town tell us how I must rule?" Cr.'s incredulous question, meant to cast doubt on Hae.'s assertion, flatly contradicts his own announced principles (178–90).

Tassein, lit., "to draw up for battle," "to order." Again he sees his rule in terms of military order (see nn. on 640, 660). An.'s early reference (8) to him as *stratēgos* suggests she understood this aspect of his character.

735. Hae. distinguishes between *neos*, "young," and *agan neos*, "too young," "immature," "childish."

736. *Chrē* usually implies moral necessity (see 89 n.). *Tēsde chthonos*, "this earth." Cr. thinks of his city as an inanimate clump of earth (see Hae.'s retort at 739); the Cho. in the Ode on Man 368–69 and An. use *chthōn* as deserving of great reverence.

737. *Andros . . . henos* contains an effective ambiguity. It can mean a city belonging to one man (genitive of possession) and a city composed of one man (genitive of content). Cf. Aeschylus

Suppliants 370: "You are the *polis*. You are the people." Also Shakespeare's *Julius Caesar* 1–2. The Cr. of Soph.'s later *Oedipus Tyrannos* takes the opposite position against Oedipus: "It is my city too, not yours alone" (*Oedipus Tyrannos* 630). Athenian democracy, both in theory and in practice, consistently denied the tyrants' claim that the city belonged to them. Cf. Aeschylus *Persians* 242; Thucydides 2. 37. 1; also Euripides *Suppliants* 404–5, "No single man is ruler. Our city is free." At 1163 the messenger unwittingly describes the true nature of Cr.'s rule with the words *pantelē monarchiān*, "absolute power," a phrase that would cause a shudder in the Athenian audience. *Monarchiā* had a more despotic ring than *tyrannis*.

738. Here it is clear that "Creon no longer speaks and acts for the *polis* as a whole; he speaks for no one but himself" (Knox, p. 108). The possessive genitive *tou kratountos* "possession of the ruler," strongly emphasizes Cr.'s claim of ownership. *Nomizdetai*, "is considered," has an ominous double meaning here, since the verb contains the noun *nomos* "law." Thus, it also can mean: "Does not the city get its *nomoi* from the ruler?" (Goheen p. 151, n. 23).

739. Hae., now for the first time sarcastic (such is the force of *ge* here), makes one of his most effective retorts. *Erēmos* properly means empty. "You would make a splendid monarch of a desert." Note the recurrence again of the emptiness theme (cf. 709 n.). An. uses *erēmos* to express her painful isolation (919).

740. *Symmachei*, "is in league with." Kitto's translation captures the political and military allusion: "This man, it seems, is the ally of the woman." See 678–80 n.

741. *Prokēdomai*, "I care for." With this word that, like *philein*, suggests deep personal concern, Hae. reasserts (701–4) his devotion to his father. The *gar oun* throws strong emphasis onto *sou*, "you." At 549, An. ironically accuses Ism. of making Cr. her concern. An. and Cr. thus both consign their friendly advisors to "the enemy," whereas Hae. continues to try to mediate.

742. *Pankakiste*, "utterly vile." With this word and *miaron*, "abominable" (746), Cr. expresses his contemptuous renunciation of his son. *Pankakistos* is Medea's strongest epithet for the vile Jason (Euripides *Medea* 465–66).

744. "Am I not right in respecting my constitutional preroga-

tives" (*tās emās archās*)? Cr. tries to invoke his kingly rights and duties, the proper execution of which he earlier (177) said revealed a true king. An. however, unmasked his rule (506–7): "Tyranny is blessed in many other ways, but especially since it has the power to do and say what it will."

745–46. Each speaker echoes a word from the previous line. Hae. thus challenges his father's conception of *dikē*, "justice," and *eusebeia*, "piety." In 745, he accuses his father of blasphemy. *Ge* gives the phrase the sense: "*when* you trample on the gods' prerogatives" (Denniston, p. 143). *Patōn*, "walking," is commonly used for blasphemous trampling on sacred things (e.g., Aeschylus *Agamemnon* 369). Cr. is trampling on the gods in that he ignores their jurisdiction over the dead and acts as though his jurisdiction over the *polis* extends to the realm below (361–62 n.). On *tīmās*, "honor," see nn. on 5, 77. Cr.'s apparently irrelevant retort at 746, accusing Hae. of being a woman's lackey, shows his realization that his son agrees with An.'s system of values (77 n.), not his own. The Cho. evidently remains with Cr. (794). On the theme of piety, see the Intro., this chap.; on *hamartanō*, the verb "to offend," twice used here, see 926.

747. *T(oi)*, properly an ethical dative together with the *ge* underlines Hae.'s conviction that the real slavery is to dishonor.

749. *Theōn* . . . *nerterōn*, "for the gods below," shows Hae.'s acceptance of another aspect of An.'s value system.

750–52. Cr.'s unnecessarily heartless remark leads his son to a slightly veiled warning of his own death 751, but Cr. takes it as a threat of rebellion (768).

752. *Ka(i) epapeilōn*. Cr. compresses a whole thought (are you threatening me?) into a participle. *Expexerchei* is a military term, lit., "are you making a sally?" For the meaning of *thrasys*, see "Vocabulary," chap. 8.

753. *Pros kenās gnōmās* "against empty judgments." Hae. finally understands his father's hollowness (cf. 709 n.). The changes in meaning of *gnōmē* are an index of the changes of Hae.'s understanding of his father. At 176, Cr. piously spoke of a man of judgment, *gnōmēn;* Hae.'s opening line (635) extols his father's *gnōmās* . . . *chrēstās*, good judgment, Cr. accepts the compliment, counseling his son to stand behind his father's *gnōmēs*, judgment. Finally here

Hae. regards his father's judgments as hollow aphorisms.

756. The abstract noun *douleuma,* "a slave-thing," is a more insulting word than *doulos,* the concrete noun "slave." *Mīsos* (760) and *parankalisma* (650) are other instances of the use of neuter nouns to convey contempt. *Kōtille,* "wheedle," perhaps an animal image here (Goheen, p. 136, n. 36).

760–61. Here Cr. is again shown relying on the physical organ of sight and on multiple words of physical presence (see 184 and 688 n.).

760. W. J. Ziobro (pp. 81–85) argues that this command results in An.'s reentry onto stage after Hae.'s angry exit (766). The more usual view is that she does not reenter until after the next ode. *To mīsos,* "the hated thing." See 756 n.

762–66. Hae. speaks pleonastically (especially at 764), using pathetically redundant visual words in imitation of his father's mode of communication, even though he has now lost all hope of reaching his father.

765. At the end of the Prologue, Ism. still promised love to the sister she could no longer understand, but An. utterly rejected both the offer and the sister who offered it. At the end of this episode, the gentle Hae. tragically becomes like his unbending fiancée, consigning Cr. to the love of those who can endure (*tois thelousi*) his madness. Cr. now joins the parade of madness (see 631; also at 135, Polynices was reported as raving.) Thus, this episode which began with Hae.'s avowal of filial piety ends with the complete rupture of the relationship between father and son. After Hae.'s abrupt departure, Cr. makes a concession that may perhaps show that Hae. did slightly penetrate Cr.'s defenses. In any case, it is a concession entirely appropriate to his legalistic understanding of piety. An. need not die; instead, she is to suffer a living death, entombed with enough "fodder" so that the city may avoid *miasma* (773–76, and see 172, 1284 n.). Such is his concession to piety. The episode ends with his invitation to An. to continue her vain reverence for Hades (777–80). The irony of these last lines becomes fully apparent at 1284 (see n. there).

GRAMMATICAL NOTES

631. εἰσόμεσθα = εἰσόμεθα, οἶδα: fut. perf. 1 pl.; μάντεων, μάντις: gen. pl.

632. τελείαν ψῆφον, τέλειος, ψῆφος: acc. sing.; κλύων . . . λυσσαίνων, κλύω, λυσσαίνω: pres. partic.

633. τῆς μελλονύμφου, ἡ μελλόνυμφος: gen. sing., objective gen. with ψῆφον; πατρί, πατήρ: dat. sing.; πάρει, πάρειμι: pres. 2 sing.

634. ἡμεῖς, ἐγώ: nom. pl. (royal pl. for sing.); δρῶντες, δράω: pres. partic. nom. pl. m.

635. γνώμας, χρηστάς, γνώμη, χρηστός: acc. pl. dir. obj. of both ἔχων and ἀπορθοῖς; ἔχων, ἔχω: pres. partic.

636. ἀπορθοῖς, ἀπορθόω: pres. 2 sing.; αἷς, ὅς: dat. pl. f. with ἐφέψομαι; ἐφέψομαι, ἐφέπομαι: fut. 1 sing.

637. ἀξιώσεται, ἀξιόω: fut. pass. 3 sing.

638. μείζων, μέγας: comparat.; φέρεσθαι, φέρω: pres. mid. inf. depending on μείζων; ἡγουμένου, ἡγέομαι: pres. partic. gen. sing. in gen. with σοῦ (σύ).

639. διὰ στέρνων ἔχειν: lit., "to be disposed in one's breast," i.e., "to feel," since στέρνον was considered the seat of the emotions.

640. γνώμης πατρῴας, γνώμη, πατρῷος: gen. sing.; πάντ(α), πᾶς: acc. pl. n.; ἑστάναι, ἵστημι: 2 perf. inf.

641. τούτου, οὗτος: gen. sing. m.; οὕνεκ(α) = οὗ ἕνεκα: prep. taking preceding gen.; εὔχονται, εὔχομαι: pres. 3 pl.; γονὰς = (παῖδας)κατηκόους, γονή, κατήκοος: acc. pl.

642. φύσαντες, φύω: aor. partic. nom. pl. m.; δόμοις, δόμος: dat. pl.

643. ἀνταμύνωνται, ἀνταμύνομαι: pres. subj. 3 pl.

644. τιμῶσιν, τιμάω: pres. subj. 3 pl.; ἐξ ἴσον, ἴσος: gen. sing.; πατρί, πατήρ: dat. sing.

645. ἀνωφέλητα . . . τέκνα, ἀνωφέλητος, τέκνον: acc. pl.

646. τόνδ(ε), ὅδε: acc. sing. m.; εἴποις, λέγω, εἶπον: aor. opt. 2 sing.; ἄλλο, ἄλλος: acc. sing. neut.; αὑτῷ = ἑαυτῷ, ἑαυτοῦ: dat. sing. m.; πόνους, πόνος: acc. pl.

647. φῦσαι, φύω: aor. inf.; πολὺν . . . γέλων, "occasion for much laughter," γέλων: poetic acc. of γέλως; τοῖσιν ἐχθροῖσιν = τοῖς ἐχθροῖς, ἐχθρός: dat. pl.

648. μή: neg. with ἐκβάλῃς; φρένας, φρήν: acc. pl.

649. γυναικός, γυνή: gen. sing., obj. of prep. οὕνεκ(α); ἐκβάλῃς, ἐκβάλλω: 2 aor. subj. used for neg. imper.; εἰδώς, οἶδα: perf. partic. regularly used as pres.

650. γίγνεται, γίγνομαι: pres. 3 sing.

651. ξύνευνος = σύνευνος.

652. γένοιτ(ο), γίγνομαι: 2 aor. opt. 3 sing.; μεῖζον, μέγας: comparat. adj. nom. neut. modif. ἕλκος.

653. πτύσας, πτύω: aor. partic.; δυσμενῆ, δυσμενής: acc. sing. f.; μέθες, μεθίημι: 2 aor. imper. 2 sing.

654. παῖδ(α), παῖς: acc. sing.; Ἄιδου, Ἄιδης: gen. because the full expression would be "in the house of Hades"; τήνδε, ὅδε: acc. sing. f.; νυμφεύειν, νυμφεύω, inf. with dat. τινί: "for someone to marry."

655. αὐτήν, αὐτός: acc. sing. f.; εἶλον, αἱρέω: 2 aor. 1 sing.

656. πόλεως . . . ἐκ πάσης, πόλις, πᾶς: gen. sing.; ἀπιστήσασαν, ἀπιστέω: aor. partic. acc. sing. f. with αὐτὴν . . . μόνην.

657. ψευδῆ ἐμαυτόν, ψευδής, ἐμαυτοῦ: acc. sing. m.; καταστήσω, καθίστημι: fut. 1 sing.

658. κτενῶ, κτείνω: fut. 1 sing.; ταῦτα, οὗτος: acc. pl. neut.; ἐφυμνείτω, ἐφυμνέω: imper. 3 sing.; Δία ξύναιμον, Ζεὺς σύναιμος: acc. sing.

659. ἐγγενῆ, ἐγγενής, ἄκοσμα, ἄκοσμος: Cr. uses acc. pl. neut. in place of acc. pl. m.; φύσει, φύσις: dat. sing.

660. θρέψω, τρέφω: fut. ind.; τούς: supply ἀκόσμους; γένους, γένος: gen. sing.

661. οἰκείοισιν = οἰκείοις, οἰκεῖος: dat. pl.

662. φανεῖται, φαίνω: fut. mid. (it means "appear" in the mid.); πόλει, πόλις: dat. sing.; ὤν, εἰμί: pres. partic.

663. ὑπερβάς, ὑπερβαίνω: aor. partic.; βιάζεται, βιάζω: pres. mid. 3 sing. (it means "do violence to" in the mid.).

664. τοῖς κρατύνουσιν, κρατύνω: pres. partic. dat. pl. (ἐπιτάσσειν takes dat.); νοεῖ, νοέω: pres. 3 sing.

665. ἐπαίνου, ἔπαινος: gen. sing. with τυχεῖν; τοῦτον, οὗτος: acc. sing. m., subject of inf.; τυχεῖν, τυγχάνω: 2 aor. inf.

666. ὅν, ὅς: acc. sing. m.; στήσειε, ἵστημι: aor. opt. 3 sing.; τοῦδε, ὅδε: gen. sing. with κλύειν

667. σμικρά = μικρά . . . δίκαια . . . τὰ (ἐ)ναντία, μικρός, δίκαιος, ἐναντίος: acc. pl. neut.

94

668. τοῦτον τὸν ἄνδρα, οὗτος ὁ ἀνήρ: acc. sing.; θαρσοίην, θαρσέω: aor. opt. 1 sing.

669. μὲν . . . δέ: balance the two inf. phrases, ἄρχειν and ἄρχεσθαι (both these inf. depend on the inf. θέλειν, θέλω); ἄρχεσθαι, ἄρχω: pres. pass. inf.

670. δορός = δόρατος, δορύ: gen. sing.; χειμῶνι, χειμών: dat. sing.; προστεταγμένον, προστάσσω: perf. pass. partic. acc. sing. modif. ἄνδρα, 668.

671. μένειν, μένω: pres. inf.; παραστάτην, παραστάτης: acc. sing.

672. ἀναρχίας, ἀναρχία: gen. sing., gen. of comparison; μεῖζον . . . κακόν, μέγας (comparat.), κακός: nom. sing. neut.

673. αὕτη, οὗτος: nom. sing. f. referring to ἀναρχία; πόλεις, πόλις: acc. pl.; ὄλλυσιν, ὄλλυμι: pres. 3 sing.; ἥδε, ὅδε: nom. sing. f. balancing αὕτη; ἀναστάτους οἴκους, ἀνάστατος οἶκος: acc. pl.

674. τίθησιν, τίθημι: pres. 3 sing.; μάχῃ, μάχη: dat. sing.; δορός = δόρατος, δορύ: gen. sing.

675. τροπάς, τροπή: cognate acc. to an idea implied in καταρρήγνυσι, i.e., "causes routs by breaking ranks"; καταρρήγνυσι, καταρρήγνυμι: pres. 3 sing.; ὀρθουμένων, ὀρθόω: pass. partic. gen. pl.

676. σώζει, σώζω: pres. 3 sing.; πολλὰ σώματ(α), πολύς, σῶμα: acc. pl.

677. ἀμυντέ(α) = ἀμυντέον: verbal expressing obligation with ἐστι (like the Latin gerundive) "to be defended"; τοῖς κοσμουμένοις, κοσμέω: pres. partic. dat. pl. with verbal.

678. γυναικός, γυνή: gen. sing., with ἡσσητέα; ἡσσητέα, ἡσσητέον, ἡσσάομαι: verbal expressing obligation.

679. κρεῖσσον = κρεῖττον, ἀγαθός: comparat. nom. sing. neut.; ἀνδρός, ἀνήρ: gen. sing.; ἐκπεσεῖν, ἐκπίπτω: 2 aor. inf.

680. γυναικῶν, γυνή: gen. pl. (of comparison); ἥσσονες, ἥσσων: nom. pl. m., comparat. of κακός; καλοῖμεθ(α), καλέω: pres. opt. pass 1 pl.

681. ἡμῖν, ἐγώ: dat. pl.; κεκλέμμεθα, κλέπτω: perf. pass. 1 pl.

682. λέγειν, λέγω: pres. act. inf.; ὧν, ὅς: gen. pl. with πέρι, elliptical for περὶ τούτων περὶ ὧν; δοκεῖς, δοκέω: pres. 2 sing.

683. φύουσιν, φύω: pres. 3 pl.; φρένας, φρήν: acc. pl.

684. ὅσ(α), ὅσος: nom. pl. neut., subject of ἐστί (neut. pl. subject takes sing. verb); πάντων χρημάτων, πᾶς, χρῆμα: gen. pl.; ὑπέρτατον,

ὑπέρτατος: acc. sing. neut.

685. τάδε, ὅδε: acc. pl. neut.

686. δυναίμην, δύναμαι: pres. opt. 1 sing.; οὔτε the first neg. indicates an assertion of fact; the second neg. μήτε indicates a prayer; ἐπισταίμην, ἐπίσταμαι: pres. opt. 1 sing.

687. γένοιτο, γίγνομαι: 2 aor. opt. 3 sing.; ἔχον, ἔχω: pres. partic. nom. sing. neut.

688. πέφυκας, φύω: perf. 2 sing. with pres. meaning; προσκοπεῖν, προσκοπέω: pres. inf.; πάντα . . . ὅσα, πᾶς, ὅσος: acc. pl. neut.

689. πράσσει = πράττει, πράσσω: pres. 3 sing.; ψέγειν, ψέγω: pres. inf.

690. ἀνδρί, ἀνήρ: dat. sing.; δημότῃ, δημότης: dat. sing. (Pearson following Dindorf believes a line is missing here.)

691. οἷς, ὅς: dat. pl. m.; τέρψῃ, τέρπω: aor. mid. 2 sing.; κλύων, κλύω: pres. partic.

693. τὴν παῖδα ταύτην, ἡ παῖς, οὗτος: acc. sing. f.; ὀδύρεται, ὀδύρομαι: pres. 3 sing.

694. πασῶν γυναικῶν, πᾶς, γυνή: gen. pl.; ἀναξιωτάτη, ἀνάξιος: superl. nom. sing. f.

695. κάκιστ(α), κακῶς: superl. adv.; εὐκλεεστάτων, εὐκλεής: superl. adj. gen. pl. modif. ἔργων.

696. ἥτις, ὅστις: nom. sing. f.; αὐτῆς, ἑαυτοῦ: gen. sing. f.; φοναῖς, φονή: dat. pl.

697. πεπτῶτ(α), πίπτω: perf. partic. acc. sing. m.; κυνῶν, κύων: gen. pl. with ὑπό

698. εἴασ(ε), ἐάω: aor. 3 sing.; ὀλέσθαι, ὄλλυμι: aor. mid. inf.; οἰωνῶν, οἰωνός: gen. pl.; τινός, τις: gen. sing.

699. ἥδε, ὅδε: nom. sing. f.; χρυσῆς . . . τιμῆς, χρυσός, τιμή: gen. sing.; ἀξία, ἄξιος: nom. sing. f.; λαχεῖν, λαγχάνω: 2 aor. inf.

700. τοιάδ(ε) = τοιήδε, τοιόσδε: nom. sing. f.; ἐρεμνή, ἐρεμνός: nom. sing. f. modif. φάτις; ὑπέρχεται, ὑπέρχομαι: pres. 3 sing.

701. σοῦ, σύ, πράσσοντος = πράττοντος, πράσσω (pres. partic.): gen. sing.

702. οὐδέν, οὐδείς, τιμιώτερον, τίμιος (comparat.): nom. sing. neut. modif. κτῆμα.

703. πατρός, πατήρ: gen. sing.; θάλλοντος, θάλλω: pres. partic. gen. sing.; εὐκλείας, εὔκλεια: gen. of comparison

704. μεῖζον, μέγας (comparat.): nom. neut. modif. ἄγαλμα; παίδων, παῖς: gen. pl.; πατρί, πατήρ: dat. sing.

705. ἕν, εἷς: acc. neut. modif. ἦθος μοῦνον = μόνον; σαυτῷ, σεαυτοῦ: dat. sing.; φόρει, φορέω: imper. 2 sing.

706. φής, φημί: pres. 2 sing.; οὐδέν, οὐδείς, ἄλλο, ἄλλος: nom. sing. neut.; ὀρθῶς: adv. with adjectival force with inf. ἔχειν.

707. φρονεῖν, φρονέω: pres. inf.; δοκεῖ, δοκέω: pres. 3 sing.

708. ἥν, ὅς: acc. sing. f.

709. οὗτοι, οὗτος: nom. pl. for nom. sing.; διαπτυχθέντες, διαπτύσσω: aor. pass. partic. nom. pl. m.; ὤφθησαν, ὁράω: aor. pass. 3 pl. (gnomic aorist expressing a general truth); κενοί, κενός: nom. pl. m.

710. ἄνδρα, ἀνήρ: acc. sing.; εἰ replaces the usual ἐάν; ᾖ, εἰμί: pres. subj. 3 sing. in a present general condition; τὸ μανθάνειν, τὸ τείνειν, μανθάνω, τείνω: subject of understood verb ἐστί.

711. πόλλ(α), πολύς: acc. pl. neut.

712. ὁρᾷς, ὁράω: pres. 2 sing.; ῥείθροισι = ῥείθροις χειμάρροις, ῥεῖθρον, χειμάρροος: dat. pl.; ὅσα, ὅσος: nom. pl. neut.

713. δένδρων, δένδρον: gen. pl.; ὑπείκει, ὑπείκω: pres. 3 sing.; κλῶνας, κλώνη: acc. pl.; ἐκσώζεται, ἐκσώζω: mid. 3 sing.

714. ἀντιτείνοντ(α), ἀντιτείνω: pres. partic. nom. pl. neut.; ἀπόλλυται, ἀπόλλυμι: pres. pass. 3 sing.

715. ναός = νεώς, ναῦς: gen. sing.; ἐγκρατῇ, ἐγκρατής: acc. sing. m. proleptically modif. πόδα; πόδα, πούς: acc. sing.

716. τείνας, τείνω: aor. partic.

717. στρέψας, στρέφω: aor. partic.; ὑπτίοις ... σέλμασιν, ὕπτιος, σέλμα: dat. pl.; ναυτίλλεται, ναυτίλλομαι: pres. 3 sing.

718. εἶκε, εἴκω: imper. 2 sing.; θυμῷ, θυμός: dat. sing., indir. obj. of δίδου; μετάστασιν, μετάστασις: acc. sing.; δίδου, δίδωμι: imper. 2 sing.

719. ἐμοῦ, ἐγώ: gen. sing.; νεωτέρου, νέος: comparat. gen. sing.

720. πρόσεστι, πρόσειμι: pres. 3 sing.

721. φῦναι, φύω: aor. inf.; τιν' ἄνδρα ... πλέων, τις ἀνὴρ πλέως: acc. sing.

722. φιλεῖ, φιλέω: pres. 3 sing.; τοῦτο, οὗτος: nom. sing. neut.; ταύτῃ, οὗτος: dat. sing. f.

723. λεγόντων, λέγω: pres. partic. gen. pl.; καλόν, καλός: nom. sing. neut. with ἐστι understood.

724. τι καίριον, τις, καίριος: acc. sing. neut.

725. μαθεῖν, μανθάνω: 2 aor. inf.; τοῦδε, ὅδε: gen. sing.; εἴρηται, λέγω: perf. pass. 3 sing.; διπλῇ, διπλόος: dat. sing.

97

Guide to Sophocles' ANTIGONE /

726. οἱ τηλικοίδε, ὁ τηλικόσδε: nom. pl. m.; διδαξόμεσθα = διδαξόμεθα, διδάσκω: fut. mid. 1 pl.

727. φρονεῖν, φρονέω: pres. inf.; ἀνδρὸς τηλικοῦδε, ἀνὴρ τηλικόσδε: gen. sing.; φύσιν, φύσις: acc. sing.

728. μηδέν . . . δίκαιον, μηδείς, δίκαιος: acc. neut. object of understood verb of learning.

729. ἔργα, ἔργον: acc. pl.; σκοπεῖν, σκοπέω: pres. inf.

730. τοὺς ἀκοσμοῦντας, ἀκοσμέω: pres. partic. acc. pl.

731. κελεύσαιμ(ι), κελεύω: aor. opt. 1 sing.; εὐσεβεῖν, εὐσεβέω: pres. inf.; ἐς (= εἰς) τοὺς κακούς, κακός: acc. pl. m.

732. ἥδε, ὅδε: nom. sing. f.; τοιᾷδ(ε) . . . νόσῳ, τοιόσδε, νόσος: dat. sing.; ἐπείληπται, ἐπιλαμβάνω: perf. pass. 3 sing.

733. φησι, φημί: pres. 3 sing.; Θήβης, Θήβη = Θῆβαι (normally pl.): gen. sing.; τῆσδ(ε), ὅδε: gen. sing. f.; ὁμόπτολις λεώς = λαός: nom. sing.

734. ἡμῖν, ἐγώ: dat. pl., royal pl. used alongside the sing. form ἐμέ; ἅ (ἐ)μέ, ὅς, ἐγώ: ἅ, acc. pl.; ἐμέ, acc. sing. subject of inf.; τάσσειν = τάττειν, τάσσω: pres. inf.; ἐρεῖ, λέγω: fut. 3 sing.

735. ὁρᾷς, ὁράω: pres. 2 sing.; τόδ(ε), ὅδε: acc. sing. neut.; εἴρηκας, λέγω: perf. 2 sing.

736. ἄλλῳ, ἄλλος: dat. sing.; (ἐ)μοί, ἐγώ: dat. sing.; με, ἐγώ: acc. sing.; τῆσδ(ε) . . . χθονός, ὅδε, χθών: gen. sing. with inf. ἄρχειν

737. ἥτις, ὅστις: nom. sing. f.; ἀνδρὸς . . . ἑνός, ἀνὴρ εἷς: gen. sing.

738. κρατοῦντος, κρατέω: pres. partic. gen. sing.; νομίζεται, νομίζω: pres. pass. 3 sing.

739. ἐρήμης . . . γῆς, ἐρῆμος, γῆ: gen. sing.; ἄρχοις, ἄρχω: pres. opt. 2 sing.

740. ἔοικε, ἔοικα: perf. (with pres. meaning) impers. 3 sing.; τῇ γυναικί, ἡ γυνή: dat. sing.; συμμαχεῖ, συμμαχέω: pres. 3 sing.

741. σοῦ, σύ: gen. sing.

742. παγκάκιστε, παγκάκιστος: superl. noun of address; ἰών, εἶμι: pres. partic.; πατρί, πατήρ: dat. sing.

743. δίκαια, δίκαιος: acc. pl. neut.; ἐξαμαρτάνοντ(α), ἐξαμαρτάνω: pres. partic. acc. sing. m.

744. ἐμὰς ἀρχάς, ἐμός, ἀρχή: acc. pl.; σέβων, σέβω: pres. partic.

745. τιμάς, τιμή: acc. pl.; πατῶν, πατέω: pres. partic.

746. μιαρὸν ἦθος . . . ὕστερον, μιαρός, ἦθος, ὕστερος: noun of address; γυναικός, γυνή: gen. sing.

98

747. ἕλοις, αἱρέω: aor. opt. 2 sing.; ἥσσω = ἥττω, ἥσσων, used as comparat. of κακός: acc. sing. m.; γε emphasizes the whole phrase "slave to dishonor" as γε (749) emphasizes "on *your* behalf"; αἰσχρῶν, αἰσχρός: gen. pl. neut.

748. σοι, σύ: dat. of possession; κείνης, (ἐ)κεῖνος: gen. sing. f.

749. σοῦ κα(ὶ) (ἐ)μοῦ, σύ, ἐγώ: gen. sing.; θεῶν τῶν νερτέρων, θεὸς νέρτερος: gen. pl.

750. ταύτην, οὗτος, ζῶσαν, ζάω (pres. partic.): acc. sing. f.; ποτέ: the strange position stresses the fact that he'll never be able to marry *her* at any time; γαμεῖς, γαμέω: fut. 2 sing.

751. θανεῖται, θνήσκω: fut. 3 sing.; θανοῦσ(α), θνήσκω: aor. partic. nom. sing. f.; ὀλεῖ, ὄλλυμι: fut. 3 sing.; τινά, τις: acc. sing. m.

752. (ἐ)παπειλῶν, ἐπαπειλέω: pres. partic.; ἐπεξέρχῃ, ἐπεξέρχομαι: pres. 2 sing.; θρασύς, predicate adj. used as adv.

753. κενὰς γνώμας, κενός, γνώμη: acc. pl.

754. κλαίων, κλαίω: pres. partic.; φρενώσεις, φρενόω: fut. 2 sing.; ὤν, εἰμί: pres. partic. (also line 756); φρενῶν, φρήν: gen. pl.

755. ἦσθ(α), εἰμί: impf. 2 sing. in contrary-to-fact clause; εἶπον, λέγω: 2 aor. 1 sing.; φρονεῖν, φρονέω: pres. inf.

756. γυναικός, γυνή: gen. sing.; κώτιλλε, κωτίλλω: imper. 2 sing.

757. βούλῃ, βούλομαι: pres. 2 sing.; λέγων, λέγω: pres. partic.; μηδέν, μηδείς: acc. sing. neut.

758. ἄληθες, ἀληθής: neut. as adv.; τόνδ(ε) Ὄλυμπον, ὅδε Ὄλυμπος: acc. sing.; ἴσθ(ι), οἶδα: imper. 2 sing.

759. χαίρων, χαίρω: pres. partic.; ψόγοισι = ψόγοις, ψόγος: dat. pl.; δεννάσεις, δεννάζω: fut. 2 sing.

760. ἄγετε, ἄγω: imper. 2 pl.; ὄμματ(α), ὄμμα: acc. pl.

761. παρόντι, πάρειμι: pres. partic. dat. sing.; θνήσκῃ, θνήσκω: pres. subj. 3 sing.; πλησία, πλήσιος: nom. sing. f.; νυμφίῳ, νυμφίος: dat. sing.

762. ἔμοιγε, ἐγώ + γε: dat. sing.; τοῦτο, οὗτος: acc. sing. neut.; δόξῃς, δοκέω: aor. subj. = imper. 2 sing.

763. ἥδ(ε), ὅδε: nom. sing. f.; ὀλεῖται, ὄλλυμι: fut. mid. 3 sing.; πλησία, πλήσιος: nom. sing. f.

764. τὸ (ἐ)μὸν κρᾶτ(α), ἐμός, κρᾶτα: acc. sing. The whole phrase is emphatic for "me"; ὁρῶν, ὁράω: pres. partic.; note the pleonism: "you will see, seeing with your eyes."

765. τοῖς θέλουσι, (ἐ)θέλω: pres. partic. dat. pl. m.; μαίνῃ, μαίνομαι: pres. subj. 2 sing.; συνών, σύνειμι: pres. partic.

99

6

Antigone's Last Speech

[891 – 928]

Introduction

The Fourth Episode has three parts: The kommos between
An. and the Cho., the impatient order from Cr. (883–90), and
finally, An.'s speech (891–943) before the guards lead her away
to her death. The Commentary and Grammatical Notes included
below (891–928) are for most of the third part.

A kommos is a dirge, usually sung by the surviving members
of a family after the death of a loved one.[1] Since An. considers
herself the last of the house, she sings her own lament, one of
the most lyrical *kommoi* of Greek tragedy, chanting it alternately
with the unresponsive Theban elders instead of with a more suppor-
tive chorus of her own sex.

In beautiful, emotional lyrics, she laments her fate as a "metic,"
a foreigner with no home (852), like the foreign settlers in Athens
who had no rights of citizenship. The word *metoikos*[2] poignantly
expresses her realization that she is a citizen of neither Thebes
nor the nether world. She has unwittingly become the *hypsipolis-
apolis* figure that the Cho. sang of in the Ode on Man, the patriot
without a city. She laments, too, her friendless state (846, 876 ff.),
but mostly she expresses her obsession with one theme: her loss
of the joys of marriage (813–76). All the suppressed desire of the
young girl now bursts forth in anguished lyrics.[3] She does not

100

mention her lover by name—thus contributing to the pattern of utter isolation even in her references to marriage.

As the elders chastise her, their judgment inadvertently evokes the audience's admiration and pity for An: she is *autonomos* (821), "following her own law," a word conveying both blame and admiration; [4] she is presumptuous, they frigidly observe, in comparing herself to Niobe who, unlike An., was of divine parentage (834); [5] she is pitiable in that she is paying for Oedipus' sin; but, like Oedipus, she has rushed to the limit of rashness (853).[6] Their most complimentary remark is their grudging admission that there is a certain reverence in her reverent action (872) in burying her brother; but they immediately retreat, blaming her self-willed temper (*autognōtos . . . orga*) for her destruction since authority "cannot brook such disobedience" (873–75).[7] Their cold unsympathetic attitude adds to our feeling for the isolated girl.

Creon returns to the stage long enough to command the guards to remove An. immediately and entomb her "alone, deserted" (*monēn erēmon,* 887) to live or die, but in any case to be without *metoikia,* the rights of a resident alien. The guards refrain from immediate action, however, tacitly granting An. time to give her last speech (891–928) after which Cr. reappears to see to the execution of his command.

In such a setting, An. begins her last speech. It is an emotional apostrophe to her tomb-bridal chamber, and yet it is spoken in the reflective, analytic iambic meter (891 ff.) instead of the earlier emotional lyric of the kommos. She expresses her overwhelming desire for union with her family who are all dead and for whom she has sacrificed herself. But the lines contain, too, a love of life and a desire for marriage absent from the twentieth-century existential An. of Anouilh. Where the latter rejects life because it does not live up to the absoluteness of her demands, Soph.'s heroine embraces death as the only embrace of love left to her.[8]

In this speech, the two central images for An., those of marriage and death, that began to converge in the preceding kommos finally unite. *Ō tymbos, Ō nympheion,* "O tomb, O bridal chamber," eloquently expresses her realization that her love will be consummated only in death.

Later, the messenger's report of the double death of the entombed lovers (1155 ff.) gives dramatic realization offstage to these lyrics.[9] In the *tymbos* she will find union not only as she expects with her family, but also beyond expectation with her spouse.

In the Creon-Haemon Debate, Hae. applied An.'s word for "isolated," *erēmos*, to his father (739). The father, in turn, uses it of An. in 887, where he consciously willed her complete isolation. Now, at 919, An. herself again expresses her desolation, as she is bereft of all *philoi*, "dear ones," and of divine assistance (921–26). For one whose whole stance has been based on *philia* and *erōs*, and on assurance that *philia* is true piety, such isolation is the ultimate woe [10] and is a necessary psychological precondition for her suicide.[11]

It is in the context of utter spiritual and human desolation that she pronounces the passage (904–15 or 904–20) that so offended Goethe,[12] and which has exasperated admirers of An. to the present day.[13] The great editor, Jebb, bracketed the lines 904–20 in his text as spurious, and he marshaled a series of reasons to bolster his conclusion that the passage was an interpolation by some post-humous editor or actor, perhaps by Soph.'s own son, who is known to have edited his father's works.[14]

Goethe hoped that scholars would find reason to reject the passage. As if in answer to his prayer, scholars did find that the passage is related to and perhaps even borrowed from a passage in Herodotos' history. In the Herodotean passage (3. 119), Inta-phernes' wife is pleading with King Dareios to save her still living brother: "O King, if the gods will, I may have another husband and other children when these are gone. But as my father and mother are no longer living, it is impossible that I should have another brother." The passage, though sophistic, is effective and appropriate in the Herodotean setting; the Sophoclean "adapta-tion," if it is such, is disappointing not only because An. seems to lose her grip, but because the argument is far less appropriate for a *dead* brother, especially because it seems to vitiate her earlier motivations.

Soph. and Herodotos were both writing about the same time; and although Herodotos had not yet published his *History* in 441, Soph. may have complimented him with this infelicitous borrowing (there is absolutely no proof of this); or both may have used a common source in contemporary Ionian folklore, since the story especially as Soph. uses it illustrates the contemporary Greek penchant for bolstering the feelings of the heart with some cerebral argument. Knox's explanation of the passage captures the mood and motives of An. here:

This is the moment when in the face of death nothing matters but the truth. She is not trying to justify her action to others, she is trying to understand it herself. In the loneliness of her last moments in the sunlight, all that was secondary in her motives . . . dissolves before her eyes. . . . The gods she championed have failed her. . . . Antigone is given no sign of approval. . . . She is reduced to purely human feelings; all that is left her is the love she bears the dead of her own blood. . . . For [Polynices] she has sacrificed her life as a woman—the husband and children she might have had. In the almost hysterical hyperbole of her claim that she would not have run such a risk for that husband and those children she will now never live to see, she is telling Polynices that no other lover . . . could surpass her love for him. The illogicality of her explanation cannot be denied. . . . But the illogicality can be understood; for Antigone the distinction between living and dead has ceased to exist . . . she is dead and about to be entombed in the land of the living, he is alive in the world of the dead.[15]

Knox perhaps overstates An.'s rejection of her husband and children. After all, she only touches upon this thought in a contrary-to-fact clause (see 905 n.). She does not have a husband or children; she has not experienced the physical or psychological fulfillment of Hae.'s love. She must now cling to the one love she has known, especially since she lacks the knowledge that Hae. has championed her cause.

I retain this illogical passage first because there is no convincing evidence that it is an interpolation; second because, although the argument is unsatisfying and even embarrassing to our way of thinking, there is evidence in Bacchylides that An.'s way of thinking was not unique in classical Greece.[16] But I retain these strange lines also because they are an appropriate demonstration of her androgynous nature. Throughout the play, she has proven herself the "masculine" doer, darer, and hunter after impossibilities. Now, like the enlightened men of Pericles' Athens, she instinctively feels the need to find a compelling rational explanation for her deed of love. And Soph. gives her this bit of contemporary sophistry, a crass "masculine" exercise in mental gymnastics. But An. is no sophist. Here she is pure woman, trying to justify herself to herself. Because her reason is not logical but instinctive, her analysis can only produce a formal "masculine" tone and an illogical, inappropriate syllogism. The rhythm she employs shows she is trying to be "masculine": she has put aside the lyrical meters of the kommos for the composed iambs of discursive analysis. The form and the matter are thus the "masculine" elements in the scene. But the anguish the words convey reveals her full femininity.[17]

Her religious instinct, too, here proves to be "feminine." Jebb objected to this passage because "her feet slip from the rock on which they were set; she suddenly gives up that which, throughout the drama, has been the immovable basis of her action—the universal and unqualified validity of the divine law." [18] But even in the passage in which she attested to the universal and unqualified validity of the *agrapta nomima* (450–70), even there she gave every indication that she came to perceive their validity as they were fleshed out in the corpse of her brother (see 465–68 n.). She never gives the impression that she proceeds from the universal to the concrete, but that, in the face of the concrete needs of one she loves, she comes to understand and believe in the universal law. At this later moment, then, as she stares down the parodos to her Death, she does not back down in her concern and belief in her loved ones, but she does momentarily lose sight of the connection that she earlier perceived between the concrete and the universal. It is one thing to perceive and believe the great religious truths when there is still some distance between one and death; it is quite another to have the strength to believe *in articulo mortis.* Soph. shows how deeply he understood human psychology in allowing his heroine this moment of doubt when the gods' laws escape her and the gods themselves seem to desert her (921 ff.). Only after this moment of doubting sophistry does her vision clear again. She faces Death down, recovers her autonomy as a truly liberated whole human being,[19] firm in her pious belief despite the gods' silence (943). Camus's complaint against a certain school of artists is applicable here. Faced with absurdity, they will not cry: "Absurd!"

they cry: "God!" [20] The heroine now has recouped her androgynous strength despite—no, *because of* her loneliness. In the labored prose of psychiatrist Robert Weiss, loneliness is "a deficit condition, a response to the absence of specific relational provisions." An.'s anguish stems from the lack of any divine or human "relational provisions." However, the poet understands what the psychiatrist apparently does not: this "deficit condition" is not a disease to be cured but a necessary element in all heroism, indeed in all self-knowledge. Delphi would now approve: she knows herself. The Cho. was right: she is *autognōtos* (875).

COMMENTARY

891. *Ō tymbos, Ō nympheion,* "O tomb, O bridal chamber." An. now sees the fulfillment of her love in the embrace of death. This expression foreshadows the messenger's report of Hae. embracing her in death (1220 ff.). The images of love and death, associated with her throughout the play, begin to converge (see 1284 n.).

Kataskaphēs, lit., "deep dug," i.e., in a dungeon or vault. Later (1216) Cr. tells his men to enter through the opening made between the rocks. The poet seems to picture a roughly constructed stone chamber in a hillside with some entrance way (1217) through which Cr. and his servants would pass before finding An. and Hae.

892. *Aieiphrouros,* "ever-guarding." The epithet suggests that An. is aware that her escape from Cr.'s tyranny has, in a sense, placed her under the yoke of a new master, the inanimate tomb that will oversee her forever.

894. *Phersephass(a)* or Persephonē, traditionally identified with Korē, the goddess of vegetation carried off by Hades to be Queen of the underworld, is here the receiver of the dead.

895–96. *Loisthiā (e)go,* "I, the very last remnant." Earlier (599–600) the Cho. spoke of "the last root" of the house of Labdakos, a phrase which may have included Ism. as well as An. However, ever since Ism. rejected the rights of her family (41 ff.), An. has considered herself the lone survivor. She is a true *metoikos* (see Intro., this chap.), a foreigner on earth since her *philoi* are all in Hades (see 898–99).

898–99. *Philē . . . prosphilēs . . . philē.* Soph. again (cf. 73) uses anaphora, the repetition of a word in the initial position, to demonstrate that love is An.'s guiding principle and motive. Cf. *Oedipus at Kolonos* 1698, where An. recalls Oedipus' last embrace with a tender double use of *philos.*

899. *Kasignēton kara,* "dear brother." An. is probably referring to Eteocles, the brother who received proper burial since she singles out Polynices by name at 902. Yet there is an inconsistency appropriate to her confused state of mind here because An. did not personally attend to the burial of Eteocles (23 ff.) as she claims in 900–901. Some critics take this inconsistency as an argument for deleting 900–928 (see Intro., this chap.).

900–901. *Thanontas . . . hymās,* "you . . . dead." According to the action of this play, this could refer only to An.'s father and mother, Oedipus and Jocasta, since she had only *heard* of the libations for her brother Eteocles. In Soph.'s later play, An. was not allowed to pour libations for Oedipus either; see *Oedipus at Kolonos* 1758 where Theseus denies her request merely to *see* his tomb. Such alterations of the myth are frequent and need not be evidence of interpolation since the poets felt themselves free to alter details in accordance with their dramatic purposes.

Autocheir, "with my own hand." This word resonates throughout this play and the later *Oedipus Tyrannos,* though with different meanings in each. In the later play, it is a semitechnical term for the one who actually does the deed but who does not intend the patricide and marriage with his mother. In this play the word is used of various characters acting with full knowledge but with differing motivations. An. here uses her hand in loving care for the corpses of her dead relatives; her motive, then, is the same as Eurydice's at 1315–16 (see notes) when the queen's own hand struck her heart in suicide. The word was used too of Hae.'s suicide when the messenger described his motive as a mixture of love of An. and anger against his father (1175–77). See also 43 n. and 172. *(E)kosmēsa,* "I dressed, honored," (lit., "put in order,"). By An.'s use of a form of Cr.'s word for "order," *kosmos,* the poet shows the difference in the two characters' conception of proper order (see Intro., chap. 5).

901–2. *Ka(i) (e)pitymbious . . . edōka,* "and I poured drink-offerings at your graves." At 431, she poured the triple libation for the dead Polynices. This triple libation of honey and milk, then wine, and finally water was considered a necessary service to the dead (see 44 and n.).

903. *Peristellousa*, "laying out for burial." The word connotes her loving concern for her brother's corpse.

904. ff. See the Intro., this chap., for the reasons why I retain this embarrassing (i.e., from a modern viewpoint) passage which many critics and some editors have judged spurious. Jebb rejected 904–20; some editors have rejected 900–928; Campbell and the more recent editors (Pearson [1924] and Dain-Mazon [1967]) retain the whole passage, as do most recent critics (except Müller, Linforth, and Whitman). See Intro., this chap., (n. 14) for various critical judgments and for the relationship of the passage to the Ionian folk story recorded in Herodotos (3. 119). Linforth (p. 229) argues that this speech must be an interpolation because Cr. never would have allowed An. to speak for so long. The passage could have been an editor's interpolation or even an actor's insertion, a practice common enough to prompt Lykurgos to pass a law in 338 B.C. forbidding actors to add speeches they liked. Still, I contend (see Intro.) that Soph. himself wrote it.

904. Depending upon the way the actor phrases this line, it can mean "I was right in honoring you, as the wise realize" or "the wise will say I did honor you." On the ethical-religious as well as the intellectual meaning of *tois phronousin*, see nn. on 95, 176, and 354–55.

905–7. This strange sophistic argument is expressed elliptically; "If I had been a mother of children," i.e., "and if I had lost a child." In An.'s defense here, it should be noted that her only rejection of husband and children is couched in a contrary-to-fact clause.

906. *Etēketo*, lit., "melted," here describes the falling away of dead flesh.

907. *Biāi politōn*, "against the will of the citizens." Ism. vainly tried (79) to restrain An. in the Prologue by claiming she would be acting *biāi politōn*. The verbal echoing in phrases such as this is certainly Sophoclean, but it is debatable whether this particular repetition is a valid argument for authenticity as Kirkwood contends (p. 239).

908, 913–14. *Tinos nomou*, "in deference to what law." *Toiōide*

. . . *nomōi,* "by such a law." These are rhetorical commonplaces that An. employs in her attempt to find cerebral justification for her instinctive belief (see the Intro., this chap.). Her repetition of the key word of her defense of the unwritten laws, i.e., *nomos,* together with words pertaining to nature (905 and 912), hearkens back to the fusion of *nomos* and *physis* in that earlier passage (see Intro., chap. 4).

909. Jebb's most convincing stylistic argument for his position that these lines are borrowed by an inferior interpolator from Herodotos (3.119) centers on *katthanontos* with an understood genitive from the noun *posis,* making up a genitive absolute here. A comparison with Herodotos shows a dependence in form as well as in subject matter here, and Jebb conjectures that the interpolator tried to "impart a touch of tragic dignity" by substituting *posis* for the more prosaic word for "husband," *anēr.* Since *anēr* is such a common word in this play (see "Vocabulary," chap. 8), its absence here may be significant.

912. She says: "There is no brother who could come into being," when she means: "There is no way a brother could come into being." Her illogical phrasing adds to the pathos.

913–14. *Toiōide. . . nomōi.* See 908 n. This expression is a commonplace for summing up the debate. The formal style and confused logic continue.

915. *Deina tolmān,* "to dare terribly." This is pure An.; she returns to two of the key words of the Ode on Man and uses the phrase with the same irony she exhibited in the Prologue (see 96 n.). Both words have a pejorative connotation for Cr., but they define An.'s heroism. Soph. avails himself of the ambiguity present in both words: each connotes both heroic virtue as well as rashness deserving censure. See nn. on 332, 372, and 1339.

916. An.'s desire for marriage and motherhood here indicates a will to life that contradicts her earlier will to death (891–902), where, poised between life and death, she turned toward the realm of death (Reinhardt, p. 92). Yet there is logic to the seeming contradiction: "Her sense of clan is so deeply involved with her sense of life . . . that in this . . . situation her death wish and her clan feeling merge and lead to her dramatic action in which they become one" (Hamburger, p. 157). On her sense of clan see 48 n.

917-18. Though An. does not mention Hae. by name, each of the four units in these two lines alludes to the marriage her act has denied her. A Victorian editor, Dindorf, censured her reference to children as "unmaidenly." Sophoclean heroines are consistently "unmaidenly" (cf. *Electra* 963-66).

919. On the importance of the isolation theme for An. and Oedipus in *Oedipus at Kolonos*, see Intro. this chap. Anouilh's An. experiences a similar total isolation (200). *Pros philōn:* The unnecessary preposition *pros* emphasizes An.'s isolation from her loved ones.

920. The juxtaposition of *dzōs(a)* and *es thanontōn* expresses An.'s acute awareness that she is condemned to a living death. See 72 and n. Later (1167) the messenger calls Cr. "a breathing corpse," *empsychon nekron.*

921-23. *Poiān . . . ti chrē?* The suddenness of these transitions has been taken as evidence of interpolation, but it can also be indicative of An.'s emotional state (cf. the awkwardness of 1-4).

Poiān . . . dikēn, "what kind of justice" suggests that there is no divine justice (cf. 451). *Poiān* expresses her indignant surprise and pain at feeling that even the gods have rejected her, a pain that is particularly poignant in view of her firm conviction that her act was in conformity with divine law. Or one may interpret this line differently. It may simply assert both An.'s belief that she has broken no law of the gods and her confidence that she has acted properly. Either way, there is a poignancy in her feeling that the gods have abandoned her.

Knox observes (p. 106) that a Christian martyr "secure in his faith and remembering that Christ rebuked those who demanded a 'sign' as a 'wicked and adulterous generation,' does not expect a miracle to save him. . . . But the ancient Greek did. The world was full of signs and portents, omens and miracles. . . . But Antigone is given no sign of approval or support." Thus, the condition of isolation which she describes is somewhat analogous to but more complete than "the dark night of the soul" described by John of the Cross, a darkness that comes from the mystic's feeling that even God has deserted him.

922. *Ti chrē?* "Why is it necessary?" (i.e., "What moral reason is there?"). On *chrē* as indicating conformity to the moral law, see 89 n. Her dilemma is complete: she now feels deserted by the

very gods from whom she drew her moral imperative. She calls herself *dystēnos,* a word with many nuances but always, in Soph.'s usage, describing the genuinely tragic. An. is the "ill-starred" daughter of an "ill-starred" father (379); An. called herself *dystēnos* twice in this scene (850 and here); the messenger speaks of Hae.'s "ill-fated" marriage (1225) and still later reports that "poor" Eurydice has died (1283). Similarly, in *Oedipus Tyrannos* (1071–72), Jocasta calls Oedipus *dystēnos* when she is about to commit suicide.

923. *Tin(a). . . xymmachōn,* "which (of the gods) as allies." The partitive genitive instead of the more usual accusative "which god" dramatizes her separation from all the gods.

923–24. *Epei . . . ektēsamēn.* She juxtaposes *dyssebeiān* and *eusebous(a),* "impiety" and "being pious." The Cho. at 872 grudgingly admitted some connection between her pious act *sebein* and the state of being pious *eusebeia tis;* now she realizes that her very piety has gained her the reputation, it seems even with the gods, of impiety. The particle *dē* emphasizes the poignancy of her self-knowledge. As Denniston remarks (p. 214): *dē* is "at home in the great crises of drama, above all at moments when death or ruin is present or imminent." On the meaning of *eusebeia,* see 74 n.

925–26. The emphatic position of *pathontes* and of *pathoien* (928) implies "only *after* I have suffered, not before." Campbell takes the two lines as meaning: "If, after all, this course of theirs is approved in heaven, when I have suffered I suppose I shall acknowledge my fault."

926–27. *Hēmartēkotes . . . hamartanousi.* See "Vocabulary," chap. 8, for the various meanings of *hamartanō,* the verb "to go astray," and the nouns *hamartēma* and *hamartia.* P. Ricoeur (pp. 108 ff.) distinguishes two directions of *hamartia* in Soph., the one toward an excusable fault in *Oedipus at Kolonos,* the other toward guilt. Here An. uses the words ironically of her own guilt, and accuses her judges of guilt in condemning her. Later, the Cho. joins the words *atē,* "ruin, delusion," and *hamartōn,* when it finally accuses Cr. of guilt for his act: the misfortune does not come from another (*ouk allotriān atēn*) but from his own fault (*all(a) autos hamartōn,* 1259–60). So, whereas the elder Soph. uses *hamartia* of an excusable fault since he pictures Oedipus as a victim of *atē,* divine infatuation, and human misfortune, the word is used in the *An.* of the fault or transgression for which the human agent must bear responsibility. (See notes on 1315, 1318, and 1340 for Cr.'s admission of guilt.)

927. *Hoide,* "they." The word may refer to Cr., to the citizens or to the combination of citizens and Cr. who condemned her. The vagueness of the word seems indicative that she does not know who shared Cr.'s viewpoint despite her earlier claim (509) that the citizens were with her. From her present position between life and death as *metoikos,* a resident alien, the curse she calls down on her malefactors is that they suffer a fate equal to hers.

GRAMMATICAL NOTES

892. αἰείφρουρος (> ἀεί, "always," and φρουρός, "guard"): a Sophoclean coinage.

893. ἐμαυτῆς, ἐμαυτοῦ: reflex. pron. gen. sing. f.; ὧν, ὅς: relative pron. gen. pl.; ἀριθμόν . . . πλεῖστον, ἀριθμὸς πλεῖστος (superl. of πολύ): acc. sing.; νεκροῖς, νεκρός: dat. pl.

894. δέδεκται, δέχομαι: perf. 3 sing.; Φερσέφασσα = Περσεφόνη, Hades' queen whose name had many forms; ὀλωλότων, ὄλλυμι, 2 perf. act. partic. gen. pl. with mid. meaning

895. ὧν, ὅς: gen. pl.; λοισθία, λοισθίος = λοιπός −ή −όν: nom. sing. f.; μακρῷ, μακρός: dat. of degree of difference.

896. μοῖραν, μοῖρα: acc. sing. subject of the inf.; ἐξήκειν, ἐξήκω: pres. inf.

897. ἐλθοῦσα, ἔρχομαι: 2 aor. partic. nom. sing. f.; ἐλπίσιν, ἐλπίς: dat. pl.

898. φίλη, φίλος: nom. sing. f.; ἥξειν, ἥκω: fut. inf.; πατρί . . . σοί, πατήρ, σύ: dat. sing.

900. θανόντας, θνήσκω: 2 aor. partic. acc. pl.; ὑμᾶς, σύ: acc. pl.

901. ἔλουσα . . . ἐκόσμησα, λούω, κοσμέω: aor. 1 sing.; (ἐ)πιτυμβίους χοάς, ἐπιτύμβιος, χοή: acc. pl.

902. ἔδωκα, δίδωμι: aor. 1 sing.; τὸ σὸν δέμας: acc. sing. neut.

903. περιστέλλουσα, περιστέλλω: pres. partic. nom. sing. f.; τοιάδ(ε), τοιόσδε: acc. pl. neut.

904. ἐτίμησα, τιμάω: aor. 1 sing.; τοῖς φρονοῦσιν, φρονέω: pres. partic. dat. pl.

905. τέκνων, τέκνον: gen. pl.; ἔφυν, φύω: 2 aor. 1 sing.

906. κατθανών, καταθνήσκω: 2 aor. partic.; ἐτήκετο, τήκω: impf. pass. 3 sing.

907. βίᾳ πολιτῶν: cf. 79 for the identical phrase; τόνδε, ὅδε: acc. sing. m.; ἠρόμην, αἴρω: imperf. mid. 1 sing.; πόνον, πόνος: acc. sing.

908. τίνος νόμου, τίς νομος: gen. sing.; χάριν, χάρις: acc. sing.

909. κατθανόντος, καταθνήσκω: 2 aor. partic. gen. in gen. absolute with τοῦ πόσεος understood (i.e., my first husband); ἦν, εἰμί: impf. 3 sing.

910. ἄλλου φωτός, ἄλλος φώς: gen. sing.; τοῦδε, ὅδε: gen. sing. with ἤμπλακον; ἤμπλακον, ἀμπλακίσκω: 2 aor. 1 sing.

911. κεκευθότοιν, κεύθω: perf. partic. gen. dual in gen. absolute with μητρός (μήτηρ) καὶ πατρός (πατήρ)

912. βλάστοι, βλαστάνω: 2 aor. opt. 3 sing.

913. τοιῶδε . . . νόμῳ, τοιόσδε νόμος: dat. sing.; ἐκπροτιμήσασα, ἐκπροτιμάω: aor. partic. nom. sing. f.

914. Κρέοντι, Κρέων: dat. sing.; ἔδοξ(α), δοκέω: aor. 1 sing.; ἁμαρτάνειν, ἁμαρτάνω: pres. inf.

915. δεινά, δεινός: acc. pl. neut.; τολμᾶν, τολμάω: pres. inf.

916. ἄγει, ἄγω: pres. 3 sing.; χερῶν, χείρ: gen. pl.; λαβών, λαμβάνω: 2 aor. partic.

917. ἄλεκτρον, ἀνυμέναιον, ἄλεκτρος, ἀνυμέναιος: acc. sing.; του γάμου, τις γάμος: gen. sing.

918. λαχοῦσαν, λαγχάνω: 2 aor. partic. acc. sing. f.; παιδείου τροφῆς, παίδειος τροφός: gen. sing.

919. φίλων, φίλος: gen. pl.

920. ζῶσ(α), ζάω: pres. partic. nom. sing. f.; θανόντων, θνήσκω: 2 aor. partic. gen. pl.; κατασκαφάς, κατασκαφή: acc. pl.

921. ποίαν . . . δίκην, ποῖος, δίκη: acc. s.; παρεξελθοῦσα, παρεξέρχομαι: 2 aor. partic. nom. sing. f.; δαιμόνων, δαίμων: gen. pl.

922. με τὴν δύστηνον, ἐγώ, δύστηνος: acc. sing. f.; ἐς = εἰς θεούς, θεός: acc. pl.

923. τίν(α), τίς: acc. sing.; αὐδᾶν, αὐδάω: pres. inf.; ξυμμάχων, ξύμμαχος: gen. pl.

924. τὴν δυσσέβειαν, δυσσέβεια: acc. sing; εὐσεβοῦσα, εὐσεβέω: pres. partic. nom. sing. f.; ἐκτησάμην, κτάομαι: aor. 1 sing.

926. παθόντες, πάσχω: 2 aor. partic. nom. pl. m. (Masculine is commonly used in tragedy instead of feminine when a woman speaks

of herself in the plural.); ζυγγνοῖμεν, συγγιγνώσκω: aor. opt. 1 pl.;
ἡμαρτηκότες, ἁμαρτάνω: perf. partic. nom. pl. m.
927. οἵδε, ὅδε: nom. pl. m.; πλείω κακά, πολύς (comparat.)
κακός: acc. pl. neut.
928. πάθοιεν, πάσχω: 2 aor. opt. 3 pl.; δρῶσιν, δράω: pres. 3 pl.

7

Creon's Lament

[1284 – 1353]

INTRODUCTION

IN THE FINAL portion of the play (for which Commentary and Grammatical Notes are provided below), the focus is entirely on King Creon and his responsibility for the corpse that he carries (i.e., his son's) and for the corpse that soon confronts him (i.e., his wife's).

Significantly, Cr. returns without An.'s body, and no one mentions her either in this final kommos or in the earlier scene when the messenger reports the deaths of Hae. and An. The poet and his characters enter into a remarkable conspiracy of silence about An. during the last two episodes. The spectator has to infer that the person who dies with Hae. is An. Only feminine modifiers of a suppressed antecedent identify the second victim as An. (1221 ff.). And the audience is left to surmise that her body suffers the same indignity as her brother's. Such is the supreme irony in a play whose whole action grows out of An.'s refusal to leave her brother's body unburied. She lies at play's end in a climate of total neglect.[1]

What led the poet to allow this strange neglect? What made him focus all eyes on Cr.'s disintegration instead of alternating the focus as he did in the first three quarters of the play? I suggest that the poet's ironic imagination[2] induced him to take the gamble—a successful one, I believe—that the inspiration of the heroine would dominate the conclusion despite his characters' utter neglect of her body, her memory, and the principle for which she died. The gamble succeeds because An.'s integrity in her catastrophe is continuously heightened in the spectator's imagination by its contrast with the king's unmasking. Both An. and Cr. suffer catastrophe that entails external event and internal despair. It is in their respective manners of coping with their despair that her wholeness inspires, whereas his emptiness merely instructs and evokes the sympathy one reserves for a moral midget.

In the case of An., her brother's rotting body elicits from her the act which results in her living death, entombment in "the ever-guarding prison" (892). Internal despair follows external event. She experiences that terrible isolation of one with no external support: family dead, Ism. rejected, fiancé silent, finally even the assurance of divine aid withdrawn. This final dark night brings her to the depths of despair out of which she achieves what Kierkegaard calls "the movement of infinite resignation" (937–43).

> O city of my fathers in the land of Thebes
> O ancestral gods!
> I go forth now and brook no more delay.
> Look at me, you princes of Thebes,
> Observe the last daughter of the king's household.
> See what I suffer—and from whose hands—
> because I revered reverence!

She has regained her pride in the fullness and integrity of her being. She does not exemplify the eternal feminine figure who foregoes the political for the human and religious. She is the true citizen, male or female, whose *philia* leads her to see and perform her moral duty despite the consequences. She is in charge of her own destiny and yet submissive to the greater power of the gods. The line "I go forth now and brook no more delay" (939) elucidates this. The usual translation of this line ("I am led forth now and am no longer (merely) about to be led away") does not convey the ambiguity inherent in the sentence. Commentators take *agomai dē* in its normal passive sense but it can also have a middle sense: "I go away." The second half of the line, with its proud assertion, favors that sense. Yet, this is admittedly against the normal first reading of the line. Soph. avails himself of the ambiguity of language: An. is freely taking herself away—these guards have no power over her—and yet there is a transcendent power that does. She knows that in one very real sense she is being led away. She is led away by that power she alludes to in her last line (*tēn eusebiān sebisāsa,* "revering reverence," 943). The final movement to self-recovery seems to have come from those very gods whose aid she could not feel (923–24).

Cr. too faces catastrophe as external event and as inner despair. When the seer Tiresias' threats finally penetrate his armor of hybris, he collapses (1095 ff.). The man has no inner resources with which to meet the subsequent assaults of his son's bestial death and his wife's accusatory suicide. Stripped of all the trappings of office and deserted by his bombastic rhetoric, he stands there naked, one of T. S. Eliot's "hollow men." Some critics argue that one pities the man because he has at last shown his humanity. If so, it is mankind's empty side that he displays, the tendency in all of us to bury authentic human possibilities under the death mask of inauthentic pomp.

So, Hae.'s metaphor of the writing tablet which, when opened, is devoid of contents (707–9) becomes the perfect symbol for his father. We have seen its aptness in Cr.'s relationship with Hae. and with his nieces (see Intro., chap. 5). Why does it apply to his other relationships? Precisely, I believe, because his words and actions throughout the play have shown him to be so devoid of the human dimension extolled in the Ode on Man. The Cho. boasted there that Man has taught himself the temper that makes communal life possible (*astynomous orgās,* 355–56). This crowns his other achievements over the animal world (341 ff.). But Cr. has reversed the direction. Far from achieving the glories of communal life, he has destroyed the fundamental balance between humanity and the animal. His inhumane neglect of the putrifying corpse gives domination back to the carrion-eating birds. Man does not "ensnare the nimble tribe of birds" (342 f.), as the Cho. suggested, but birds mangle the remains of a man.

So, it is hardly surprising that his relationship with the divine world in the person of Tiresias, the priest of Delphi, is also awry.

When the seer warns him that he has sinned, Cr. responds with the same groundless charges of bribery that he used earlier (294 ff.) against the bumptious guard. He could not endure the guard's news of disobedience to his edict; still less can he face the priest's condemnation. In both cases, with arms flailing, he reduces a well-meaning opponent into a greedy assailant. Delphi is no less corrupt than the ordinary citizen. And as if to dramatize that point, he warns the priest that he will prevent the burial even if Zeus' eagles seek to lift the remains to the Olympian throne (1039-43).

Thus, the cycle is complete. If humanity is measured, as the Ode on Man indicates, by one's relationships with the animal world and with divinity, but especially with one's fellowmen, Cr.'s tablet is devoid of contents.

Therefore, even Cr.'s admission of guilt lacks the promise of a new beginning. Emptiness cannot grow. It can only direct the spectator's thoughts back to its opposite, i.e., to the heroine's *philia*. Cr. cannot evoke "the pity and fear" that Aristotle required of a tragic character. Instead, he comes the closest of any major Sophoclean character to exemplifying Aristotle's extremely bad man who proceeds from happiness to misery, a structure which may arouse sympathy (*to philanthrōpon*) in us but neither pity nor fear (*Poetics* 1453a1-4).

Thus Soph.'s structural technique is paratactical, his method ironically antithetical. The diptych arrangement allows him in a few short scenes to depict authentic human conviction, nobly accepting its own autonomy within a structure of faith; this alongside the less tense, less interesting unveiling of the inauthentic king. "Attention must be paid" to the Willy Lomans and the Creons. Yet Soph. does not, like Arthur Miller, make Cr. his tragic figure or centerpiece.[3] Rather, the assignment of almost half of the play to the unmasking of the king's illusions is the poet's sardonic reminder that life is like that: the ironic faith of life's tragic heroes is a rare and, he suggests, brief experience that escapes the notice of the prosaic. Far more of life is concerned with the sardonic irony embodied in the Creons. The young man in Eliot's *Family Reunion* speaks to life's Creons: "You are all people to whom nothing has happened, at most a continual impact of external events." The playwright understood that the revelation of the nontragic "breathing corpse" greatly illuminates the tragic grandeur of the dead, unburied heroine.

COMMENTARY

1284 ff. This is the first antistrophe of the final kommos. (On the meaning of kommos, see Intro., chap. 6). This kommos consists of strophes and antistrophes sung in the excited dochmaic meter with interruptions by the Cho. and messenger speaking in the more discursive iambic trimeter. The *oi*'s and *ai*'s are cries of despair and intense grief (e.g., *aiai aiai*). The dochmaic is a syncopated rhythm which achieves its emotional effect by distorting the regular iambic line.

1284. *Dyskathartos Haidou limēn:* "Inexorable harbor of Hades" is the unifying symbol of the play, since the images of marriage and death, sea, and disease all converge in this phrase (Goheen, p. 43). An. has found Hae.'s embrace in the house of death (1240–41) and reunion with her *philoi*. Irony can go no further: the fullness of love and the emptiness of death coexist in this couple. But for Cr., the harbor of Hades is *dyskathartos,* 'a word that lit. means "hard to cleanse," and thus may imply that the harbor is choked with the dead (Campbell); but it more naturally connotes "hard to satisfy by purification or atonement" and thus suggests that Hades relentlessly refuses to purify Cr. of his *miasma* (see 172 and 765 n.). The theme of pollution is not as pervasive in this play as in the *Oedipus Tyrannos,* but the infection is in one sense deeper, since Cr. is personally responsible for the pollution he caused in a way that Oedipus is not. Cr. claims that An. is diseased (732), but Tiresias exposes the truth: it is Cr.'s decision not to allow burial for Polynices and his companions that carried "polluting odor to each city that has an altar" (1083). And Soph. suggests in the Ode on Man that the nobility of the *deinos anthrōpos* (An.?) can cure the city of impossible diseases (361–64) although it cannot overcome the ultimate disease of death.

1291–92. *Sphagion . . . moron?* lit., "a violent womanly death heaped onto destruction?" Cr. uses the abstract for the concrete as a way of dulling his recognition of the new horror. He lacks Macduff's simple directness: "My wife killed too?" (*Macbeth* 5. 1.

212). *Amphikeisthai*, "heaped onto," is properly used of a wall "set around" a city.

The figure of Eurydice suffers from her late introduction into the action (she speaks only nine lines and listens to fifty). It is difficult for the audience to take the fate of such a latecomer seriously. Did Soph. perceive her as a second Hae. tortured by Cr.'s inhumanity to a point beyond what humanity can endure, thus intending her suicide to be the climax of Cr.'s ruin (Kitto, *Form*, p. 175); or as a second An., a pale reflection of the noble woman who uses her hand (see 1315 and 900) against the tyrant? It is true that the queen's words and act serve to keep the young princess' spirit before the audience (see subsequent notes), but a less commonly observed link between An. and the Eurydice scene is Pallas Athena, the goddess whose shrine Eurydice was about to visit when she was stunned by news of her son's death (1184–85). Athena was traditionally the martial goddess (pictured with helmet, spear, and shield); the goddess who was called "mother" and yet was the virgin-goddess (as the name Pallas may suggest); the patroness of all arts and crafts, especially spinning and weaving; the goddess of wisdom who taught heroes the difference between true and apparent heroism; and, incidentally, the goddess who sometimes transformed herself into a bird. By Eurydice's abortive visit to Athena's shrine Soph. may be recalling the spirit of the androgynous An., the maiden of martial deeds and "feminine" warmth, the weaver of the divine and human law (368 n.), the mother bird intent on protecting her young (424–28), and the one who intuitively knows true wisdom (see nn. on 95 and 1347). See Braun's perceptive n. on 1362 ff., p. 92. A more conventional explanation of the Athena reference here is simply that it was appropriate to give thanks to this war goddess, especially revered in Thebes, after the city's decisive victory.

1293. The line is an implicit stage direction, *parepigraphē*, common in classical drama. Eurydice's body is revealed either simply by opening the central doors so that it could be seen within or, more probably, by the *ekkyklēma*, a platform which wheeled the body into the orchestra, setting it perhaps behind Hae.'s body. The *ekkyklēma* was a stage convention for bringing an interior scene out where the audience could see it.

1295. Cr. is now surrounded by the bodies of his wife and son, the two monuments to his unreason as the choral leader put it (1258–60). The irony of the king's neglect to bring back the body of the girl who gave her life so that her brother's body might not suffer a similar neglect is not lost on the audience. Yet, the absence of An.'s body clearly indicates the poet's decision to shift the focus of the action away from An. to Cr. and his pathetic downfall.

1295–99. Cr.'s customary limitation to that which can be seen or touched becomes pathetic here.

1300. *Māter athliā,* lit., "struggling mother." Eurydice, like An., resisted Cr. with her only weapon, her suicide.

1301. The text is corrupt here. The speaker, *the Exangelos,* "a messenger who comes out," is a functionary in Greek tragedy who reports violent interior scenes not represented on stage. This messenger has entered from the palace at 1278. Soph. does not develop his personality or that of the earlier messenger (perhaps the same person—one cannot tell). The messenger(s) and the far more developed guard in the first episode resemble Cr. in their platitudinous language. Thus, the poet again identifies Cr. with the mediocre and unheroic.

1303. "Megareus who died previously." The fact that Eurydice blamed Cr. for her other son's death may have come as a surprise to the ancient as well as the modern audience. This may be an original Sophoclean addition to the myth. The tradition on Megarus is unclear: in Aeschylus *Seven against Thebes* 474, he is a valiant warrior; Euripides' later *Phoenissae* (930–1018) follows a significantly different version, since there, when Cr. refuses to comply with Tiresias' warning that one of his sons must be sacrificed, Megareus (there called Menoeceus) nobly kills himself. Here *paidoktonos,* "son-slayer" (1305) is ambiguous (it can refer to son or sons), but Eurydice clearly holds Cr. responsible for both deaths (1312–13).

1305. *Ephymnēsasa.* The word can mean "chanting over" but is better taken as "cursing" here, thus recalling Cr.'s scornful use of the word at 658.

1308. *Aneptān,* "I fly away." Cr., who has earlier treated An. and Hae. as animals (see 202 n.), is himself now like a frightened bird.

1310–11. *Deilaios. . . deilaiāi.* The word properly means "sorry" or "paltry" and is perhaps an extension of the monetary theme.

Dyāi, "misery," is Cr.'s companion. Cf. 95 where An. ironically takes *dysboulia,* "folly," as her companion.

1312–13. *Tōnde . . . morōn,* i.e., the deaths of Hae. and Megareus. See 1303 n.

1314. *Ka(i) (a)pelūsat(o).* I follow the MSS reading here rather than Pearson's strange emendation. The whole line somewhat awkwardly interrupts the king's lament with a factual question.

1315. *Autocheir,* "her own hand." At 900 (see n. there), An. uses this word in telling how she lovingly adorned her dead relatives' bodies "with her own hand." Here, An.'s word is repeated, this time of another woman whose love of her dead son Hae. (1316) led her hand to suicide. The love motive links the acts of the heroine and the queen; both women commit suicide, and by their acts almost incidentally destroy Cr.; for both women, the primary motive is not destruction but *philia,* love of one's own. This incidental destruction of Cr. by yet a second woman adds an ironic footnote to Cr.'s earlier admonition (677–78): "we must never be defeated by a woman."

1318. Guilt "fits" (*harmosei*) him, Cr. again admits. *Aitia* here is guilt for a criminal misdeed quite different from the *aitia* of Oedipus in *Oedipus Tyrannos* who was *autocheir* (see 900 n.), the one whose hand committed the deed but who did not intend the act of patricide (see 926–27 n.). In a subtle Sophoclean wordplay, *harmosei* echoes the word Ism. used to describe the suitability of An. and Hae. for each other (570). So the two lovers are suitably united in Hades and the king is suitably joined to guilt.

1319. *Egō . . . (e)kanon.* Cr. accepted responsibility for Hae.'s death (1262 ff.) and now for his wife's. Significantly he never mentions An.'s death or his responsibility for it. The pathetic repetition of *egō* underlines Cr.'s attempt to come to terms with his first insight, i.e., the first judgment that he makes without ocular proof. But one must question the depth of the insight. Is he aware that he has made morally sinful judgments in not respecting divine laws and human rights, or is he simply aware that his policies have not worked? Did he bury Polynices out of respect for An.'s values or merely from superstitious fear of divine retribution and/or from political fear of the *epigoni?* (According to a myth recorded in a lost Theban epic and familiar to Soph.'s audience from *Iliad*

4. 406, the *epigoni* or sons of the seven against Thebes were successful where their fathers had failed in storming the city.) Most critics agree with Reinhardt's estimate (p. 102): "He is left overwhelmed by misfortune rather than touched at the very root of his being."

1320 ff. Now Cr., like Tiresias earlier, must lean on servants. Still, Goheen (p. 86) overstates the similarity in a remark more applicable to Oedipus in the *Oedipus Tyrannos*, "in part he has assumed the posture of the blind seer." Cr.'s insight is too short-lived (see 1341 n.) and shallow to justify Goheen's claim.

1322. Having driven out of his life everyone he loved, Cr. finally realizes he has no home, is no one, and can only ask to be taken *ekpodōn*, "out of the way" (an adverb pathetically echoed at 1339). He still uses spatial words for a spiritual reality (cf. *empedois*, 169).

1325. *Ton . . . mēdena*, "absolutely nobody." All of Cr.'s counting in the play adds up to his being worth a cipher. The Cho. accepts his monetary self-evaluation in the next line.

1329–32. This passage has troubled critics, since *moros* denotes a violent fate. Yet Cr. means exactly what he says: a violent end would be happiest for him. Cr.'s prayer here parallels the opening lines of the parodos (100 ff.) where the Cho. welcomed "the ray of the sun, the fairest that ever dawned on Thebes." Now it is the day of death that will be *to kalliston*, "the fairest."

1332. Cr. renounces the physical sight which has proven to be a fatal guide. See 1319 n.

1334–35. *Mellonta . . . prassein*, "this lies in the future; the present must be our concern." Soph. uses asyndeton, the absence of normal connectives, to emphasize the contrast between the present *mellonta* and the future *prokeimenōn*. Since Greek is so rich in connectives, this absence of connectives is more striking than in other languages.

1335. *Hotoisi chrē melein*. This Cho. earlier (211–14) thought Cr. had power over both the living and the dead. Now it entrusts both to more mysterious powers, powers that are left vague. Whereas Euripides, for instance, probably would have named specific divine powers, e.g., the fates or the gods below, Soph. is characteristically vague and mysterious about divinity.

1336. *Erōmen*, lit., "we desire passionately." Cr. adopts the word that was much more appropriately used of An. (see 90 n.). If the text is correct, the mixture of singular and plural verbs here is hard to explain.

1337–38. Campbell thinks this advice of the Cho. reflects "the rationalism of the day." Jebb sees it as an exhortation to recognize "with pious resignation, the fixity of the divine decrees." Such pious reflections are typical of the choruses at the conclusion of the plays and are not unambiguous reflections of the poet's judgment.

1338. *Apallagē,* "means of escape." In the Ode on *Atē,* the Cho. sang (596): "There is no release from generation to generation." Part of the irony of that ode is that the Cho.'s words then seemed applicable only to An.; their relevance to Cr.'s fate as well is clear to the audience in hindsight.

1339. *Mataion,* "vain," "rash," reintroduces two earlier themes: i.e., emptiness and rashness. Hae.'s conclusion that his father's counsels were empty (753 n.) finds an echo in Cr.'s words here. More important, the deeper meaning of the poet beneath the pious musing of the Cho. at the end of the Ode on Man (370–72) is now evident. There, the Cho. sang: "Without a city (*apolis*) is the man who rashly dwells with sin." The Cho., superficially at least, was retreating from its wondering admiration of the daring man (332 ff.). But for the poet, there are two types of daring, the one that dares the noble impossibility (see 90–96 n.), the other that is reckless because it is ignoble. Once again, the audience is led to reflect on the "rash man" as the cityless Cr. is now rash by his own admission. See also 915 n.

1340. *Ouch hekōn,* "not purposely." Cr. seems to retreat from his earlier full acceptance of responsibility for the deaths at 1318 and especially at 1261–69 where he acknowledged the blindness of his decisions (*bouleumata*) and where he admitted Hae. died because of *emais . . . dysbouliais,* "my own folly" (see 95 n.). At 1242, the Cho. finally saw that the lack of good sense, *aboulia,* embodied in Cr. is mankind's greatest curse.

1341–46. Note Cr.'s return to his ocular vocabulary. If he seemed momentarily (see 1319 and 1332 n.) to abandon sense perception for An.'s intuitive way of judging, the insight is not long-lived. Yet, the images and the action of the play vindicate An.'s way (Goheen, p. 93).

1345. *Lechria,* lit., "oblique," i.e., "awry." The word is an ironic reminder of the results of Cr.'s "straight" sailing (162 ff.). *Ta (e)n cheroin,* "that which is in my hands," *ta d(e),* "and that." Jebb takes the first phrase as referring to Hae. and the second as referring to Eurydice and An. If so, it is Cr.'s only mention of An. in the exodos. However, the second phrase must refer only to the second body on stage (i.e., that of Eurydice), a sufficient physical reminder of the heroine for the playwright, if not for the critics. The messenger as well as Cr. are purposely made to avoid mention of An. Jebb, like Cr., seems to require ocular evidence, whereas the poet keeps An.'s spirit before the audience in many ways, most notably by the inversion of images and themes, as Goheen's study first demonstrated.

1345-46. *Epi . . . eisēlato:* "A crushing fate has dashed down upon my head." The image of fate or the gods swooping down upon man and/or crushing him resonates through the play. Earlier (278), the Cho. hesitantly suggested that the first burial of Polynices was a "god-driven" (*the-ēlaton*) deed. In the Ode on *Atē,* the Cho. sang of divinely sent *atē,* doom or disaster by which some god dashed man down (*ereipei,* 598). Then, at 1260–75, even while Cr. admitted that his own poor judgment and blindness were responsible for his downfall, he insisted that some god smote him from above (*epaisen*) and hurled him into savage ways (*eseisen*). See 453–55 n. This imagery is even more pervasive in the *Oedipus Tyrannos* (see, e.g., 28, 255, 417, and *the-ēlaton manteuma deinon,* "the god-driven dreadful oracle," at 992).

1347–53. Cr. has now been escorted inside and the Cho., with marching anapests (a meter that was intermediate between the lyric meters and spoken iambs), recites its final "tag." This statement touches upon many of the themes of the play but limits itself to the pedestrian insights of the Cho. as they reflect not on An.'s tragedy but only on Cr.'s downfall. The Cho. discourses in its usual banal way on wisdom (1346 and 1353); piety, which is a form of wisdom (1349–50); arrogance, which is the absence of wisdom (1350–51); and the role of suffering in learning wisdom (1352–53). Thus, although the Cho. mentions key themes, its usual obtuseness prevents it from coming to terms with the meaning of the action (see 724–25 n.).

However, with the double recurrence of *to phronein*, "wisdom," the Cho. reinforces Cr.'s own admission (1260–69, see 1340 n.) that he was indeed guilty of *dysboulia*, "folly," and that his boasted *euboulia* (684 and n.) was a disastrous miscarriage of the rational process. The audience is left to consider whether An.'s symbiotic union with folly, *dysboulia* (95 n.), is not really *euboulia*, the kind of reasoning that Tiresias called mankind's greatest possession. The audience must also decide whether her impiety (see 74 n. and Intro., chap. 1) was not true *eusebeia*, piety (see 923–24). No one, least of all the Cho., says so, but An.'s last words called on all to see what she suffered because she revered reverence (*tēn eusebiān sebisāsa*, 942–43).

1350–51. *Megaloi . . . megalās plēgas . . . hyperauchōn:* "Big (i.e., proud, haughty) words bring down big (i.e., heavy) blows upon the proud." The ironic repetition of Cr.'s favorite "value" word (see 637 n.) underscores the fallacy of his system of values (see nn. on 183, 652, and 1325).

1353. *To phronein edidaxan*, "these teach wisdom." This phrase is a bitter answer to the question Cr. earlier thought rhetorical (727): "Am I to be taught wisdom from boys of his age?" The so-called gnomic aorist, *edidaxan*, is best translated by the present tense. This final maxim recalls Aeschylus' famous dictum (*Agamemnon* 177) *pathei mathos*, "wisdom comes through suffering," but the phrase, so integral to Aeschylus' drama, is hardly appropriate as a "lesson" of this play. The play reveals little evidence that Cr. has learned wisdom, and An.'s tragedy shows that she suffers *because* she is wise, not in order to become wise.

GRAMMATICAL NOTES

1284. Ἅιδου, Ἅιδης: gen. sing.

1285. ὀλέκεις, ὀλέκω: pres. 2 sing.

1286. κακάγγελτα, κακάγγελτος: acc. pl. neut.

1287. προπέμψας, προπέμπω: aor. partic.; ἄχη, ἄχος: acc. pl.; τίνα . . . λόγον, τίς λόγος: acc. sing.; θροεῖς, θροέω: pres. 2 sing.

1288. ὀλωλότ(α) ἄνδρ(α), ὄλλυμι (perf. mid. partic., meaning "perish") ἀνήρ: acc. sing.; ἐπεξειργάσω, ἐπεξεργάζομαι: aor. 2 sing.

1289. φής . . . λέγεις, φημί, λέγω: pres. 2 sing.; τίνα . . . νέον, τίς νέος: acc. sing. m., modif. μόρον (1292).

1291–92. σφάγιον . . . γυναικεῖον . . . μόρον, σφάγιος γυναικεῖος μόρος: acc. sing.; ὀλέθρῳ, ὄλεθρος: dat. sing.; ἀμφικεῖσθαι, ἀμφίκειμαι: pres. inf.

1293. ὁρᾶν, ὁράω: pres. inf.; πάρεστιν, πάρειμι: pres. 3 sing.; μυχοῖς, μυχός: dat. pl.

1295. κακὸν τόδ(ε) ἄλλο δεύτερον, κακὸς ὅδε ἄλλος δεύτερος: acc. sing. neut.

1296. περιμένει, περιμένω: pres. 3 sing.

1297. χείρεσσιν = χερσί, χείρ: dat. pl.

1299. ἔναντα: adv.; νεκρόν, νεκρός: acc. sing.

1300. μᾶτερ (= μῆτερ), ἀθλία, μήτηρ, ἄθλιος: noun of address.

1301. ἡμένη . . . βωμία, ἧμαι (pres. partic.), βώμιος: nom. sing. f.

1302. λύει, λύω: pres. 3 sing.; κελαινὰ βλέφαρα, κελαινός, βλέφαρον: acc. pl.; κωκύσασα, κωκύω: aor. partic. nom. sing. f.

1303. τοῦ . . . θανόντος Μεγαρέως, ὁ θανὼν (θνήσκω, aor. partic.) Μεγαρεύς: gen. sing.; κενὸν λέχος, κενός, λέχος: acc. sing.

1304. τοῦδε, ὅδε: gen. sing.; κακὰς πράξεις, κακός, πρᾶξις: acc. pl.

1305. ἐφυμνήσασα, ἐφυμνέω: aor. partic. nom. sing. f.; τῷ παιδοκτόνῳ, ὁ παιδοκτόνος: dat. sing.

1308. ἀνέπταν = ἀνέπτην, ἀναπέτομαι: 2 aor. pass. 1 sing. (trag. aor.); φόβῳ, φόβος: dat. sing.; ἀνταίαν, ἀνταῖος: acc. sing. (supply πληγήν, "blow").

1309. ἔπαισε(ν), παίω: aor. 3 sing.; ἀμφιθήκτῳ ξίφει, ἀμφίθηκτος ξίφος: dat. sing.

1310. δειλαία . . . δύᾳ = δύῃ, δείλαιος, δύη: dat. sing.; συγκέκραμαι, συγκεράννυμι: perf. 1 sing.

1312. ὡς αἰτίαν, αἰτία: acc. sing.; ἔχων, ἔχω: pres. partic.; τῶνδε κα(ὶ) (ἐ)κείνων, ὅδε, ἐκεῖνος: gen. pl. (poetic pl. for sing.).

1313. τῆς θανούσης τῆσδ(ε), θνήσκω (aor. partic.), ὅδε: gen. sing. f.; ἐπεσκήπτου, ἐπισκήπτω: impf. pass. 2 sing.; μόρων, μόρος: gen. pl. (poetic pl. for sing.)

1314. ποίῳ . . . τρόπῳ, ποῖος τρόπος: dat. sing.; (ἀ)πελύσατ(ο), ἀπολύω: aor. mid. 3 sing. The mid. shows she brought about her own release. I follow the MSS reading with most modern editors rather than Pearson's strange emendation. φοναῖς, φονή: dat. pl. for sing.

1315. παίσασ(α), παίω: aor. partic. nom. sing. f.; αὐτήν = ἑαυτήν, ἑαυτοῦ: acc. sing. f.

1316. παιδός, παῖς: gen. sing.; τόδ(ε) . . . ὀξυκώκυτον πάθος, ὅδε, ὀξυκώκυτος, πάθος: acc. sing.; ἤσθετ(ο), αἰσθάνομαι: aor. 3 sing.

1317. τάδ(ε), ὅδε: nom. pl. neut.; ἄλλον, ἄλλος: acc. sing. m.; βροτῶν, βροτός: gen. pl.

1318. ἐμᾶς ἐξ αἰτίας, ἐμός, αἰτία: gen. sing.; ἁρμόσει, ἁρμόζω: fut. 3 sing.

1319. (ἔ)κανον, καίνω: aor. 1 sing.

1320. φάμ(ι) = φημί; ἔτυμον, ἔτυμος: acc. sing. neut.; πρόσπολοι, πρόσπολος: noun of address, pl.

1321. ἀπάγετε . . . ἄγετε, ἄγω: pres.imper. 2 pl.; ὅτι τάχος = ὡς τάχιστα; ἐκποδών: adv.

1325. τὸν . . . ὄντα . . . μηδένα, ὁ ὢν (partic. of εἰμί) μηδείς: acc. sing. m. μηδείς here means "absolutely nobody," "counting as nobody."

1326. κέρδη, κέρδος: acc. pl.; παραινεῖς, παραινέω: pres. 2 sing.; κακοῖς, κακός: dat. pl. neut.

1327. βράχιστα (superl. of βραχύς) . . . κράτιστα (used as superl. of ἀγαθός); τ(ὰ) . . . κακά (ὁ κακός): nom. pl. neut.; (ἐ)ν ποσίν, πούς: dat. pl.

1328. ἴτω, εἶμι: pres. imper. 3 sing.

1329. φανήτω, φαίνω: aor. pass. imper. 3 sing.; μόρων . . . ἐμῶν, μόρος ἐμός: gen. pl.; κάλλιστ(α), καλός: superl. adv. emphatic, with the force of a predicate.

1330–31. ὁ . . . ἄγων (ἄγω: pres. partic.) ὕπατος: modif. μόρος understood; τερμίαν . . . ἀμέραν, τέρμιος, ἡμέρα: acc. sing.

1332. ἆμαρ = ἦμαρ = ἡμέρα, ἄλλο, ἄλλος: acc. sing.; εἰσίδω, εἰσοράω: aor. subj. 1 sing.

1334. μέλλοντα (ἐστὶ) ταῦτα, μέλλω (pres. partic.), οὗτος: nom. pl. neut.; τῶν προκειμένων = τῶν παρόντων, πρόκειμαι: pres. partic. gen. pl. with τι.

1335. μέλει, μέλω: impers. verb, 3 sing.; τῶνδ(ε) (supply τῶν μελλόντων), ὅδε: gen. pl. with μέλει; ὅτοισι = ὅτοις (= τούτοις ὅτοις μέλει), ὅστις: dat. pl.

1336. ὧν, ὅς: gen. pl.; ἐρῶμεν, ἐράω: pres. 1 pl. (supply τυχεῖν, "to happen"); συγκατηυξάμην, συγκατεύχομαι: aor. 1 sing.

1337. νυν: enclitic common with imperatives; προσεύχου,

προσεύχομαι: pres. mid. imper. 2 sing.; μηδέν, μηδείς: acc. sing. neut.; πεπρωμένης, πέπρωται (no pres. form): perf. partic. gen. sing. f., modif. συμφορᾶς (συμφορά).

1338. θνητοῖς, θνητός: dat. pl.

1339. ἄγοιτ(ε), ἄγω: pres. opt. 2 pl.; μάταιον ἄνδρ(α), μάταιος ἀνήρ: acc. sing.

1340. κατέκανον, κατακτείνω: 2 aor. 1 sing.

1343. σέ... τάνδ(ε) = τῆνδε, σύ, ὅδε: acc. sing. f.

1344. πότερον, πότερος: acc. sing.; ἰδῶ... κλιθῶ, ὁράω, κλίνω: aor. subj., one act., one pass., deliberative after ἔχω; πᾷ = πῇ: interrog. particle

1344–45. πάντα... λέχρια τ(ά), πᾶς, λέχριος: nom. pl. neut.; χεροῖν, χείρ: dat. dual; τὰ δ(έ): refers to the deaths of Eurydice and An., whereas τὰν χεροῖν refers to Hae.'s death; κρατί, κράς = κάρα: dat. sing.

1346. εἰσήλατο, εἰσάλλομαι: aor. 3 sing.

1348. πολλῷ, πολύς: dat. sing.; τὸ φρονεῖν, φρονέω: inf. with article as a noun, subject of ὑπάρχει (ὑπάρχω).

1349. ἔς = εἰς θεούς, θεός: acc. pl.

1350. ἀσεπτεῖν, ἀσεπτέω = ἀσεβέω: pres. inf.; μεγάλοι... λόγοι, μέγας λόγος: nom. pl.

1351. μεγάλας πληγάς, μέγας, πληγή: acc. pl.; τῶν ὑπεραύχων, ὁ ὑπέραυχος: gen. pl., gen. of possession with λόγοι and objective gen. with πληγάς.

1352. ἀποτείσαντες, ἀποτίνω: aor. partic. nom. pl. m.

1353. γήρᾳ, γῆρας: dat. sing.; τὸ φρονεῖν, φρονέω: inf. used as object of ἐδίδαξαν; ἐδίδαξαν, διδάσκω: aor. 3 pl. gnomic aor. used in sententious generalizations.

128

8

Vocabulary

The numbers indicate the lines at which the words occur in the selections. See the Preface for an explanation of the various forms cited.

α

ἀγαθός, ή, όν adj., *good, brave*, 31; *valiant, well-born, gentle*, 671
ἄγαλμα, ατος, τό n., *glory, delight*, honor, 704
ἄγαν adv., *very much, too much*, 473, 711, 735, 1251, 1256
ἄγραπτος, ον adj., *unwritten*, 454
ἄγραυλος, ον adj., *dwelling in the field, rustic*, 349
ἀγρέω, *take by hunting* or *fishing, catch, snatch*, 343
ἄγριος, α, ον adj., *living in the fields, wild, savage, living in a wild state, fierce*, 344, 1231, 1274
ἀγχιστεῖα, τά n., *close kinship, rights of kin, right of inheritance*, 174
ἄγω aor. ἤγαγον (ἄξετε), *lead, carry, bring*, 202, 760, 877, 885, 916, 931, 939, 1321, 1330; *lead toward, guide, manage*, 624, 1339; *hold, estimate, treat*, 34
ἀδελφός, ή, όν adj., *brotherly, sisterly; akin, cognate*, 192
ἀδελφός, ὁ m., *son of the same mother, brother*, 13, 46, 55, 81, 517, 912
ἀεί (αἰεί) adv., *ever, always*, 76, 166, 184, 456
ἄθαπτος, ον adj., *unburied*, 205, 467, 697
ἄθλιος, α, ον adj. (ἀθλίως adv.), lit., *winning the prize* or *running for it; struggling, unhappy, wretched, miserable*, 1209, 1300; adv., 26
αἰαῖ or αἶ interj., used to express astonishment or grief
αἰεί, poetic for ἀεί
αἰείφρουρος, ον adj., *ever-watching, everlasting*, 892

Guide to Sophocles' ΑΝΤΙGONE /

αἰκίζω (αἰκισθέν), pass., *be tortured*, 206
αἷμα, ατος, τό n., *blood*, 201; *bloodshed*, *murder*
αἱρέω aor. εἷλον, perf. pass. ᾕρημαι, *take with the hand, grasp, get into one's power, catch, detect, overcome*, 493, 497, 606, 655, 747
αἴρω, mid., *begin, undertake, take upon oneself*, 907
αἰσθάνομαι (ᾔσθετο), *perceive, hear, learn, understand*, 1316
αἰσχρός, ά, όν adj., *causing shame, dishonoring, reproachful; morally shameful, disgraceful*, 5, 511, 711, 747
αἰτέω (αἰτοῦσα), *ask, beg, ask for, demand*, 65
αἰτία, ἡ f., *responsibility, guilt, blame*, 445, 1312, 1318
ἀκάματος, η, ον adj., *without sense of toil, untiring, unresting, inexhaustible*, 339, 607
ἄκλαυτος, ον adj., *unwept, without funeral lamentation*, 29, 876
ἀκμής, ῆτος adj., *untiring, unwearied*, 352
ἀκοσμέω, *be disorderly, offend*, 730; *be mutinous*
ἄκοσμος, ον adj., *disorderly*, 660
ἀκούω, *hear*, 692; *listen to; obey*, 64
ἄκρα, ἡ f., *highest or farthest point*; with κατά *from top to bottom, utterly*, 201
ἀλγεινός, ή, όν adj., comparat. ἀλγίων, *painful, grievous*, 4, 12, 64
ἀλγέω (ἤλγουν), *feel bodily pain, suffer*, 468; *feel pain of mind, grieve*
ἄλγος, εος, τό n., *pain, grief*, 466
ἀλγύνω, pass., *feel, suffer pain, be grieved* or *distressed*, 468
ἄλεκτρος, ον adj., *unwedded*, 917
ἀληθές n. adj. as adv., *indeed?, really?*, 758
ἀλίσκομαι fut. ἀλώσομαι, *be taken, be seized; be established*, 46
ἀλλά conj., *but, yet*, e.g., 35; *still, at least*, 1336; with γε, *but then, however*, 84; *well*, 89
ἀλλήλων (ἀλλήλοιν) pron., *one another, mutual, reciprocal*, 57
ἄλλος, η, ο adj. or pron., *another, other*, 646, 706, 909, 1295
ἄλλοτε adv., *at another time, sometimes*, 367
ἆμαρ, ατος, τό n., *day*, 1333
ἁμαρτάνω 2 aor. ἥμαρτον, perf. ἡμάρτηκα, *miss the mark, fail*, 1250; *be deprived of; do wrong, err, sin*, 744, 914, 926, 927, 1250, 1260
ἁμάρτημα, ατος, τό n., *failure, fault*, 1261
ἁμέρα, see ἡμέρα
ἀμήχανος (ἀμάχανος), ον adj., *without means* or *resources, helpless, incapable, awkward*, 79, 363; *hard, impossible*, 90, 92, 175
ἀμπλάκημα, ατος, τό n., *error, fault*, 51

130

Vocabulary

ἀμπλακίσκω aor. ἤμπλακον with gen., *lose, be bereft of*, 910
ἀμυντέον verbal adj. expressing necessity, *one must assist, defend*, 677
ἀμφί prep. with acc., *about, around, by, at*
ἀμφιβάλλω (ἀμφιβαλών), *emcompass, beset, surround with nets*, 343
ἀμφίθηκτος, ον adj., *sharpened on both sides, two-edged*, 1309
ἀμφίκειμαι, *lie round or upon, be heaped on*, 1292
ἀμφίλοφος, ον adj., *encompassing the neck*, 351
ἄν particle, usually an indicator that the action is limited by
    circumstances or defined by conditions
ἄναξ, ἄνακτος, ὁ m., *lord, master* (used of the king), 724, 1257
ἀνάξιος, ον adj., superl. ἀναξιώτατος, *undeserving*, 694
ἀναπέτομαι (ἀνέπτην), *fly away; be startled*, 1308
ἀναρχία, ἡ f., *lack of a leader, lawlessness, anarchy*, 672
ἀνάστατος, ον adj., *ruined, laid waste*, 673
ἀνδάνω (ἀδεῖν), *please, delight, gratify*, 89, 504
ἀνεμόεις (ἠνεμόεις), εσσα, εν, *windy, airy, high-soaring, rapid*, 354
ἀνέχομαι aor. ἠνσχόμην, *allow, suffer, bear*, 467
ἀνήρ, ἀνδρός, ὁ m., *man*, 62, 162, 175, 187, 347, 458, 484, 605, 616,
    641, 661, 668, 679, 690, 710, 721, 727, 737, 942, 1243, 1339;
    gentleman (as term of address), 162
ἄνθρωπος, ὁ m., *man* (generically), *mankind*, 334, 452, 683
ἄνους, ουν adj., *without understanding, silly, without wit*, 99
ἀνταῖος, α, ον adj., *right opposite; opposed to, hostile*, 1308
ἀντείρω (ἀντειρηκότος), *speak against, gainsay*, 47
ἀντί prep. with gen., *opposite, over against; instead of, set against,
    compared with, in preference to*, 182; *in place of*, 186
ἀντιτείνω, *stretch, strain back; act or strive against, resist*, 714
ἀνυμέναιος, ον adj., *without the nuptial song, unwedded*, 876, 917
ἀνωφέλητος, ον adj., *unprofitable, useless*, 645
ἄξιος, α, ον adj., *worthy, estimable*, 699; *worthy of, deserving*
ἀξιόω (ἀξιώσεται), *deem worthy, esteem, honor, value*, 637, 1248
ἀπαλλαγή, ἡ f., *deliverance, release, escape*, 1338
ἀπειλή, ἡ f., *boastful promise, boast, threat*, 753
ἀπεχθής, ές adj., *hateful, hostile, hated*, 50
ἀπό prep. with gen. *from, away from; sprung from*, 2, 193, *in descent
    from, by, because of, by reason of*
ἄπολις, ιδος adj., *without city, state*, or *country, outlaw, banished man,
    no true citizen*, 370
ἀπόλλυμι 2 aor. mid. ἀπωλόμην, mid., *perish, die*, 50; pass., *be*

destroyed, 714
ἀπολύω (ἀπελύσατο), mid., *release oneself, depart,* 1314
ἀπορθόω, *make straight, guide aright,* 636; *restore to health*
ἄπορος, ον adj., *without passage, having no way in, out,* or *through;*
    without means or *resources, helpless,* 360
ἀπόρρητος, ον adj., *forbidden,* 44; *not to be spoken, secret*
ἀποτίνω (ἀποτείσαντες), *repay, pay the debt, atone,* 1352
ἀποτρύω (ἀποτρύεται), *rub away, wear out,* 339
ἅπτω mid. ἅπτομαι, *fasten* or *bind,* 40; mid., *fasten oneself to, cleave to,*
    179
ἆρα interrog. particle, implying anxiety or impatience, 2
ἀράσσω (ἀράξας), *smite, dash violently,* 52
ἀρέσκω aor. pass. ἠρέσθην, *please, satisfy, conform to,* 75, 89, 211, 500
ἀριθμός, ὁ m., *number,* 893; *amount, sum*
ἀριστεύω (ἀριστεύσας), *be best* or *bravest, gain the prize for valor, gain*
    the highest distinction, 195
ἄριστος, η, ον adj., *best, noblest, bravest,* 197; *morally best,* 179; 1114
ἁρμόζω (ἡρμοσμένα) fut. ἁρμόσω, *fit together, join, suit, adapt,* 570,
    1318
ἄρνυμαι, *win, gain* (esp. of honor or reward), 903
ἄροτρον, τό n., *plough,* 340
ἀρτάνη, ἡ f., *rope, noose, halter,* 54
ἄρτι adv., *lately, newly,* 8
ἀρχή, ἡ f., *first place* or *power, sovereignty, duty of administration,* 177,
    744
ἀρχήν noun as adv., *to begin with, yes,* 92
ἄρχω fut. ἄρξω, *be first, begin; rule, govern, command,* 63, 525, 669,
    736, 739
ἀσεπτέω, *be impious, act profanely, commit sacrilege,* 1350
ἀστός, ὁ m., *townsman, citizen* (one with civil but not political rights),
    27, 186, 193
ἀστυνόμος, *protecting the city,* pertaining to *law-abiding* or *social life,*
    355
ἀσφαλής, ές adj., *not liable to fall, immovable, steadfast,* 454; *sure, certain*
ἀσφαλῶς adv., *surely, certainly, safely, firmly, steadily,* 162
ἀτάομαι (ἀτώμενος), *suffer, be in distress,* 17
ἄταφος, ον adj., *unburied,* 29
ἄτερ prep. with gen., *without, apart from, free from,* 4

Vocabulary

ἄτη, ἡ f., *bewilderment, infatuation* (caused by blindness or delusion sent by the gods), 624; *reckless guilt* or *sin, doom, ruin*, 4, 185, 533, 583, 614, 624, 625, 1260

ἀτιμάζω (ἀτιμάσασ᾽), *hold in no honor, esteem lightly, deem unworthy*, 22, 77

ἄτιμος, ον adj., *unhonored, dishonored, dishonorable*, 5, 78

αὖ adv. *again, anew, besides*, 7, 1343; *back, backward; on the other hand, in turn*, 58, 198, 601

αὐδάω, *speak to, address; invoke*, 923

αὖθις, *again, anew, in turn, hereafter*, 167, 1304

αὔλειος, α, ον adj., *of* or *belonging to the court*, 18 (here the outer door)

αὐξάνω or αὔξω, *increase, increase in power, strengthen, intend to make prosperous*, 191

αὐτάδελφη, ἡ f., *own sister*, 1

αὐτάδελφος, ὁ m., *one's own brother*, 503, 696

αὐτίκα adv., *at once, in a moment*

αὐτοκτονέω, *slay one another*, 56

αὐτόπρεμνος, ον adj., *together with the root, root and branch*, 714

αὐτουργός, όν adj., *self-working*, 52

αὐτόφωρος, ον adj., *self-detected*, 51

αὐτόχειρ, −χειρος adj., *with one's own hand, creative*, 900; *murderous* (esp. of murder committed by one's own kinsman), 172; *as noun, one's own hand*, 1315

αὔτως adv., *in this very manner, even so*, 85

ἀφαγνίζω (ἀφαγνίσαι), *purify, consecrate*, 196

ἄφθιτος, ον adj., *undecaying, imperishable, unchanging, unchangeable*, 339

ἄχος, εος, τό n., *pain, distress*, 1247, 1287

β

βαίνω (βεβῶσι), *walk; in perf., stand, be*, 67

βέλος, εος, τό n., *missile*, esp. *arrow, dart*, 359

βία, ἡ f., in dat., *against the will of, in spite of*, 59, 79, 907

βιάζω, mid., *overpower, press hard, do violence by*, 663; pass., *be constrained to*, 66

βίος, ὁ m., *mode of life, manner of living; life*, 54, 896

βλαστάνω (βλάστοι), *bud, sprout, come to light, be born*, 912

βλέπω, *see, have the power of sight,* 1264, 1295; *look; look to, rely on,* 923
βλέφαρον, τό n., *eyelid, eye,* 105, 1302
βορά, ἡ f., *food,* (of carnivorous beasts), 30
βούλευμα, ατος, τό n., *resolution, purpose,* 179, 1265
βούλομαι, *will, wish, be willing,* 757
βραχύς, εῖα, ύ adj., superl. βράχιστος, *short,* 1327
βροτός, ὁ m., *mortal man,* 1276, 1317
βώμιος, α, ον adj., *at the altar,* 1301

γ

γαμέω, *marry,* i.e., *take a wife,* 750
γάμος, ὁ m., *wedding, marriage, wedlock,* 637, 917
γάρ casual conj., normally introducing the reason or cause for what
    precedes *for; yes! since, why, what;* other uses noted in context
γε particle, usually emphasizing the previous word
γέλως, −ωτος, ὁ m., *laughter; occasion of laughter,* 647
γένος, εος or ους, τό n., *race, stock, kin, clan, house, offspring, family,* 174,
    341, 584, 596, 660
γῆ, ἡ f., *earth, land, country, native land, city,* 199, 338, 518, 739, 937
γῆρας, γήραος, τό n., *old age,* 1353
γίγνομαι aor. ἐγενόμην, *come into being, be born, become,* 650; in past
    tenses, *be,* 374; *be produced, take place, come to pass, be,* 652, 687
γιγνώσκω, *come to know, perceive, recognize,* 188
γλυκύς, εῖα, ύν adj., *sweet to the taste* or *smell,* 29
γλῶσσα, ης, ἡ f., *tongue,* 180, 505; *talking, speech, language,* 708
γνώμη, ἡ f., *organ of perception, a means of knowing, intelligence, thought,*
    judgment, opinion, 42, 176, 635, 640, 719, 753, 1250, *maxim,* 753
γονή, ἡ f., *offspring, children,* 641
γοῦν restrictive particle, *at least, then, at any rate,* 45; *for indeed,* 489,
    771; indicates an incredulous question, 734
γυναικεῖος, α, ον adj., *of* or *belonging to women, feminine,* 1292
γυνή, γυναικός, ἡ f., *woman, mistress, lady,* 61, 525, 649, 651, 678, 680,
    694, 740, 741, 746, 756, 1244; *wife, spouse,* 53, 651

δ

δαίμων, ονος, ὁ m., *god, goddess, the divine power,* 921

Vocabulary

δέ particle, used to answer μέν; alone, used to express opposition

δεῖ impers., *there is need, one must, it is needful* or *fitting*, often expressing inevitability, 75, 679

δείδω perf. (δείσασα), *fear, be alarmed, be anxious, dread*, 459

δείκνυμι fut. δείξω, aor. ἔδειξα, *bring to light, show forth, point out, show*, 37, 1242

δείλαιος, α, ον adj., *wretched, sorry, paltry*, 1310, 1311

δεινός, ή, όν adj., *fearful, terrible, marvelously strong, powerful, wondrous, marvelous, strange, awful, mighty, rigid*, 96, 332, 690, 915; *clever, skillful*; comparat., 333

δέμας, τό n., *bodily frame, corpse*, 205, 903

δένδρον, τό n., *tree*, 713

δεννάζω (δεννάσεις), *abuse, revile*, 759

δεῦρο adv., *hither, here*, 33

δεύτερος, α, ον adj., *second*, 1295

δέχομαι (δέδεκται), *take, accept, receive*, 894

δή temporal particle, *at this point, now, then, already, at length, of course*

δηλόω, *make visible, make clear*, 20, 471

δημόλευστος, ον adj., *publicly stoned; by public stoning*, 36

δημότης, ου, ὁ m., *one of the people, commoner*, 690

δῆτα adv., lengthened and more emphatic form of δή, in answers, *yes, indeed*; in questions, *then, so, of course*

διά prep. with gen. and acc., *right through*

διαπτύσσω (διαπτυχθέντες), *open and spread out, unfold, disclose*, 709; *split open*

διδάσκω fut. mid. διδάξομαι, aor. ἐδίδαξα, aor. mid. ἐδιδαξάμην, *instruct, teach*, 1353; mid., *teach oneself, learn*, 356, 726

δίδωμι fut. δώσω, aor. ἔδωκα, *give freely, offer*, 902; *grant, allow, bring about*, 718; *pay*, 460

δίκαιος, α, ον adj., *observant of custom, rule*, or *duty* (to gods and men), *righteous*, 24, 662, 671, 728, 743

δίκη, ἡ f., *custom, usage; order, right, justice*, 23, 94, 369, 451, 742, 921, 1270; *atonement, penalty*, 459

δικτυόκλωστος, ον adj., (of a net) *woven in meshes*, 346

διόλλυμι (διώλετο), pass., *perish utterly*, 168

διπλόος, η, ον (διπλοῦς, ῆ, οῦν) adj., *twofold, double*, 14, 53, 170, 1233; pl., *two, both*, 51

δίχα adv., *in two, divided, apart, aloof*, 164

135

δοκέω fut. δόξω, aor. ἔδοξα, *expect, think, suppose, imagine*, 707, 762; with inf., *seem, pretend*, 181, 469, 682, 914; with inf. and dat., *seem, seem good, be resolved on*, 71, 76, 98, 622

δόμος, ὁ m., *house*, 600, 651; *household, family*, 583, 600, 642

δόρυ, δορός, τό n., *plank, shaft of a spear, spear*, 195, 670, 674

δούλευμα, ατος, τό n., *service, slave*, 756

δοῦλος, ὁ m., *born slave, slave*, 479, 517

δουλόω (δουλώσας), *enslave*, 202

δράω (δρῶ, δρῶντες, δρῴην), perf. δέδρακα (ἐδεδράκη), *do, accomplish*, esp. *do some great thing good* or *bad*, 35, 70, 79, 442, 443, 482, 483, 507, 928; *try, act*, 469, 634; partic., *the doer, culprit*, 634

δύα, ἡ poetic, *misery, anguish*, 1311

δύναμαι, *be able, strong enough*, 90, 455, 686

δύο, δυοῖν adj., *two*, 13, 55

δύσαυλος, ον adj., *bad for lodging, inhospitable*, 356

δυσβουλία, ἡ f., *ill-counsel*, 95, 1269

δυσκάθαρτος, ον adj., *hard to purify, hard to purge, hard to satisfy by purification* or *atonement*, 1284

δυσκλεής, ές adj., *inglorious, infamous, shameful*, 50

δυσκόμιστος, ον adj., *hard to bear, intolerable*, 1346

δυσμενής, ές, *hostile, enemy*, 187, 653

δύσμορος, ον adj., *ill-fated*, 919

δύσνους, ουν adj., *ill-disposed, disaffected*, 212

δύσομβρος, ον adj., *stormy*, 359

δυσσέβεια, ἡ f., *impiety, ungodliness*, 924

δύστηνος, ον adj., *wretched, unhappy, unfortunate, disastrous*, 379, 850, 922, 1225, 1283

ε

ἐάν contr. ἤν and ἄν conj. with subj., *if, if ever*

ἑαυτοῦ, ῆς, οῦ contr. αὑτοῦ reflex. pron. of 3d person, *of himself, herself, itself, themselves*

ἐάω (ἐῶ, ἐᾶν) aor. εἴασα, *suffer, permit, allow*, 95, 698; *let alone, let be*, 29, 205

ἐγγενής, ές adj., *native, of the race* or *country*, 199; *born of the same race, kindred*, 659

ἐγγύτατος, η, ον superl. adj., *nearest;* 933

Vocabulary

ἐγκλείω (ἐγκλήσας), *shut in, close, confine*, 180, 505

ἐγκρατής, ές adj., *in possession of power, holding fast*, 715, 474

ἐγώ ἐμέ, με, ἐμοῦ, μου, ἐμοί, μοι pron. of the 1st person, *I*

ἔγωγε, *I at least, for my part, indeed, for myself*, 636

ἐθέλω (θέλω) aor. ἠθέλησα, *consent, be willing, wish*, 45, 69, 200, 201, 669, 765; with neg., *be able*

ἔθνος, εος, τό n., *body of men, band; swarms, flocks*, 344

εἰ, *if; whether*; other uses noted in context

εἰδώς, see οἶδα

εἴη, see εἰμί

εἰκός, ότος adj., *like truth, likely, probable, reasonable*, 724

εἴκω, *give way, retire, yield*, 472, 718

εἶμι (ἰών), *come, go*, 42, 472, 1328, 1331

εἰμί (εἶναι,'ἴσθι, ἦν, ὤν) fut. ἔσομαι, *be*

εἰν, see ἐν

εἴπερ or εἴ περ, *if really, if indeed*, 679, 741, *even if, even though*

εἴργω, *shut out or in, bar one's way*, 48

εἴρηκα, εἴρημαι, see λέγω

εἷς, μία, ἕν (ἑνός, μιᾶς) adj., *one, single*, 14, 55, 170, 705, 737

εἰς or ἐς prep. with acc., of place, *into, to*; of time, *up to, until, within, for, on*; of measure or limit, *as far as, as much as*; of relation, *toward*, 922; *in regard to*, 731; "etos eis etos," *year after year*, 340

εἰσακούω (εἰσήκουσας), *hear, perceive*, 9

εἰσάλλομαι (εἰσήλατο), *spring or rush into, leap into*, 1346

εἰσοράω (εἰσίδοις, εἰσίδω), *look into, behold, gaze upon steadily*, 30, 476, 1332

εἶτα adv., *then, next; soon; therefore*

εἴτε conj. generally doubled, *either . . . or, whether . . . or*

ἐκ, ἐξ prep. with gen., of place, *from, out of*; of position, *outside of, beyond, apart from*; of time, *from*, 12; *for, since, after*; *out of*, of cause or means, *by*; *on account of*, 180; *by* (agent), 63, 93; *from source, origin, parents*, 466

ἐκβάλλω (-εβάλης), *throw away, cast aside, reject*, 649

ἐκδίκως adv., *lawlessly, unjustly*, 928

ἐκεῖ adv., *there, in that place; in another world*, 76

ἐκεῖνος, η, ο (κεῖνος) demonstr. pron., *the person there, that one*

ἐκκηρύσσω (ἐκκεκηρῦχθαι, ἐκκεκήρυκται), *proclaim by the voice of a herald*; pass., *be banished by proclamation*, 27, *be proclaimed*, 203

137

ἐκμανθάνω (ἐκμαθεῖν), in past tenses, *to have learned thoroughly, know full well,* 175

ἐκπέμπω, *send out, call outside,* 19

ἐκπίπτω (ἐκπεσεῖν), *fall out of, be displaced, be banished,* 679

ἐκποδών adv., *away from the feet, out of the way, away,* 1321, 1339

ἐκπροτιμάω (−τιμήσασα), *honor above all,* 913

ἐκσῴζω, *preserve from danger, keep safe;* mid., *save for oneself,* 713

ἐκτός adj., *without, outside,* 18

ἑκών, ἑκοῦσα, ἑκόν adj., best translated as adv. *readily, wittingly, purposely,* 1340

ἕλκος, εος, τό n., *wound, sore, ulcer,* 652

ἐλπίς, ίδος, ἡ f., *hope, expectation, reason to expect* or *believe,* 366, 616, 897, 1246

ἐμαυτοῦ, ἐμαυτῆς reflex. pron., *of me, of myself*

ἐμέ, ἐμοῦ, ἐμοί acc., gen. and dat. of ἐγώ

ἐμμένω, *abide in, be true to, stand fast, be faithful,* 169

ἔμπεδος, ον adj., *in the ground, steadfast,* 169

ἐμφανῶς adv., *openly, without doubt,* 655

ἐν (εἰν) prep. with dat., *in, within; in the number of,* 661; *in the eyes of,* 925; *in the time of,* 16

ἐνάλιος (εἰνάλιος), α, ον adj., *in, on, of the sea,* 345

ἔναντα adv., *opposite, over against,* 1299

ἐναντίος, α, ον adj., *opposite,* 671; *opposing,* facing (in battle)

ἔνδικος, ον adj., *according to right, just, legitimate, upright,* 208; *legal*

ἔνερθεν adv., *from beneath, up from below, beneath, below;* esp. of the underworld, 25

ἐνεστί impers., *it is in, it is in one's power,* 213

ἐνθάδε adv., *in this world, here,* 75

ἐννοέω, *have in one's thoughts, reflect, understand,* 61

ἔνορκος, ον adj., *having sworn, bound by oath, included in a treaty, that to which one is sworn,* 369

ἔντιμος, ον adj., *in honor, honored with, honored,* 25, 77

ἐντριβής, ές adj., *proved by rubbing, versed or practiced in,* 177

ἐξαμαρτάνω, *miss the mark, fail, miss one's aim; err, do wrong,* 743

ἐξήκω, *have reached; have run out, have expired,* 896

ἔξοιδα perf. in pres. sense (ἐξῄδη), *know thoroughly, know well,* 460

ἐξορθόω, *set upright; set right, correct,* 83

ἔξω prep. with gen., *outside,* 660

Vocabulary

ἔοικε impers. perf. with pres. sense, *it seems*, 740

ἐπάγω (ἐπάξεται), mid., *bring to oneself, procure for oneself, devise, invent*, 362

ἔπαινος, ὁ m., *approval, praise, commendation*, 665

ἐπαπειλέω, *hold out as a threat to, threaten*, 752

ἐπεί conj., *after, since, when*, 15, 168, *from the time when, ever since*, 655

ἔπειτα adv., *thereupon, thereafter, afterward, then*, 53, 63, 611

ἐπεξεργάζομαι (−ειργασάσω), *effect besides, accomplish*, 1288; *slay over again*, 1288

ἐπεξέρχομαι, *march out, attack, proceed to an extremity*, 752

ἐπί prep., with gen., *upon, on*; with dat., *upon, in, at, near, by, on, over, for*; with acc., *upon, onto, to, as far as*

ἐπιλαμβάνω (ἐπείληπται), *lay hold of, seize, attack*, 732

ἐπισκήπτω, *denounce, blame, accuse*, 1313

ἐπίσταμαι, *know, be able, be capable*, 686

ἐπίστημος, ον adj., *knowing*, 721

ἐπιτάσσω, *put upon as a duty, enjoin, impose commands*, 664

ἐπιτύμβιος, ον adj., *at or over a tomb*, 901

ἔπος, εος, τό n., *word, utterance, tale*, 20, 53, 621

ἐράω, *love, be in love with, love or desire passionately*, 90, 1336

ἔργον, τό n., *work, deed, action, thing, matter*, 85, 695, 729, 730, 1228; *mischief, trouble*, 1225

ἔρδω poetic, *do*, 375; *offer*

ἐρεμνός, ή, όν adj., *murky, black, dark*, 700

ἐρῆμος, ον or η, ον adj., *empty, desolate, lonely, solitary*, 739, 887, 919

ἕρπω, *move slowly*, 584, 1213; *go forth, come suddenly*, 367

ἔρχομαι 2 aor. ἦλθον, *start, set out, come, go*, 99, 360, 897, 920; *happen to*, 197

ἐρῶ, see λέγω

ἐς = εἰς

ἐσθλός, ή, όν adj., *brave, stout, noble*, 38; *morally good, faithful*, 38, 245, 367, 622

ἔσται fut. of εἰμί

ἑτέρως adv., *in one or the other way, otherwise than should be*, 687

ἔτι adv., *yet, still*

ἔτος, εος, τό n., *year*, 340

ἔτυμος, ον adj., *true*, 1320

εὖ adv., *well, thoroughly, competently*, 166, 669

εὐγενής, ές adj., *well-born, noble, noble-minded, generous*, 38
εὐδαιμονία, ἡ f., *prosperity, good fortune, true, full happiness*, 1347
εὐθύνω, *guide straight, direct, make* or *put straight*, 178, 1164
εὐκλεής, ές adj., *of good report, famous, glorious*; superl., 695
εὔκλεια, ἡ f., *good repute, glory*, 703
εὐμενής, ές adj., *well-disposed, kindly, friendly*, 212, 1200
εὔνους, ουν adj., *well-disposed, kindly, friendly*, 209
εὐσέβεια, ἡ f., *reverence toward the gods* or *parents, piety* or *filial respect, loyalty*, 872, 943
εὐσεβέω, *live* or *act piously, reverence*, 731, 924
εὐτυχέω, *be prosperous, fortunate, be well off*, 17
εὐτυχῶς adv., *successfully, fortunately*, 701
εὔχομαι, *pray, utter in prayer, wish for, boast*, 641
ἐφέπομαι fut. ἐφέψομαι, *follow, obey, attend to*, 636
ἐφυμνέω aor. −ύμνησα, *chant at, utter over*, 658, 1305; *sing a dirge, repeatedly invoke (a scornful word)*, 658; *curse*, 1305
ἐχθαίρω fut. mid. with pass. sense, ἐχθαρεῖ, pass., *be hateful*, 93
ἐχθές = χθές adv., *yesterday*, 456
ἐχθρός, ά, όν adj., *hated, hateful*, 94; comparat., *more hated*, 86; as noun, *enemy*, 10, 522, 643, 647
ἔχω 2 aor. ἔσχον, *have, hold; possess mentally, understand, know of*, 9, 366, 1341; *be, be engaged* or *busy, hold oneself, keep*, 639, 706; with adv., 706

ζ

ζάω (ζώσαιν), *live*, 3, 210, 214, 457, 464, 525, 750, 888, 920; *be in force*, 457
ζυγόν, τό n., *yoke*, 351

η

ἤ conj., *or; than, as*
ἦ adv., *in truth, although*
ἡγέομαι (ἡγουμένου), *go before, lead the way*, 638
ἡδονή, ἡ f., *enjoyment, pleasure, delight*, 648
ἡδύς, ἡδεῖα, ἡδύ adv., *sweet, pleasant, welcome*, 12; adv., *pleasantly, with pleasure, gladly*, 70

Vocabulary

ἦθος, εος, τό n., *custom, usage, disposition, character,* 705, 746
ἦλθον, see ἔρχομαι
ἦμαι (ἡμένη), *be seated, sit, lurk at,* 1301
ἡμεῖς, ἡμᾶς, ἡμῶν, ἡμῖν pl. 1st person pron., *we*
ἡμέρα (ἀμέρα), ἡ f., *day,* 14, 55, 171, 1330
ἦν impf. of εἰμί
ἡνίκα adv., *at the time when, whenever, when*
ἧπαρ, ατος, τό n., *liver, the seat of passions, anger, fear,* etc., 1315
ἦσαν 3d person pl. impf. of εἰμί
ἡσσητέος, α, ον verbal adj., *must be beaten,* 678
ἥσσων, ἧσσον gen. −ονος used as comparat. adj. of κακός, *inferior,
    weaker, worse,* 680; *yielding, a slave to, unable to resist,* 747

θ

θάλλω, *bloom, sprout, grow, thrive, flourish, be prosperous,* 703
θάνατος, ὁ m., *death,* 933
θάπτω fut. θάψω, *honor with funeral rites, bury,* 44, 72
θαρσέω (θαρσοίην), *be of good courage, have no fear of, believe
    confidently, make bold,* 668, 935
θέλω, see ἐθέλω
θεός, ὁ m., *god, the deity,* 77, 162, 199, 337, 369, 451, 454, 459, 597,
    601, 607, 624, 683, 745, 749, 922, 925, 938, 1218, 1273, 1349
θερμός, ή, όν adj., *hot,* 88, 619; *hot headed, hasty,* 88
θήρ, θηρός, ὁ m., *beast of prey,* esp. *a lion, beast,* 344, 350
θηράω, *hunt, chase; hunt after, pursue eagerly,* 92
θησαυρός, ὁ m., *store, treasure,* 30
θνήσκω (θνήσκω) fut. θανοῦμαι, aor. ἔθανον, perf. τέθνακα, pres. and
    impf., *die a natural* or *violent death,* 72, 460, 462, 512, 522, 761;
    aor. and perf., *be dead* or *be put to death,* 14, 94, 97, 209, 214, 467,
    751, 900, 920, 1268, 1282, 1313
θνητός, ή, όν adj., *liable to death, mortal, human,* 455, 614, 1338
θρασύς, εῖα, ύ adj., *bold, full of confidence; rash, arrogant, insolent,* 752
θροέω, *cry aloud, scare, terrify,* 1287
θρόνος, ὁ m., *seat, chair, throne, chair of state,* 166, 173, 1041
θυμός, ὁ m., *soul, spirit* (as the principle of life); *the seat of anger,
    anger, wrath,* 718

ι

ἱκνέομαι aor. ἱκόμην, *arrive at, come, reach, attain,* 12, 165
ἵππειος, α, ον adj., *of a horse,* 341
ἵππος, ὁ m., *horse,* 351, 478
ἴλλω, *wind, turn around,* 340
ἴσος, η, ον adj., *equal, like,* 374, 644; *equal in rights;* n. as adv.,
    equally, likewise, 489
ἵστημι aor. ἔστησα, 2 perf. ἔστηκα, *stand, be set* or *placed, take up an
    attitude, stand idle,* 640; *set up, appoint,* 666
ἴσχω = ἔχω, *have, hold,* 66
ἰώ exclamation used when invoking aid and as an expression of grief
    or suffering, *oh! ah!*

κ

καί conj. and adv., *and, but, even, also, just;* when duplicated, or
    with te, *both . . . and*
καίνω (ἔκανον), *kill, slay,* 1319
καίριος, α, ον adj., *in season, timely,* 724
καίτοι conj., *and indeed, and further, and yet*
κακάγγελτος, ον adj., *caused by ill tidings, ill tidings,* 1286
κακός, ή, όν adj. (κακίων, ον; κάκιστος, η, ον), *bad, base, morally evil,
    diseased,* 38, 208, 463, 472, 495, 582, 651, 652, 731, 1243, 1245,
    1280, 1281, 1304; as n. noun, 2, 6, 10, 367, 520, 622, 643, 672,
    927, 1295, 1326, 1327; comparat., 1281; superl., 181, 489, 695,
    895; superl. as adv., 59
καλέω, pass., *be called,* 680
καλός, ή, όν also ά, όν adj., superl. adv. κάλλιστα, *beautiful* (of form);
    morally beautiful, noble, honorable, 72, 723, 925; as n. noun, *beauty,
    virtue, honor, nobility,* 370; as adv., *well, rightly, happily, fairly,* 18,
    97, 638, 669, 687, 739; superl., *most happily,* 1329
καλύπτω (καλύψαι), *cover, hide, conceal,* 1254; of death, *to be buried,* 28
καλχαίνω, *make purple; make dark and troublous, brood,* 20
κἀμέ = (καὶ ἐμέ) *and me*
κάρα, τό n., lit., *head,* 441, 1272; *dear,* 1, 899, 915
καρδία, ἡ f., *heart,* 88, 1254; *inclination, desire, purpose, mind*
κάρτα adv., *extremely, very much,* 660, 897

Vocabulary

κασιγνήτη, ἡ f., *sister*, 49

κασίγνητος, ὁ m., *brother, born from the same mother*, 21, 899, 915

κατά (καθ᾽, κατ᾽) prep., with gen., *down from, down into, under*, 24, *by, in respect of, concerning*; with acc., *down, on, over, throughout, in*, 55, *in accordance with*, 174, *before*, 760

καταθνήσκω (κατθανών), *die away, be dying*, 464, 515, 906, 909

κατακαίνω (κατακτείνω) aor. κατέκανον, *kill, slay*, 1340

κατάκρας adv., *from top to bottom, utterly*, 201

καταρρήγνυμι, (of armies) *break up and turn to flight*, 675

κατασκαφή, ἡ f., *grave*, 920

κατασκαφής, ές adj., *dug down, deep-dug*, 891

καταυδάω *speak out plainly*, 86

κάτειμι *go, come down*, 896

κατεργάζομαι (κατειργάσαντο), *effect by labor, achieve, finish*, 57

κατέρχομαι (κατελθών), *come back, return* (esp. from exile), 200

κατήκοος, ον adj., *hearing, obedient*, 642

κἄτι (καὶ ἔτι), *and still, and yet*

καθίστημι fut. καταστήσω, *set in order, array, arrange, make*, 657

κάτω adv., *downward*, 716; *beneath, below*, 75, 451

κεῖμαι fut. κείσομαι, *lie, lie outstretched, remain*, 73, 76, 485, 1197, 1240

κεῖνος, see ἐκεῖνος

κελαινός, ή, όν adj., *black, dark, murky*, 590, 1302

κελεύω (κελεύσαιμι), *urge, drive on, exhort, bid*, 69, 731

κενός, ή, όν adj., *empty*, 709, 753, 754, 1303; *destitute, bereft, devoid of wit, vain, pretentious*, 709

κέρδος, εος, τό n., *gain, profit*, 326, 462, 464, 1061, 1326

κεύθω (κεκευθότοιν), *cover, hide, conceal*, 85; intr., *be concealed, be hidden*, 911

κήρυγμα, ατος, τό n., *that which is cried by a herald, public announcement, proclamation*, 8, 454

κηρύσσω fut. κηρύξω, aor. ἐκήρυξα, aor. pass. ἐκηρύχθην, *proclaim, announce, command publicly*, 32, 87, 192, 450, 447

κινδύνευμα, ατος, τό n., *hazard, venture*, 42

κλαίω, *cry, lament*; partic. *to your sorrow* or *loss, at your peril*, 754

κλέπτω (κεκλέμμεθα), *steal, deceive, cheat*, 681

κλίνω (κλιθῶ), pass., *lean, stay oneself*, 1344

κλύω, *hear, attend to*, 19, 632, 691, 757; *comply with, obey*, 666

143

κλών, κλωνός, ὁ m., *twig, spray, slip*, 713
κοινός, ή, όν adj., *common*, 57; *connected by common origin, kindred*, 1, 202
κοσμέω aor. ἐκόσμησα, *order, arrange* (esp. set an army in array), 677; *adorn, dress*, 901
κοσμούμενα, τά n., see also κοσμέω, *orderly institutions*, 677
κουφίζω (κουφιεῖς), *lighten, make light, lift up, raise*, 43
κουφόνοος, ον adj., *light-minded, thoughtless*, 342, 617
κράς, κρατός, ὁ m., *head*, 764, 1345
κρατέω, *be strong, be powerful, rule, be lord* or *master of*, 347, 738; *conquer, get the upper hand, be superior*, 347
κράτιστος, η, ον superl. adj., *strongest, mightiest, best, most excellent*, 1327
κράτος, εος, τό n., *strength, might, power, rule, authority*, 60, 166, 173, 485, 873
κρατύνω, *rule, govern*, 664
κρείσσων, ον gen. −ονος comparat. adj. of ἀγαθός, *stronger, mightier* (esp. in battle), 63, 679; *better*
κρύπτω aor. ἔκρυψα, *hide, cover*; *cover in the earth, bury*, 25, 196
κρυφῇ adv., *secretly, in secret, obscurely*, 85
κτάομαι (ἐκτησάμην), *procure for oneself, acquire, win*, 924
κτείνω (κτενῶ), *kill, slay, put to death*, 658
κτερίζω, *bury with due honors*, 204
κτῆμα, ατος, τό n., *anything gotten, piece of property, possession*, 702
κύων, κυνός, ὁ m., *dog*, 206, 697
κωκύω aor. ἐκώκυσα, *shriek, wail over one's dead* (always of women), 28, 204, 1302
κωτίλλω, *cajole, beguile with fair words, tease by prating*, 756

λ

λαγχάνω aor. ἔλαχον, *obtain by lot, obtain as one's portion*, 699, 918
λαμβάνω (λαβών), *take, take hold of, grasp, seize, take by violence*, 916
λανθάνω, *escape notice*, 9
λασιαύχην, ενος adj., *with rough shaggy neck*, 350
λέγω fut. λέξω, (ἐρῶ) aor. εἶπον, perf. εἴρηκα, perf. pass. εἴρημαι, *say, speak*; *count, tell*, 183; *wish to say, mean*, 198; *proclaim, order*, 725, 734, 735

Vocabulary

λείπω (λελειμμένα), pass., *be left, left behind*, 58, 1202

λέχος, εος, τό n., *couch, bed, marriage bed, marriage, spouse*, 629, 1225, 1303; *nest*

λέχριος, α, ον adj., *slanting, crosswise, awry*, 1345

λεώς, λαός, ὁ m., *people assembled, the people*, 733

λιμήν, ένος, ὁ m., *harbor, haven of refuge; gathering place, receptacle*, 1284

λόγος, ὁ m., *verbal utterance, word*, 691, 748, 1350; *common talk, news*, 1287

λοιπός, ή, όν adj., *remaining over, remaining*, 941; as n. noun, *the rest*, 717

λοίσθιος, α, ον adj., *remaining over, that which remains*, 895, 1220; as adv., *lastly*, 1304

λούω aor. ἔλουσα, *wash, purify*, 901, 1201

λυσσαίνω, *rave madly*, 633

λύω, of things, *loosen, unbind*, 40; *relax, close*, 1302

λωβάομαι, *outrage, maim, bring to a shameful end*, 54

μ

μαίνομαι, *rage with anger, be furious, be mad*, 135, 765, 1152

μακρός, ά, όν adj., *great, far*, 895

μάλιστα superl. adv., *most of all, especially*, 89, 474

μᾶλλον comparat. adv., *more, rather*, 17, 729, 1325

μανθάνω (μαθεῖν), *learn* (esp. by study), *understand*, 710, 723, 725

μάντις, εως, ὁ m., *diviner, seer, prophet*, 631, 1212

μάταιος, α, ον adj., *empty, foolish, rash, irreverent*, 1339

μαχανόεις (μηχανόεις), εσσα, εν adj., *ingenious*, 365

μάχη, ἡ f., *battle, combat*, 674

μάχομαι (μαχουμένα), *fight, struggle against*, 62

μέ, μοῦ, μοι, see ἐγώ

μέγας, μεγάλη, μέγα adj., superl. μέγιστος; comparat., see μείζων, *big, great, might*, 797, *strong, crushing*, 1273, 1351; *haughty, proud*, 1350; superl., 1243

μεθίημι (μέθες), *set loose, let go, release, dismiss*, 653

μείζων, ον gen. −ονος comparat. adj. of μέγας, *greater, more important, of higher authority*, 182, 497, 638, 652, 672, 704

μέλει impers., *it is of concern*, 873, 1335

145

μέλεος, α, ον adj., *idle, useless; unhappy, miserable*, 1319, 1341

μελλόνυμφος, ον adj., *about to be betrothed* or *wedded*, 633

μέλλω, *be destined* or *likely to, be about to*, 448, 458, 939; n. partic. used as noun, *future, things to come*, 361, 611, 1334

μέν particle, commonly used to point out that the word or clause with which it stands is correlative to another following word or clause which is introduced by de

μέντοι, conj., *yet, nevertheless*, 687, 897; adv., *of course, well* (marking a new stage in the progression of an argument), 913

μένω, *stand fast* (in battle), 671, 169

μέρος, εος, τό n., *share, portion, one's part*, 918

μετά or μέτα prep., with gen., *in the midst of, among, between, along with, with, together with*; with dat., *between, among*; with acc., *into the middle of, coming into or among*

μετάστασις, εως, ἡ f., *removal, shifting, departure, change*, 718

μέτεστι impers. (μέτα), *have a share* or *claim to*, 48

μετοικία, ἡ f., *change of abode, migration, sojourn*, 890

μή neg. particle, *not*

μηδέ neg. particle, as conj., *and not, nor*; as adv., *not even, not either*

μηδείς, μηδεμία, μηδέν adj. or pron., *not one, not even one, nobody, nothing*, 84, 1325, 1337

μηκέτι adv., *no more, no longer, no further*, 1333

μήν particle, *truly*

μήτηρ (μᾱτερ), μητρός, ἡ f., *mother*, 53, 467, 899, 905, 911, 1300

μηχανή (μαχανά), ἡ f., *contrivance* (esp. machine, engine, any artificial contrivance), 349

μιαρός, ά, όν adj., *stained, defiled with blood, morally foul*, 746

μίασμα, ατος, τό n., *stain, pollution*, 172

μικρός (σμικρός), ά, όν adj., *small, little*, 477, 671

μῖσος, εος, τό n., *hate, hatred*; of persons, *hateful object*, 760

μοῖρα, ας, ἡ f., *portion, man's appointed doom, death*, 170, 896

μόνος (μοῦνος), η, ον adj., *alone, solitary*, 19, 58, 361, 508, 656, 705, 739, 941

μόρος, ὁ m., *fate, destiny, doom, death*, 56, 465, 489, 628, 1266, 1292, 1313

μοῦνος, see μόνος

μῦθος, ὁ m., *word, fact, tale*, 11

μυχός, ὁ m., *innermost part, nook, inner chamber*, 1293

μωρία, ἡ f., *folly*, 470

μῶρος, ά, όν adj., *dull, sluggish, stupid, foolish*, 469, 470

Vocabulary

ν

ναῦς, ναός, ἡ f., *ship*, 715
ναυτίλλομαι, *sail, sail on*, 717
νεκρός, ὁ m., *corpse*, 43, 1240, 1299; in pl., *the dead*, 25, 197, 893,
    1240, 1282
νέκυς, υος, ὁ m., *corpse*, 26, 467, 515
νέομαι (νεῖσθαι), *come*, 33
νέος, α, ον adj., comparat. νεώτερος, *young, youthful*, 719, 728, 735,
    749, 1266, of events, *new, unexpected, strange, evil*, 1289
νεότομος, ον adj., *fresh-cut, newly-inflicted*, 1283
νέρτερος, α, ον adj., *lower, nether, belonging to the lower world*, 602, 749
νοέω *observe, think, presume*, 664; *intend*, 44
νομίζω, *use customarily; consider as, believe*, 183, 738
νόμιμος, η, ον adj. as n. pl. noun, *usages, customs, laws*, 455
νόμος, ὁ m., *that which is in habitual practice, use*, or *possession; usage,
    custom*, 24, 59, 519; *law, principle*, 59, 177, 191, 213, 368, 449,
    452, 481, 613, 663, 908, 914
νόος, νόου, ὁ m., *mind, sense, wit, meaning*, 68
νόσος, ἡ f., *sickness, disease, plague*, 363; *disease of mind*, 732
νότος, ὁ m., *south wind*, 335
νυμφεῖον, τό n., *bridechamber*, 891, 1205
νυμφεύω, *give in marriage, betroth, marry*, 654, 816
νυμφίος, ὁ m., *bridegroom*, 761
νῦν (νυν) adv., *now; henceforth, presently, just now*; untranslated enclitic
    used with imperatives, 1337
νύξ, νυκτός, ἡ f., *night*, 16
νώ (νῷν) dual nom. and acc., *we two*, 3, 21, 50, 58

ξ

ξίφος, εος, τό n., *sword*, 1232, 1309
ξυμ–, ξυν–, see συμ– and συν–; e.g. ξύμμαχος = σύμμαχος

ο

ὁ, ἡ, τό def. article (οἱ, αἱ, τά; τόν, τήν, τό, τούς, τάς, τά; τοῦ, τῆς,
    τοῦ, τῶν, τῶν, τῶν; τῷ, τῇ, τῷ, τοῖς, τοῖς, τοῖς: dual nom. and
    acc., τώ; gen. and dat., τοῖν)
ὅδε, ἥδε, τόδε (n. pl., τάδε) demonstr. pron. which normally looks

forward in time, *this, those, these*

ὀδύρομαι, *lament, bewail, mourn for*, 693

οἶδα perf. with pres. meaning (εἰσόμεσθα, ἤδη, εἰδώς, εἰδόσιν,'ἴσθε), *see with mind's eye, know*, 2, 16, 18, 33, 89, 98, 166, 457, 631, 649, 758

οἶδμα, ατος, τό n., *swell, swelling, swollen waves*, 337, 588, *the sea*, 337

οἰκεῖος, α, ον adj., *in or of the house, domestic*, 661; *native*, 1203

ὄίκησις, εως, ἡ f., *house, dwelling*, 892

οἶκος, ὁ m., *house, home*, 674

ὄἰμοι exclamation, *ah me! oh! alas!* 49, 82, 86, 933

ὄίομαι, *think, suppose, believe*, 453

οἰωνός, ὁ m., *a large bird, bird of prey*, 29, 205, 698; *a bird of augury*, 1000

ὀλέθρος, ὁ m., *ruin, destruction, death*, 1291

ὀλέκω, *ruin, destroy*, 1285

ὄλλυμι fut. ὀλέσω, ὀλῶ, aor. ὤλεσα, fut. mid. ὀλοῦμαι, 2 aor. mid. ὠλόμην, perf. act. with mid. meaning ὄλωλα, act., *destroy, do away with, lose*, 517, 673, 751, 875, 894; mid., *perish, die*, 59, 171, 174, 195, 698, 763, 1288

ὄμμα, τό n., *eye, sight*, 690, 760

ὁμοίως adv., *in like manner with, alike, equally*

ὁμόπτολις, εως adj., *from* or *of the same city* or *state*, 733

ὅμως conj., *all the same, nevertheless*

ὀξυκώκυτος, ον adj., *wailed with shrill cries, lamented*, 1316

ὀξύπληκτος, ον adj., *struck by a sharp blow*, 1301

ὄπισθεν prep. with gen., *behind*, 640

ὁποῖος, α, ον adj., *of what sort* or *quality as*, 3, 5, 71

ὁπόσος, η, ον adj., *as many, as many as, as much as, as great as, how great*, 214

ὅπως, as adv., *as in such manner as, how, in what manner*; as conj., *in such a manner that, in order that*

ὁράω fut. ὄψομαι, aor. εἶδον, perf. ὄπωπα, aor. pass. ὤφθην, *see, look*, 6, 184, 185, 206, 709, 712, 735, 743, 764, 1293, 1342

ὀργή, ἡ f., *natural impulse, temperament, mood, disposition*, 356, 875, 1200; *anger, wrath, passion*, 875; *fits of anger*, 956

ὄρειος (οὔρειος), α, ον adj., *of the mountains, mountain-haunting*, 352

ὀρεσσιβάτης adj., *mounting-roaming*, 350

ὀρθός, ή, όν adj., *straight*, 190; *right, safe, prosperous, correct, true* ὀρθόω aor. ὤρθωσα, *set straight, set upright, set up, raise up, build, raise*, 163, 167, 675; *be prosperous*, 675

ὀρθῶς adv., *rightly, really, truly*, 99, 494, 685, 706

ὁρίζω (ὥρισεν), *ordain, determine, lay down, define, mark out*, 452

ὄρνις, ὄρνιθος, ὁ m., *bird*, 343; *bird of omen*, 1001, 1021

ὅς, ἥ, ὅ relative pron., *who, which, what*

ὅσιος, α, ον adj., *hallowed, sanctioned* or *allowed by the law of gods or of nature*, 74

ὅσος, η, ον indirect interrog. adj., *how much*, 59

ὅστις, ἥτις, ὅ τι indef. relative pron. (ὅτοισι, ὅτου etc.) *anyone who, anything which, whoever*

ὅταν adv. of time, *whenever, since, such time as*

ὅτι conj., *that; for that, because*

οὐ, οὐκ, οὐχ, οὐχί neg. particle, *not*

οὐδαμά adv., *never, not at all*, 763

οὐδαμῇ adv., *nowhere, in no place, in no direction, no way*

οὐδαμοῦ adv., *nowhere, as naught, non existent*, 183

οὐδαμῶς adv., *in no way*, 678

οὐδείς, οὐδεμία, οὐδέν adj. or pron., *no one, nothing, none*

οὐκέτι or οὐκ ἔτι adv., *no more, no longer, no further, not now*

οὐκοῦν adv., *surely then, then*

οὖν adv., *certainly, in fact, really so, then, therefore*

οὕνεκ(α) relative conj., *on account of which, wherefore*, 19, 63, 641

οὔποτε adv., *not ever, never*

οὔτε adv., *and not*; when duplicated, *neither . . . nor*

οὗτος, αὕτη, τοῦτο (pl., οὗτοι, αὗται, ταῦτα) demonstr. pron., *this, these*

οὕτως adv., *in this way, so, thus*

ὀφθαλμός, ὁ m., *eye*, 764

ὀφλισκάνω, *become a debtor, incur, get a character for*, 470, 1028

ὄψις, εως, ἡ f., *eye*, 52

π

πᾶ interrog. particle, *in which way, whither*, 1344

παγκάκιστος, ον superl. adj., *worst, utterly evil*, 742

πάγος, ὁ m., *crag, rock; frost*, 357

πάθος, εος, τό n., *experience, misfortune, calamity*, 1316

παίδειος, ον adj., *of a boy, of rearing children*, 918

παιδοκτόνος, ον adj., *slaying one's child* or *children*, 1305

παῖς, παιδός, ὁ, ἡ m. or f., *child* (son or daughter), *boy* or *girl*, 169, 193, 211, 472, 626, 632, 639, 648, 654, 693, 704, 910, 1214, 1231, 1266, 1289, 1316, 1340

παίω aor. ἔπαισα, *strike, smite*, 171, 1309, 1315; *drive, dash*, 1274

πάλαι adv., *long ago, long before now*, 181

πάλιν adv., *again, once more*, 163

πάνδημος, ον adj., *of* or *belonging to all the people, public*, 7

πανουργέω (πανουργήσασα), *to do everything*; usually used prejoratively, *play the knave*, 74

πανταχῇ, *on every side, in every direction, every way*, 634

πάντες, πάντα pl. of πᾶς

παντοπόρος, ον adj., *all inventive*, 360 (from pās, all and poros, way, road)

παρά prep., with gen., *from the side of, from beside*; with dat., *by the side of*; with acc., *beside, near, by*; *compared with, short of, lower than*

παραγκάλισμα, ατος, τό n., *that which is taken into the arms, darling*, 650

παραινέω *exhort, recommend, advise*, 1326

παραστάτης, ου, ὁ m., *one who stands by* or *near, one's comrade on the flank, supporter*, 671

πάρειμι, *be present, be near*, 633, 761, 1293

παρείρω, *thread in, insert*, 368

παρέξειμι pres. with fut. sense, *pass alongside of*; *transgress, overstep*, 60

παρεξέρχομαι (−ελθοῦσα), *slip past*; *overstep, transgress*, 921

παρέστιος, ον adj., *by* or *at the hearth*, 373

παρῆν impf. of πάρειμι

πᾶς, πᾶσα, πᾶν (πάντες, πᾶσι) adj., *all, the whole, every*

πάσχω fut. πείσομαι, aor. ἔπαθον, *have done to one, suffer, be treated, have happen*, 96, 926, 928, 942

πατέομαι (πάσασθαι), *eat, partake of, taste*, 202

πατέω, *tread, walk, tread under foot, trample on*, 745

πατήρ, πατρός, ὁ m., *father*, 49, 471, 633, 635, 644, 683, 701, 703, 704, 742, 755, 898, 911

πάτρα, ἡ f., *fatherland, native land*, 182; *fatherhood, descent from a common father*

Vocabulary

πατρῷος, α, ον adj., *of* or *from one's father, hereditary, patrimonial*,
    199, 640, 937
παύω (πεπαύσομαι), mid., *cease, have done, stop*, 91
πειθαρχία, ἡ f., *obedience to command*, 676
πείθω (πείσομαι), *persuade*, pass. and mid., *be won over, obey*, 67, 1099
πέλω, *come into existence, become, be, is wont to be*, 333, 874
πέπρωται, perf. pass., *it has been fated* (or destined), 1337
πέραν adv., *on the other side, across, over* or *across to*, 334; *over against,
    opposite*
περάω, *pass right across* or *through, traverse*, 337
περί, πέρι prep. with gen., *concerning, in regard to*, 193, 214, 678
περιβρύχιος, ον adj., *engulfing*, 336
περιμένω, *wait for, await, be in store for*, 1296
περισκελής, ές adj., *very hard*, 475; *obstinate, stubborn*
περισσός, ή, όν adj., *beyond regular number* or *size, extraordinary,
    strange; excessive, extravagant, useless*, 68; *superfluous*, 780
περιστέλλω, *dress, clothe, wrap up; lay out* (of a corpse), 903; *cherish,
    protect*
περιφραδής, ές adj., *very thoughtful, very skillful*, 347
πίμπρημι (πρῆσαι), *fill full of, satisfy, glut*, 201
πίπτω (πεπτῶτα), *fall* (in battle), *be ruined*, 697
πλείων, πλέον (πλείω) comparat. adj., *greater, more*, 74, 927; n. used
    as adv., *more*, 40
πλεκτός, ή, όν adj., *plaited, twisted*, 54
πλέω, *sail, go by sea*, 190
πλέως, α, ων adj., *full, filled*, 721
πληγή, ἡ f., *blow, stroke*, 1351
πλῆγμα, ατος, τό n., *stroke, sting, blow*, 1283
πλήν conj., *only, save, except, but*, 646
πλήσιος, α, ον adj., *near, close to*, 761, 763
πλήσσω (πληγέντες), pass., *be struck, smitten*, 172
ποιέω mid. ποιοῦμαι, *make, produce, cause; do, act*, 72, 211; mid.,
    deem, 78, *make* (for oneself), *adopt* (of children), 190
ποῖος, α, ον interrog. adj., *of what kind? what sort?* 42, 921
πολεύω, *turn up*, 341
πολιός, ά, όν adj., *grey; bright, clear, serene*, 334
πόλις, εως, ἡ f., *city*, 7, 44, 162, 167, 178, 191, 194, 203, 209, 212,
    656, 657, 662, 666, 673, 693, 734, 737, 738, 1247; *community*,

body of citizens, the public, 36
πολίτης, ου, ὁ m., citizen, freeman, 79, 907
πολύς, πολλή, πολύ adj. (most forms with double λ: e.g., πολλοί),
    much, great, mighty, many
πομπός, ὁ m., conductor, messenger, envoy, 164
πόνος, ὁ m., work, labor, trouble, 646; task, business, 907, 1276
πόντος, ὁ m., sea, open sea, 335, 345
πορεύομαι, go, walk, 81, 892
πόσις, ὁ m., husband, spouse, 906, 909, 1196
πότε (πότ', ποθ'), ποτέ, interrog., when? at what time? indef., at sometime
    or other, at anytime, ever, 42, 456, 762, 912
πότερος, α, ον adj., which of the two? 1344
πότμος, ὁ m., that which befalls one, lot, destiny, 83, 881, 1296, 1346
ποῦ interrog. adv., where? 42
που enclitic adv., in some degree, perhaps, I suppose, 214
πούς, ποδός, ὁ m., sheets of a boat, 715; foot, 1327
πρᾶγμα, ατος, τό n., deed, act, affair; concrete reality, 34
πρᾶξις, εως, ἡ f., doing; fortune; exaction of vengeance, retribution, 1305
πράσσω, achieve, be busy with, 69; manage, do, act, 68, 69, 447, 689,
    1335; fare, 625, 701
πρέπει impers., it is fitting, 92
πρεσβεύω, be older than, take the first place, rank before, 720
πρίν adv. and conj., adv., before, formerly, 1303; conj., before, until,
    176
προδίδωμι (προδοῦσα), give or deliver up (esp. give up to the enemy),
    betray, 46
προέχω (προύχω) fut. προέξω, hold before, 208; mid., put forth as a
    pretext, pretend, 80
πρόκειμαι (προκεῖσθαι), be set before one, be exposed, be exposed to, 1334;
    be set forth, be prescribed, 36, 481
προκήδομαι take care of, take thought for, 741
προκηρύσσω fut. προκηρύξω, aor. προυκήρυξα, proclaim by a herald,
    proclaim publicly, 34, 461
προμηνύω (προμηνύσῃς), denounce beforehand, indicate before, predict,
    84
προπέμπω (προπέμψας), send before; conduct, escort, 1287
πρός prep. expressing direction, with gen., from, on the side of, 704,
    at the hand of, 205; by, 727, 919; by reason of, 51; with dat., near,

with acc., *toward, to*, 893, *against*, 10, 62, 753; *on account of*, 658
προσβλέπω, *look at, regard*, 1298
πρόσειμι, *be added to, be attached to, belong to*, 720; *be present, be at hand*, 1252
προσεύχομαι, *offer prayers* or *vows, worship*, 1337
πρόσθεν prep. with gen., *before*, 462
πρόσκειμαι fut. προσκείσομαι, *be involved in, be bound up with, be added* or *attached to*, 94, cf. also 1223, 1243
προσκοπέω, *watch, act as spy*, 688
προσοράω (προσόψει), *look at, behold*, 764
πρόσπολος, ὁ m., *servant, attendant*, 1320
προστάσσω (προστεταγμένον), *place, attach to, assign to, station*, 670
προστίθημι (προσθείμην), *hand over*, mid., *bring* or *take upon oneself*, 40
προσφιλής, ές adj., *dear, beloved*, 898
προταρβέω, *fear beforehand, fear* or *be anxious for*, 83
προτίω (προτίσας), *prefer in honor, prefer, deem more worthy*, 22
πρῶτος, *the very first, principal, primary*, 1349
πτύω (πτύσας), *spit out* or *up, spit*, 653, 1232; *with loathing*, 653, 1232
πύλη, ἡ f., *house door, gate*, 18
πῦρ, πυρός, τό n., *fire*, 200, 475, 619

ρ

ῥεῖθρον, τό n., *that which flows, a river, stream*, 712
ῥέπω, *turn the scale, sink; incline one way or the other*, 722

σ

σάλος, ὁ m., *tossing motion, rolling swell, tossing on the sea*, 163
σαυτοῦ, ης (σεαυτοῦ) reflex. pron., *of yourself*, 705
σαφῶς adv., *clearly, plainly, distinctly*, 34
σέβω, *worship, honor, respect, approve*, 166, 511, 730, 744, 745, 872, cf. also 943
σείω aor. ἔσεισα, aor. pass. ἐσείσθην, *shake, move to and fro*, 163; *agitate, disturb*; pass., *be shaken* (to its foundations), 583, 1274
σέλμα, ατος, τό n., *the upper planking of a ship, deck, rowing benches*, 717

σθένω, *have strength, have power, be able,* 91, 453

σιγάω, *keep silent,* 87

σῑγῇ adv., *in silence, in a whisper, secretly,* 700

σιωπάω (σιωπήσαιμι), *keep silence,* 185

σκοπέω, *behold, consider, examine,* 41, 58, 729

σμικρός, see μικρός

σός, ή, όν possessive adj. of the 2d person, *your, yours*

σοφός, ή, όν adj., *skilled in any handicraft or art, clever in practical matters, wise, prudent, shrewd, worldly-wise,* 365; *learned, wise, ingenious,* 710

σπεῖρα, ή f., *anything twisted or wound, rope, cord, fold,* 346

στείχω, *walk, march, approach,* 10, 98, 186

στέλλω aor. ἔστειλα, *make ready, summon, bring,* 165; as a nautical term, *gather up, furl*

στερέω (ἐστερήθημεν), pass., *to be deprived or robbed,* 13, 890

στέρνον, τό n., *breast, chest, heart,* 639

στρατηγός, ὁ m., *general, commander, governor, magistrate, king,* 8

στρατός, ὁ m., *army, host,* 15

στρέφω (στρέψας), *turn about or aside, overturn, upset,* 717

σύ, σέ, σοῦ, σοί pron. of the 2d person, *you*

συγγιγνώσκω (συγγνοῖμεν), *think with, be conscious, acknowledge, own, confess,* 926

σύγγνοια = συγγνώμη, ή f. (only used here), *fellow feeling, forbearance, lenient judgment, allowance,* 66

συγκατεύχομαι (συγκατηυξάμην), *join in praying for, pray together with,* 1336

συγκεράννυμι (συγκέκραμαι), pass., *be commingled, be blended,* 1311

συμμαχέω, *be an ally, help, assist,* 740

σύμμαχος, ον adj., *fighting along with, allied with,* 923

συμπονέω (ξυμπονήσεις), *toil or suffer with or together, take part in,* 41

συμφορά, ή f., *fortune, misfortune,* 1338

συμφράζομαι (ξυμπέφρασται), *join in considering, take counsel with, contrive,* 364

σύν (ξύν) prep. with dat., *with*; as an adv., *together, at once*

σύναιμος (ξύναιμος), ον adj., *of common blood, kindred,* 488, 659, Zeus xynaimos as presiding over kindred, 659; as substantive, *kinsman, kinswoman* (esp. brother or sister), 198

σύνειμι, *be with, be joined with, be acquainted with, be engaged in,* 372, 765

Vocabulary

συνεργάζομαι (ξυνεργάσῃ), *work with, cooperate, contribute, take part in,*
     41
σύνευνος (ξύνευνος), ὁ, ἡ m. and f., *bed fellow, consort,* 651
σύνοικος (ξύνοικος), ον adj., *living in the same city or country, fellow*
     inhabitant, 451
σφάγιος, α, ον adj., *slaying, slaughtering, fatal, deadly,* 1290
σφεῖς (σφέ, σφε) pron. of 3d person, *him, her,* 44, 772
σχεδόν adv., *about, approximately, more or less, almost,* 470
σχέτλιος, α, ον adj., *able to hold out, unwearying, unflinching,* 47;
     cruel, merciless, headstrong, 47
σῴζω, *keep safe, save from death or destruction,* 189, 676
σῶμα, ατος, τό n., *body, life, person, human being,* 676
σωτηρία, ἡ f., *deliverance, safety, well-being,* 186

τ

τάδε, see ὅδε
ταλαίπωρος, ον adj., *suffering, distressed, miserable,* 56
ταλαίφρων, ονος adj., *much-enduring, wretched,* 39, 877
τάλας, τάλαινα, τάλαν adj., *suffering, wretched* (either describing a
     passive victim or a daring, reckless one), 82, 880, 1211, 1295, 1298
τάσσω, *draw up in order of battle; rule, impose,* 734
ταῦρος, ὁ m., *bull,* 352
ταῦτα, see οὗτος
τάφος, ὁ m., *funeral rites, rites of burial, grave, tomb,* 21, 28, 80, 196,
     203, 490, 503, 1215
τάχα adv., *quickly, presently,* 631; *perhaps, probably*
ταχύς, εῖα, ύ adj., *swift, sudden; in haste,* 37
τε enclitic particle as conj., *and;* with kai or another te, *both . . . and*
τείνω, *stretch, pull tight, keep taut,* 711, 716
τέκνον, τό n., *child,* 645, 703, 905, 1230, 1247, 1297, 1299
τέλειος, α, ον adj., *perfect, fully constituted, valid, authoritative,*
     final, 632
τελέω (τελεῖ), *fulfill, accomplish, execute, perform,* 3
τέρμιος, α, ον adj., *at the end, last, of death,* 1330
τέρπω (τέρψει), *delight, gladden, cheer,* 691
τέχνη, ἡ f., *art, skill, cunning of hand, craft,* 366; *set of rules, system,*
     method
τήκω (ἐτήκετο), pass., *melt away, be consumed, fall away,* 906

155

τηλικόσδε, −ήδε, −όνδε adj., *of such an age, so old*, 726; *so young*, 727

τίθημι (θεῖναι, θείμην), *set, put, place*, 504; *lay down, give*, or *make* (a law), 8, 674; *hold, regard as*, 188

τιμάω (τιμήσεται, ἐτίμησα), *honor, revere, bestow honors, reward*, 210, 514, 516, 644, 904

τιμή, ἡ f., *worship, esteem, honor, due regard*, 208, 699, 745; *value, price, worth*, 208

τίμιος, α, ον adj., comparat. τιμιώτερον, *valued, held in honor, worthy, valuable, prized, honorable, dear*, 702

τίς, τί interrog. pron. (τοῦ, τίνος, τῷ, τίνες, τίσι, etc.) *who? which? what? τί, why? how?*

τις, τι indef. pron. τοῦ, etc. *anyone, anything; someone* (referring to a definite person one wants to avoid naming), 751

τόδε, see ὅδε

τοιόσδε, −άδε, −όνδε demonstr. pron., *such as this*, 732, 903, 913

τοιοῦτος, τοιαύτη, τοιοῦτο demonstr. pron. *such as this, such*

τόλμα, ης, ἡ f., *courage, hardihood, nerve, daring; recklessness*, 372

τολμάω, *dare, bring oneself to, to have courage* or *grace*, 449, 915

τοσοῦτος, αύτη, οῦτο demonstr. adj., *so great, so large, so tall; so much*

τοτέ adv., *at times, now and then*; τοτὲ μὲν . . . ἄλλοτε *at one time . . . at another*, 367

του (τινός) gen. sing. of τις

τοῦτο, ταῦτα, see οὗτος

τρέφω (θρέψω), *cause to grow, bring up, rear*, 660

τρίτον adv., *thirdly*, 55

τροπή, ἡ f., *the turning about of the enemy, putting to flight* or *routing*, 675

τρόπος, ὁ m., *way, manner*, 1314

τροφή, ἡ f., *nurture, rearing*, 918

τυγχάνω, 2 aor. ἔτυχον, *happen to be at, happen to, come to*, 469; *succeed, obtain*, 665; *hit upon, meet*, 465

τύμβος, ὁ m., *sepulchral mound, tomb, grave*, 886, 891, 1203

τύραννος, ὁ m., *an absolute ruler, monarch, tyrant, chief, despot*, 60, 1056, 1169

τώ, dual of ὁ, ἡ, τό

τῷ (τινί), see τις

υ

ὑμεῖς (ὑμῶν, ὑμῖν, ὑμᾶς) pl. pron. of the 2d person, *you*

ὑπάγω (ὑπαξέμεν), *lead under yoke, bring under one's power*, 351

156

Vocabulary

ὑπαίθριος, ον adj., *under the sky, in the open air, in public*, 357
ὑπάρχω *begin, be*, 1349
ὕπατος, η, ον adj., *highest, uppermost, the very top*, 1331
ὑπείκω, *retire, withdraw, depart; yield, give way, comply*, 713, 716
ὑπέρ prep., with gen., *over, above, beyond; in defense of, on behalf of*,
    748; *in the name of;* with acc., *beyond*, 364
ὑπέραυχος, ον adj., *overboastful, overproud*, 1351
ὑπερβαίνω, (ὑπερβάς), *step over, transgress, go beyond*, 449, 481, 663,
    cf. also 605
ὑπερδείδω, ὑπερδέδοικα perf. with pres. meaning, *fear for, fear
    exceedingly, be in exceeding fear*, 82
ὑπερμαχέω, *fight for* or *on behalf of*, 194
ὑπέρτατος, η, ον adj., *uppermost, highest, eldest*, 338, 684
ὑπέρτερον adj. as adv., *better than*, 16, 631
ὑπερτρέχω (ὑπερδραμεῖν), *run beyond, outrun, prevail against; excel,
    surpass*, 455
ὑπέρχομαι, *go under, creep, insinuate*, 700
ὑπό (ὑπ’, ὑφ’) prep., with gen., *from under, in, with;* of agent, *by*,
    with dat., *under;* with acc., *toward, under*
ὕπτιος, α, ον adj., *laid on one's back, upturned, upside down*, 716
ὕστερος, α, ον adj., *latter, behind; inferior in age, worth* or *quality,
    second, below*, 746
ὑψίπολις, ιδος adj., *high in the city, citizen of a proud city*, 370

φ

φαίνω, fut. φανῶ, 2 aor. pass. ἐφάνην, perf. pass. πέφασμαι, *bring to
    light, show forth*, 177, 621; mid. and pass., *come to light, appear,
    become*, 457, 662, 1329
φάτις, ἡ f., *common talk, rumor*, 700
φέρω, *bear* or *carry, convey*, 464, 1279; mid., *win for oneself, gain*, 638
φεῦ, exclamation expressing grief or anger *alas!* 1300
φεύγω, *flee, take flight, avoid, escape, shun*, 359
φεῦξις, εως, ἡ f., *refuge, escape*, 362
φημί (φησί, φασί etc.), *say, affirm, assert*
φθέγμα, ατος, τό n., *sound of the voice, voice, language, speech*, 354
φθίνω, *decay, wane, pass away*, 695
φιλέω, *love, regard with affection*, 524; *be fond, be used to*, 493, 722
φίλος, η, ον adj., *one's own, relative, beloved, dear*, 99, 898, 899
φίλος, ὁ m. or φίλη, ἡ f., *dear one, relative, friend, ally*, 10, 11, 73,

157

99, 183, 187, 190, 522, 634, 644, 652, 765, 882, 919
φίλτατος, η, ον superl. adj., *one's nearest and dearest*, 81, 572
φιτύω, *sow, plant, beget*, 645
φόβος, ὁ m., *panic, flight, fear, terror, dread*, 180, 505, 1308
φονή, ἡ f., *carnage, bloodshed*, 696, 1314
φόνος, ὁ m., *murder, slaughter, death as a punishment*, 36
φορέω, *wear, hold, bear*, 705
φρενόω (φρενώσεις), *make wise, instruct, inform, teach*, 754
φρήν, φρενός, ἡ f., *midriff, heart, mind, will, purpose*, 492, 603, 623,
    648, 683, 754, 1261
φρονέω aor. ἐφρόνησα, *have understanding, be wise, be prudent, think*,
    49, 510, 707, 755, 904, 1347, 1353; *learn wisdom*, 727
φρόνημα, ατος, τό n., *mind, spirit*, 176, 473; *thought, purpose, will*,
    169, 207, 355, 459; *pride, arrogance*, 459
φρονούντως adv., *wisely, prudently*, 682
φροῦδος, η, ον adj., *fled, departed*, 15
φυγάς, άδος, ὁ m., *fugitive, exile, deserter*, 200
φυγή, ἡ f., *flight* (in battle), *escape, avoidance*, 363, 1234
φῦλον, τό n., *race, tribe, class*, 342
φύσις, φύσεως, ἡ f., *origin, nature, birth, age*, 659, 727; *kind, species*,
    345
φύω, aor. ἔφυσα, 2 aor. ἔφυν, perf. πέφυκα, *bring forth, produce*,
    beget, 642, 647, 683; pass. meaning in 2 aor., *be begotten, be
    descended from*, 62; pres. sense in 2 aor. and perf., *be by nature*,
    be, 38, 79, 501, 523, 688, 721, 905
φώς, φωτός, ὁ m., *man*, 910; *hero*, 107

χ

χαίρων partic., *safe and sound, with impunity*, 759
χάρις, χάριτος, (χάριν) ἡ f., *a gratification, a delight*, 30; acc. sing.
    as prep. with gen., *for the sake of, in compliance with*, 908, 372
χείμαρρος, ον adj., *winter-flowing, swollen by rain and melted snow*, 712
χειμέριος, α, ον adj., *wintry, stormy, cold, raging*, 335
χειμών, ῶνος, ὁ m., *winter; stormy weather, storm*, 670
χείρ, χειρός (χερί, χεροῖν, etc.) ἡ f., *hand*, 14, 43, 52, 57, 916, 1258,
    1297, 1345
χθών, χθονός, ἡ f., *earth* (esp. its surface originally), 1203, but more

Vocabulary

commonly in the An., *the maternal depths beneath the surface*, 24, 368; *those in the shades below*, 65; *land, country, city*, 187, 368, 736

χοή, ἡ f., *drink-offering, libation*, 902

χόω (χώσουσα), *throw* or *heap up* (of earth), *form with heaped-up ashes*, 81, 1204

χράομαι (χρῆσθαι, χρησθείς), with dat., *treat, regard*, 24; *use*, 213

χρή impers., *it is necessary, one must* or *ought* (freq. implying a moral imperative), 61, 89, 639, 666, 729, 734, 736, 922, 1099, 1334, 1335, 1349

χρῆμα, ατος, τό n., *property, possession*, 684

χρηστός, ή, όν adj., *useful, good of its kind, serviceable*, 636, 622; *morally good*, 520, 636

χρόνος, ὁ m., *time*, 74, 461, 608, 625; *lifetime, age*, 681, 729

χρύσεος, η, ον adj., *golden, fine, wealthy, noble*, 699

χωρέω, *go, journey, travel*, 336

ψ

ψέγω, *blame, censure*, 689

ψευδής, ές adj., *lying, false, untrue*, 657

ψῆφος, ἡ f., *a small pebble used in voting, the vote, judgment*, 60, 632

ψόγος, ὁ m., *blameable fault, blemish, flaw*; *blame, censure*, 759

ψυχή, ἡ f., *life, soul, conscious self* or *personality, self, heart, mind, wit, spirit*, 176, 708, 930

ψυχρός, ά, όν adj., *cold*, 88, 650; *cold-hearted, heartless, indifferent*

ω

ὦ expresses surprise, joy, or pain, *O!* with vocatives, a mode of address

ὠμηστής, οῦ adj., *eating raw flesh, savage, brutal*, 697

ὡς conj., with noun clauses, to express a fact, *that*; with purpose clauses, *so that, in order that*

ὡς relative adv., *as*

ὡς relative and interrog., *how*

ὡσεί adv., *as if, as though*, 653

ὥστε, adv., *as being, inasmuch as, as*, 97; conj., *so as to*, 454

Appendixes

Notes

Glossary

Selected Bibliography

Index

Appendix A

Sophocles' Relation to the Mythic Tradition

THE INTERACTION BETWEEN the creative genius of the playwright and the mythic tradition is nowhere more fascinating and instructive than in this play. Some facts on the received myth about the sons of Oedipus and, more significantly, about the daughters of Oedipus shed light on Sophocles' relation to his material.

Our knowledge of the two brothers Polynices and Eteocles is meager and mostly dependent upon Aeschylus' *Seven against Thebes,* the third part of a trilogy on the ancestral curse on the house of Laios, produced about twenty-five years before the *An.* Aeschylus' play focuses almost exclusively on Eteocles, initially the "rational," responsible, heroic leader of Thebes, who, like Cr., thinks of himself as the captain of the ship of state who must avoid female destruction, but who, unlike Cr., rises to tragic stature by his acceptance of his cursed fate as Oedipus' son (702–19). Subsequently, he goes out to meet Polynices in violent, unrestrained fratricidal conflict. Nothing in the *Seven* elucidates the political or family background of the quarrel between the brothers. Neither Aeschylus nor Soph. was interested in the reasons that Eteocles was the defender and Polynices the treasonous adversary. Nor does either play specify whether the two were twins, although the frequent use of duals may point in that direction. Only in Soph.'s much later *Oedipus at Kolonos* is a point made of their ages: there Polynices is made the elder son, presumably to strengthen his claim to the throne. Soph. appears to have introduced this alteration of the myth into the *Oedipus at Kolonos* for the sake of the dramatic idea of that play.

Polynices never appears in the *Seven,* and on the rare occasions when he is mentioned it is as the villainous traitor. Eteocles, the more objective priest (576 ff.), and the Cho. see him thus. He is the one Eteocles must defeat, a man who lives up to his name

163

(i.e., the "Much-Quarreler," 658), and yet a man whose shield claims that he like Eteocles has Justice on his side (645 ff.). The poet is not concerned to explore Polynices' claim since he focuses not on the conflict between the two but on the tragic heroism of Eteocles. When the Cho. calls Polynices an evil-spoken zealot (678), it is probably true that the phrase really characterizes both brothers.[1]

Another tradition relating to the brothers was recorded in a lost Theban myth.[2] This was the story of the *epigoni,* the sons of the Argive Seven, who unsuccessfully invaded Thebes. The sons succeeded where Polynices and their fathers failed (see n. on 1319).

Thus, as Soph. received the myth, the brothers, perhaps twins, each claimed justice in his position, each appeared to be a mixture of good and evil, but Eteocles is considered Thebes' defender and Polynices the treasonous rebel.

Soph.'s originality is far more significant in relation to the daughters of Oedipus. It is now generally agreed that he was the first to develop the story of the sisters [3] and that he was the creator of the character of his heroine. Homer, Hesiod, and Pindar do not mention the sisters at all in their accounts of the myth, and the two scenes depicting them in the *Seven against Thebes* are now widely considered spurious later imitations inspired by Soph.'s play rather than sources for Soph. as scholars used to think.[4] Many of the key themes and even the vocabulary of Soph.'s drama appear in those scenes of Aeschylus: An. will find a way (*mēchanēsomai,* 1044) to bury her brother although she does not defend his act or character; words like *anarchia* (1030), the strange (*deinon*) power of the common womb from which they come (1031), *perisson* (1049), *philia* (971), "self-willed" (1053), *autognōtos* (875) are curious echoes of the Sophoclean drama. But these themes, so integral to the *An.,* are handled as an afterthought in the *Seven.*

Therefore, may we not assume that the myth concerning An.'s defiance of the king's order was probably a local legend in Soph.'s native Kolonos, just outside of Athens? Just as the apotheosis of Oedipus at Kolonos was probably part of the local tradition first developed in Soph.'s *Oedipus at Kolonos* (in the *An.,* Oedipus is thought of as dying in Thebes), so, too, local associations are probably the poet's source for the girl's act, the seed out of which his fertile imagination created the character of the heroine and the drama of her defiance.[5] As a childhood in the shadow of Salisbury Cathedral inspired William Golding's *Spire,* so Soph. of Kolonos kept returning to the mysterious myth of his birthplace at widely separated moments in his career. He produced the *An.* in his fifties, the *Oedipus Tyrannos* over ten years later, and the *Oedipus at Kolonos* still twenty odd years after that. In all these works the mystery of birthplace and the mystery of creative genius interacted in a marvelous, one might say "deinotic" (see 332 n.) way.

Appendix B

Chronological Note

ca. 497/96 B.C.	Birth of Soph. in Kolonos.
490–79	Persian wars.
468	His first dramatic victory.
467	Aeschylus produces the *Seven against Thebes*.
460–29	Pericles leads Athens.
458	Aeschylus' *Oresteia*.
456	Death of Aeschylus.
454	Treasury of the Delian League is moved to Athens; its funds are diverted to the beautification of Athens.
450	Construction of buildings on the Acropolis at Athens begins.
447–32	Parthenon is constructed under Phidias' guidance.
446	Peace with Sparta
444 ?	Arrival of Protagoras in Athens
443–42	Pericles ostracizes his conservative rival, Thucydides (not the historian); Soph. is elected chairman of the Board of Treasurers of the Delian League.
442 or 441	Soph., author of about thirty plays before this date, produces his most popular play yet, the *An.*—there is no general agreement on the precise date nor on whether the *Ajax* is earlier or later.
441–40	Soph. is elected as one of Athens' ten generals and performs an ambassadorial role in preventing the spread of the Samian revolt.

431	Peloponnesian War begins between Athens
439	Pericles' skillful management of the Samian crisis cements his position at home; Euripides' *Alcestis*.
	and Sparta; Euripides' *Medea*.
430 ?	Soph. produces the *Oedipus Tyrannos*.
429	The Athenian plague decimates the population; Pericles dies.
428	Euripides' *Hippolytos*.
427	Birth of Plato.
415	Athens embarks on the disastrous imperialistic Sicilian Expedition
406–5	Soph. completes the *Oedipus at Kolonos;* both Soph. and Euripides die, Soph. allegedly while reciting the *An.* to friends.
405	The comedian Aristophanes produces the *Frogs,* in which Dionysos journeys to Hades to retrieve one of the dead tragedians to save Athens.
404	Athens falls and the Athenian Empire capitulates; "the Thirty," an oligarchy, is imposed.
399	Socrates dies.

THE YEARS SURROUNDING the production of the *An.* were politically active and significant years for the playwright and especially for Athens' first citizen, Pericles. "The Olympian," as Pericles was called, had put together a coalition of liberal democrats and of powerful nobles, followers of the recently deceased aristocrat, Cimon. A certain Thucydides, leader of the oligarchic pro-Spartan party, was trying to break this tenuous coalition. He opposed Pericles as a real tyrant who was misappropriating the money of Athens' allies in order to beautify the city. Pericles' quick introduction of proceedings to ostracize his conservative rival nipped the threat to his power but unsettled his Cimonian followers. Evidently as part of his plan to win back conservative support (see Ehrenberg, *Sophocles and Pericles* pp. 130–33), Pericles created a new post, Treasurer of the Delian League, to which Soph., in origin a Cimonian conservative, was elected.

That same spring or possibly the following one, Soph. produced the *An.* and its popularity insured his subsequent election as a *stratēgos,* one of the generals whose task it was to defend the city (see 8 n.). That year, war broke out between Athens and the oligarchic island of Samos, an Athenian tributary and an autonomous state with a powerful navy. Thus, faced with a serious threat to Athens' leadership in the Delian League, Pericles personally led the sixty ships that quelled both the revolt and the threat from Sparta; he also made maximum use of his nonmilitary general, Soph. by dispatching the aristocratic poet to two islands that were pro-Samian. The fact that these islands subsequently aided the Athenian cause testifies to the ambassador's success. By the harsh but generally humane terms of settlement, the Samians accepted a democratic government but escaped Athenian garrisons and tribute.

What can we conclude about 1) the relationship between Soph. and Pericles (see Ehrenberg, *Sophocles and Pericles,* passim) and 2) the relationship between Soph.'s political activities in the late 440s and the mythical world of the *An.*? Although one must be circumspect, the evidence warrants certain conclusions.

The poet and the politician evidently never had a close personal relationship, but Soph. esteemed and perhaps even admired the sagacious leader. At the very least, he was willing to put his own considerable prestige at Pericles' service on at least these two occasions.

In regard to the much more complex relationship between Soph.'s political life and the writing of the *An.,* the nature of the poetry demands a strong caveat and the evidence permits measured speculation. On the negative side, any identification between the astute Pericles and Cr., victim of his own folly, is both unhistorical and unworthy of the poetic craft; again, any identification between the autonomous An. and tiny Samos battling mighty Athens for its autonomy is similarly unjustified. Yet, on the positive side, it is fascinating to reflect that the man who was officially responsible for the collection of taxes from the Aegean tributaries, whose autonomy Athens was curtailing, was privately depicting the clash between the autonomous heroine and the tyrannical king. Like William Butler Yeats during the Irish rebellion, Soph.'s poetry grew out of his life experience. Both of these poets could have borrowed Aeneas' words, "quorum pars magna fui" (Virgil *Aeneid* 2. 6). But like all truly great poets, they universalize personal and political experience and see with frightening prophetic insight. It is almost as though Soph. were encapsulating Thucydides' account of subsequent Athenian history. One sees flashes of the ruthless demagogue, Cleon, proposing to break Mytilene by bloody reprisals (Thucydides 3. 36–41). The Melian Dialogue (Thucydides 5. 84–113) could be a commentary on Cr.'s dictum: "You must obey anyone the city appoints, in matters small and great, just and unjust" (666–67). Indeed, the unexpected collapse of the mighty Cr. held instructive parallels for the subsequent fall of the mighty Athens. One must not press such parallels. Athens was not the empty cipher within (1325) but she was fast frittering away her inner resources. And so, one may conclude that while the play offers no one-to-one historical parallels, it does exemplify poetry's gift for universalizing history.

Notes

Preface

1. Herington's article (pp. 558–68) proposed a new kind of classical commentary, one in which a Greek prose paraphrase would appear side by side with the classical Greek text. Although this *Guide* and a forthcoming work (see n. 2 below) bear little resemblance to the original proposal, I am grateful to Professor Herington for the initial impetus and for his subsequent suggestions and encouragement.

2. Joan V. O'Brien, *Bilingual Selections from Sophocles' "Antigone": An Introduction to the Text for the Greekless Reader* (Carbondale and Edwardsville: Southern Illinois Univ. Press, forthcoming). Hereafter cited as *Bilingual Selections*.

3. I have most often followed Pearson's readings, and although I have not concentrated on textual problems, I have indicated in the Commentary where and why I deviate from them.

4. One of the themes that runs through my Commentary is that An. is not only the heroine of the play but is an "androgynous heroine." See the intro. to *Bilingual Selections* for a detailed study of this neglected aspect of the play.

5. Jebb, also available in Shuckburgh. Müller has provided a scholarly, although idiosyncratic German commentary. Also Braun provides a less extensive and yet provocative commentary but without reference to the Greek text. Gellie's recent study attempts to discuss diverse elements of the poet's style, simply from an English translation which imitates as much as possible the order, sound patterns, etc., of the original (pp. 263 ff.). Müller, unlike Braun and Gellie, discusses the Greek lines in his commentary. However, he does not provide the Greek text, and so it is often difficult to determine exactly what reading he would adopt if he printed the text.

6. For a comprehensive grammar, see Smyth; for a more modest grammar, see Goodwin.

I PROLOGUE
[1 - 99]

1. See Finley, *Three Essays on Thucydides,* p. 83; also Webster, *An Introduction to Sophocles,* pp. 143–62. Campbell's (pp. 1–107) remains the best-detailed study of the playwright's stylistic usage, although Long's is an admirable study of certain elements of his style. For images of this particular play, see Goheen. Also see Gellie, pp. 261–79.

2. Plutarch *Moralia* 79b claims that Soph. himself distinguished three styles of his own work: the weight (or loftiness) of Aeschylus in his early work, the pointedness and artificiality of his own style, and finally his best and most "ethical" style (ethical in the sense of being adapted to the *ethos,* the character, of the individual speaker). It seems clear that all the extant Soph. dramas—the *An.* is perhaps his thirty-second play—belong to the third style.

3. In a detailed study of a passage from the *Oedipus Tyrannos* in English, Gellie tries to point out from an English translation such elements of Soph.'s style as simplicity of vocabulary, the structured ordering of words, the lack of stretching in his metaphors ("Sophocles tries not to think of two things at once but of one and a quarter things," p. 272), the manipulation of sound to assist and reinforce meaning.

4. Knox, pp. 79–80 has a detailed study of duals in the Prologue.

5. Braun, p. 11, observes that this play is compounded of pairs whom life sunders but whom death reunites: Eteocles and Polynices, Megareus and Hae., An. and Hae., An and her family. Cr. and Ism., the only two "alive" at the end of the play, are separate and alone. Death, not life, brings reconciliation and reunion.

6. At 300–301, the audience is reminded of the literal meaning of the word in order to heighten the ambiguity in its use in the Prologue.

7. Cf. Euripides *Medea* 583 where Medea flails the faithless Jason for his reckless villainy (*tolmāi panourgein*).

8. Opinion remains divided on the relative dating of the *Ajax* and *An.* Lesky argues persuasively on structural grounds that the *Ajax* antedates *An.*

9. Goheen, pp. 120–21, summarizes the dominant images on a convenient chart.

10. I.e., the nautical images (20, 83), the merchandising and animal images (29–30). The nautical images are generally more closely identified with Cr. except in the Ode on *Atē* (583 ff.) where the Cho. presumably alludes to An.

11. See Long, pp. 51–53.

12. Snell, pp. 4–10.

13. Méautis, p. 175. Other critics make the opposite error and attenuate her love by reducing it to an objective *philia*.

14. Knox, p. 79 ff.

15. Müller, p. 107, examines this line in context and shows the error in the recent attempts to exclude the element of her passionate nature from this line and to reduce it to an objective love of family.

16. In *Bilingual Selections,* I analyze An.'s androgyny, comparing and contrasting it with the character of Ajax, Soph.'s other hero from an extant play, *Ajax,* of the same period as the *An.* There, too, I compare An.'s androgyny with what I call Hae.'s "gynecandrism," a word coined to describe his androgyny in which the "feminine" qualities are more apparent than the "masculine." The ideas on androgyny that are summarized in these pages are documented fully there. The term androgyny is borrowed from Carolyn Heilbrun, although I reached my conclusions on the reality of androgyny in An. and Hae. before reading Heilbrun's fascinating study. See the intro. to *Bilingual Selections* for my reservations about Heilbrun's conclusions.

17. For two very different understandings of the play see Gellie, p. 45 ff., and Calder, "Sophokles' Political Tragedy, *Antigone,*" pp. 389–407. According to Gellie, An. has two different faces: one, "a sexless and self-involved creature who can be neither lovable in life nor tragic in death" in the first half of the play; the other, "all woman" in her closing lament. For Calder, Cr. is the protagonist, and the play is not primarily concerned with An. and love but is a political tragedy in which Soph. was championing the government's position, not that of the agitator, and Calder contends that Pericles would have understood it as such. Webster, *Greek Tragedy,* p. 23, retorts; "To say Perikles' sympathy would have been

with Kreon . . . is, I hope, to underrate Perikles' intelligence."
I do not therefore deny that the play is diptych in structure as
Kirkwood showed in *A Study in Sophoclean Drama*, pp. 30–98, and
that Cr. is one of the two foci of the play. The poet is concerned
with the king's pitiful downfall, but the revelation of his emptiness
serves to enhance the fulness of the heroine. Goheen's study of
the recoil of the images at the end of the play confirms the poet's
judgment that Cr.'s obstinate adherence to his shortsighted principles is the mark of a mediocre man incapable of heroic grandeur.

18. See the notes on these verses in the Comm. See also the
intro. to *Bilingual Selections* for an analysis of the androgyny in these
phrases.

2 Creon's First Speech and the
Reply of the Chorus
[161 – 214]

1. Kitto, *Form*, p. 151. For a more sympathetic treatment of
Cr., see Bonnard, *Greek Civilization*, pp. 15 ff. Bonnard contends
that Cr. is not moved by wrong principles, just by principles of
a lower order. Whereas An. is filled with love, Cr. is filled with
self-love.

2. The fact that the poet later depicts two obviously mediocre
men, the guard and the messenger, with a similar platitudinous
style confirms the impression dimly perceived here that Cr.'s apparent majesty conceals a nonheroic, ordinary man.

3. Podlecki, p. 362. Reinhardt (p. 118) observes that Cr. ap-
peals to something that was not false in itself; but there was something brutal and repellent in the *Wahrheit* by which he justifies
his ruthless decree.

4. The ship of state was not a new figure (cf. Alcaeus, frg.
18) but it was not as banal, exhausted an image as it is to the
modern audience. It was particularly appropriate for Cr. since the
superpatriot Eteocles in Aeschylus' *Seven against Thebes* used it of
his state (cf. *Seven* 1–3, 208–10). For Pericles' similar use of the
image in the Funeral Oration, see 189 n.

5. Goheen, pp. 44 ff., traces the image throughout the play.

6. See Demosthenes *On the Embassy* 246–47; *Third Philippic* 69–70; and see 179–90 n.

7. Gomme, p. 108.

8. Cf. Thucydides 1. 84. 3–4, and see Finley's analyses (*Three Essays on Thucydides*, p. 15) of the parallels between Cr.'s speeches and those of the Spartan, Archidamos. See also Herodotos 3. 80 ff. (the Debate on the Constitutions) where Herodotos puts a defense of monarchy into the mouth of the earlier Persian monarch, Dareios, a defense, however, which reflected contemporary philosophical debate. Dareios' platform resembles Cr.'s: one ruler is best, provided he is of the best character (*aristos*); his judgment (*gnōmē*) will be in keeping with his character; his administration or control of the people will be blameless; in a democracy, corrupt dealings in government service lead to close personal associations (*philiai ischyrai*) which are formed by the villainous to carry out their plots. Monarchy, Dareios concludes, made Persia free and will preserve it. Dareios, like Cr., advocates *euboulia* and *gnōmē*, the good judgment of the ruler as the safeguard of freedom. In this play, however, *euboulia* will finally be seen as the possession, not of the ruler but of the advocate of *philiai ischyrai*. The preponderance of political vocabulary in this play—there are more political concepts in this play than in any other Sophoclean drama—suggests Soph.'s concern with political theory, but his judgment seems to be that the human and religious judgments must transcend the political. See Long, pp. 54–56, on political vocabulary and Ehrenberg (*Sophocles and Pericles*) for parallels between Cr. and Pericles.

9. See the unreliable *Life of Sophocles* 14 (Pearson, p. xx).

3 ODE ON MAN
[332 – 75]

1. For a summary of the various critical judgments on the divine and human action evident in the double burial, see McCall, pp. 105–12. Most critics agree, since Reinhardt, pp. 82–86, that there is in the burial and in the play an intermingling of divine and human motivation. On the religious dimension of the ode, see O'Brien, pp. 138–51.

2. In addition to the critics cited in the Comm., see Friedländer, pp. 56–63, and MacLeish, pp. 9–11.

3. I do this 1) by exploring the relation of this ode, *Polla ta deina*, with the famous "feminine" ode of Aeschylus' *Oresteia* which begins: *Polla men gā trephei deina deimatōn achē* (*Choephoroi* 585–86); 2) by studying the "feminine" images of the ode, particularly the image of weaving, long rejected by the commentators (see 368–69 n.).

4. Kranz claims the Cho. has a triple function: 1) as a character in the play; 2) as a means of dividing the action and of deepening its significance; and 3) as spokesman for the poet. Most critics deny Kranz's third function: the Cho. of a tragedy does not serve like the chorus in the parabasis of a comedy, as an unambiguous spokesman for the poet. However, this Cho. does provide the poet with an ironic persona: although the Cho. does not understand fully its own meditation and although the poet does not share the pietistic application that it makes of its own thoughts (373–75), the poet's own profound views can be found in this ode and others like the Ode on *Atē* and the Ode on Eros.

5. See Plato *Protagoras* 320c–323a. Although the dramatic date of the dialogue was about ten years after the production of the *An.* and although Plato wrote it much later, most scholars agree that the myth presented in the *Protagoras* is faithful both to the sophist's general teaching and to the prevailing climate of Soph.'s day. The myth explains how civic virtue arose and how previously isolated men learned to band together and overcome the dangers of a hostile environment through the divine gifts of respect for others, *aidos;* a sense of justice, *dikē;* political order, *kosmos;* and finally through *philia.*

6. See 342–53 n.

7. See n. 3 above.

8. In the intro. to *Bilingual Selections,* I contrast the deinotic nature of An. with that of Ajax, the Homeric hero whom the playwright also calls *deinos.* Ajax is deinotic in a more narrowly "masculine" manner, appropriate for the individualistic glory of the Homeric hero.

9. Mouzenidis, during a lecture at Southern Illinois University at Carbondale, March 1975.

10. On metrical questions, see Pohlsander; also Raven, Dale, and Thomson. Thomson is particularly helpful for the uninitiated.

4 Defense of the Unwritten Laws
[450 – 70]

1. The debate does appear in embryonic form in Soph.'s *Ajax* 1052 ff. where Teucer like An. insists on burying the lawless Ajax despite the kings' *nomos* forbidding it. The parallels are striking. The contemptible King Menelaos has good reason to express fury toward Ajax since the latter vainly tried to murder Menelaos and his comrades. See Aeschylus *Suppliants* 673 for a religious understanding of *nomos;* Aeschylus expresses his convictions about justice more often in terms of *dikē*, justice. DeRomilly (*La loi dans la pensée grecque,* chap. 1) traces the development of the *nomos-physis* debate; Ehrenberg (pp. 22–50) compares Soph.'s usage of "unwritten laws" with that of Pericles and others.

2. Both DeRomilly (above, n. 1) and Ehrenberg give substantial evidence of this fact.

3. Several of the frgs. of Heraclitus refer to law (cf. frgs. 29, 44, 120), but frg. 114 makes divine law normative for human social activity: "Those who speak with sense must rely on what is common to all, as a city must rely on its law, and with much greater reliance: for all the laws of men are nourished by one law, the divine law; for it has as much power as it wishes and is sufficient for all and is still left over." The verb "nourish" portrays human laws as young, immature dependents on divine law that is its "nurse," guarding its integrity.

4. Ehrenberg (pp. 49–50) after an extensive comparison of Soph.'s and Pericles' use of "unwritten laws" in the Funeral Oration (Thucydides 2. 37. 3) concludes: "For the poet, the unwritten laws were the eternal and universal laws which by divine will rule the world and mankind; the statesman, if he had any definite views on them saw them as general laws of social behavior, fixed by human tradition or convention." Linforth (p. 202, n. 20) minimizes the differences between Soph. and Pericles, asserting that they arise more from the fact that one was a poet and the other an orator

177

than from a difference in basic belief. Linforth thus misses the point: the depth of the poet's vision drew him to a medium suited to express his transcendent meaning.

5. Goheen (pp. 14–30) traces the business language of gain with which Cr. weighs human nature. Tiresias later uses *kerdos*, "gain," in the meaning of spiritual gain, salvation, similar to An.'s use here. see 462–64 n.

6. The term *autonomos* had a special political and spiritual meaning for Athenians (see Intro., chap. 6). Since each *polis* had its own *nomos*, the individual *polis* had its special autonomy. An.'s autonomy would thus be analogous to that of a separate *polis* within Cr.'s kingdom. Cf. Solzhenitsyn's remark: "For a country to have a great writer is like having another government."

7. Goheen (pp. 135–36, n. 32). But the text and therefore the interpretation are doubtful.

8. Cf. also *Oedipus Tyrannos* 865 ff., where the Cho., in its ode on the sanctity of oracles sings of *nomoi hypsipodes* "high-footed laws" born in the bright sky.

9. See n. 3 above.

5 THE CREON-HAEMON DEBATE
[631 – 765]

1. In the intro. to *Bilingual Selections,* I coined the word "gyne-candrism" to describe Hae.'s variety of androgyny. Whereas An. is androgynous in such a way that the "masculine" firmness, even harshness, conceals her passionate "femininity," Hae. is more properly gynecandrous, i.e., the "feminine" qualities are more apparent in him. I analyze there, too, the complementarity of their natures. Thus, although there is no dramatization of their love in the play—a fact that distressed romantic critics—it is a fair assumption that Hae., if anyone, would be a fitting lover for An. I try to show, too, that their wholeness contrasts with the narrowly "masculine" king and the narrowly "feminine" Ism.

2. Reinhardt, p. 94, explores Hae.'s role as a *Hilfsgestalt* and shows how much more elaborate the role of the auxiliary character is here than, for instance, in the *Trachiniae.*

3. Hollowness is a constant theme in Soph.'s works (Knox, pp. 32–33). Significantly, the playwright takes up the theme again in his final work, *Oedipus at Kolonos,* with the same cast of characters. There, the noble Athenian king Theseus confirms Hae.'s judgment of Cr. here, calling him "bereft of wit" at a time of life when he should be full of wisdom (931: cf. also 359, 917–18).

4. See Intro. chap. 6. The *Oedipus at Kolonos* stresses even more the anguish of isolation for a loving hero.

5. See Kirkwood, pp. 236–39, where he traces the theme throughout the play; also see Long, p. 151, and my Comm. on lines 74, 76–77, 743–45.

6. For a different view, see Calder, "Sophokles' Political Tragedy, *Antigone,*" p. 400, n. 48. According to this distinguished scholar, Cr.'s act was simply an act of prudence quite in line with the Indo-European practice of avoiding pollution when executing maidens of the royal house.

7. See 1 above.

8. Johansen, *General Reflection in Tragic Rhesis,* p. 107.

9. See the short analysis of the ode in *Bilingual Selections.*

6 ANTIGONE'S LAST SPEECH
[891 – 928]

1. See Aristotle *Poetics* 1452b24 where kommos (a noun from the verb "to beat one's breast in grief") is defined as a dirge sung alternately by the Cho. and one or more of the characters. The meters are emotionally charged, the music and dance appropriately mournful.

2. There were in Athens perhaps fifty thousand metics, resident aliens, in Soph.'s day, and Athenian law denied them the right of citizenship. See Knox (p. 114) on *metoikia.*

3. Gellie, p. 45, objects to the "two faces of Antigone" i.e., the aggressive martyr who rejected the feelings and attitudes of her sex, the "sexless and self-involved creature" of the Prologue "who can be neither lovable in life nor tragic in death," and the An. of the kommos who "must suddenly become all woman." I suspect that many other critics would have questioned the play-

wright's understanding of human nature if the gritty earlier speeches continued here.

4. *Autonomos*, "self-legislating," was a highly charged political word in Periclean Athens (see Intro. chap. 4, n. 6). Since each *polis* had its own laws, *nomoi*, Athens had been proud in the early years of the Delian Confederacy to exercise "hegemony over autonomous allies who participated in common synods" (Thucydides 1. 97. 1). By the opening of the Peloponnesian War, less than fifteen years after the *An.* was produced, Athenian politicians admitted the confederacy had degenerated into an empire which Athens ruled as tyrant (Thucydides 2. 63. 3). At the time Soph. was writing the *An.*, Pericles was in the process of reorganizing the League so as to refute charges of tyranny. Also, within the *polis* the autonomy of the individual was a cherished ideal; the *polis* was the free men that sustained the whole (Thucydides 7. 77. 7); high treason was "deception of the people" (see Kagan, pp. 140 ff., for a general recapitulation of the climate of the day). Thus, the Athenian audience might well view the autonomous "metic" An. with the combination of admiration for a courageous fellow citizen and of fear for a rebellious tributary. It is important to remember, too, that women did not have active citizenship in Periclean Athens; thus, as woman and as metic, An. would be transgressing (see 455 n.) proper bounds even in pleading her own case. Cf. Polyxena's existential freedom as she dies in Euripides' *Hecuba* 347–552.

5. The Cho.'s sophistic distinction between the hybris of the mortal An. and the immortal Niobe is particularly inhuman, but instructive at a moment when the distraught heroine displays none of the arrogance of the earlier scenes. Niobe, the daughter of Tantalos and mother of several children, had angered Leto, mother of Apollo and Artemis, by her boast that she was superior because she had more children. As a result, Leto's children killed Niobe's children and the grieving mother was transformed into a statue of stone on Mt. Sipylos. An. recalls the similarity (833) of their "most tearful" stone prison. But the comparison goes deeper than their mutual fate and tears. The poet aptly chooses to compare his heroine to an immortal who suffered because of her indomitable family love, *philia*.

6. See 373 n. and 1339 n. on the different meanings of *tolmē*,

"courage" and "rashness," and other related words in the play.

7. Goheen, p. 73, notes the relation between *auto-gnōtos* and the religious-moral maxim of the Delphic oracle: "know thyself," *gnōthi sauton.*

8. She continuously refers to the light of the sun and the waters of her native Dirce that she must leave. For a comparison of the An. of Soph. and Anouilh's heroine, see Hamburger, p. 160 ff.

9. Goheen, pp. 38–41, traces the marriage and death symbols and notes that these symbols not only generate pathos but are part of "the portrayal of An.'s rise above the passive reception of sympathy" (p. 39).

10. See 921–23 n. Soph.'s last play, returns to the theme of isolation with even more poignancy. But, interestingly, the An. figure there learns to yield, a thing that she never does in the *An.* (*Oedipus at Kolonos* 1768–72). One can only speculate as to whether this is due to the fact that she is only a supporting character there, or whether the aged playwright longed to recast her in a more "feminine" mould.

11. Cf. Alvarez where the writer points out the terminal inner loneliness common to all suicides. Knox, pp. 32–35.

12. Goethe, reported by Eckermann, hoped scholars could find the lines are spurious (see Jebb, Appendix, p. 259).

13. Aristotle *Rhetoric* 1417a29 (written ca. 338 B.C.) knew and accepted these lines as genuine though embarrassing. Aristotle's witness is important since he was "the head of a research school which busied itself . . . with the history of tragedy" (Knox, p. 105).

14. See Jebb, Appendix, p. 259, for the stylistic awkwardness of the passage (see n. on 909) and for the inconsistency between 450–70 and this passage (see also notes on 465–68); more recently, Müller (1967) rejects the passage, but the editors Pearson (1924) and Dain-Mazon (1967) retain it *in toto.* The argument that An.'s remarks here are excessively formal is not valid since all statements in iambic trimeter are formal (cf., e.g., Medea's opening iambic speech, Euripides *Medea* 214 ff. with her opening anapests, 96 ff.). The whole point of the iambics here is that An. is attempting to be formal and rational at a moment when it is humanly impossible for her to do so. Page (*Actors' Interpolations in Greek Tragedy,* pp. 86 ff.) argues against the suitability of the passage but thinks

Soph. succumbed to the temptation to throw in these lines knowing they would not have time to jar the audience. Mazon-Dain think Soph.—not an interpolator—borrowed this from Herodotos and that the poet was fully aware of the surprising and paradoxical nature of the borrowing (pp. 66 ff.). Waldock finds the dialectic grotesque and topsy-turvy (p. 133) and the whole passage has "the tang of a fairy tale." Watling calls it "inconsistent and unworthy but dramatically correct." Bowra finds these thoughts "deeply touching and perfectly natural." Kitto, (*Form,* p. 171) insists: "Nothing is left to her but her deep instinct that she had to do it and it is neither surprising nor undramatic that she should now find what reason she can." Elsewhere (*Greek Tragedy* p. 127), Kitto calls this "the finest borrowing in literature," a superlative that few would agree with. Kirkwood (p. 165) says: "It is altogether too obscure in manner, too little explained in terms of clear development of mood, to be dramatically first rate. But it . . . is altogether appropriate to Antigone's nature." Adams who would retain the passage remarks: "The only *nomos* she knows is the *nomos* of *eros.*" Whitman and Müller and Linforth are almost alone among recent critics in rejecting the Sophoclean origin. Whitman (p. 264, n. 31) points to two "incontrovertible facts": the argument is basically sophistic whether in Herodotos or Soph.; "there is nothing in all the rest of Sophocles which is so deadly *psychron* [i.e., cold]." On the conflict between An.'s statement on the unwritten laws at 450–70 and this passage, Reinhardt (pp. 92 ff.) points to a similar conflict between the hero's ideal and personal reaction at the moment of death in Soph.'s earlier play *Ajax* 835 ff. and 479–80. Gellie (p. 4) states: "Her explanation makes nonsense of every reason An. has given . . . for her action." And he adds: "The statement betrays the wrong kind of absurdity for mental disturbance. It is not a crudely silly statement tossed off among other silly statements. It is preceded and followed by many lines of good sense, it is a developed thesis and it has a spiky logic of its own. In fact it is the only attempt made by the play to answer precisely and rationally the question with which Soph. has been grappling throughout: how could a girl prefer a dead brother to a live husband?"

15. Knox, pp. 106–7.

16. There is a similarly "strange" sister-brother attachment in a poem of Bacchylides (Ode 5. 136–54) where Althaia decides to kill her *son* because he killed her *brothers* in battle; cf., too "Hesiod," *Shield* 1–22, when Alkmene marries her *father's* slayer but refuses intercourse with him until he has avenged her *brothers'* deaths. (I am grateful to Professor Mary Lefkowitz for pointing out these earlier examples.) Thus, An.'s remarks probably sounded less strange in the ancient setting than they do before a modern audience.

17. Cook (p. 115) concurs, noting "the leap from the tense logic of her argument in the second episode to the dreamlike extremes of these final utterances. Here she shows herself to be the woman whom the devotion of Haemon and the ode to Eros call up."

18. Jebb, Appendix, p. 259.

19. Alvarez notes that suicide in classical Greece was not considered an act of cowardice but of courage: "But the suicides retained at least one last shred of freedom: they took their own lives. In part, this is a political act, both a gesture of defiance and a condemnation of the system. . . . It is also an act of affirmation: the artist values life and his own truths too much to be able to tolerate their utter perversion" (p. 250). Socrates' death forty years after Soph. wrote the *An.* illustrates the Athenian respects for suicide even though it is true that the philosopher's calm, reasonable approach to death would hardly be typical of that of the ordinary Athenian.

20. Lynch, p. 27, describes the path of the imagination in such cases as a plunge through or down into the real contours of being but in such a way that the plunge down causally generates a plunge up into insight.

7 CREON'S LAMENT
[1284 – 1353]

1. Consider, too, the dramaturgic effect of the king's confession of guilt as he is flanked *only* by his son's and his wife's body; also see 1319, 1340–41 (cf. 1261–69) for Cr.'s failure to include An.'s death among his transgressions.

2. See Lynch for a significant discussion of the ironic imagination. The discussion is applicable to this play although Lynch does not make the application.

3. Many fine critics disagree with this statement and believe Cr. is the centerpiece. See Kitto, *Form,* p. 176; see also n. 17, chap. 1.

APPENDIX A: *Sophocles' Relation to the Mythic Tradition*

1. Rosenmeyer makes this suggestion in "Seven against Thebes: The Tragedy of War" (p. 57), in McCall, *Aeschylus.*

2. *Iliad* 4. 406 contains a memory of the destruction of Thebes recorded in that epic. The epic is believed to reflect the historical destruction of Thebes in Mycenaean times.

3. According to the Argument of Salustius (a fifth-century A.D. rhetorician) which Jebb quotes on p. 5 of his text of the *An.,* Mimnermus, a late seventh-century B.C. lyric poet, wrote of the murder of Ismene at Thebes. Salustius also reported that Ion of Chios, writing a few years before the *An.* (c. 450 B.C.) has both sisters burned in the Theban temple of Hera by Eteocles' son when the *epigoni* took Thebes. Jebb argues that the fact that this Ionian contemporary did not know of An.'s deed indicates that her defiance is of Attic origin (i.e., from around Kolonos).

4. See Dawson (pp. 23–25) for a summary of the arguments and bibliography.

5. Our knowledge of the plot of Euripides' *An.* is meager (see Jebb, pp. 1–2) but that plot further demonstrates Soph.'s originality. In the Euripidean version the love interest and apparent happy ending are sharply at odds with Soph.'s drama. Hae., in Euripides' play, apparently refused to kill An.; instead he fathered a child by her who was subsequently recognized by Cr., whereupon, the king ordered the execution of both Hae. and An., a dire extremity that was prevented by a deus ex machina.

GLOSSARY

The numbers refer to the lines in the selections at which the name is mentioned, the person is referred to, or the character appears.

Acheron, 812, 816
Antigone, 1–99, 450–70, 653–660, 692–99, 740, 748, 891–928
Argives, 15
Athena, 1291 n.
Cadmeans, 508
Creon, 8–10, 21, 31, 162–214, 631–765, 914, 1284–1353
Dikē (Justice), 450 n.
Erinys (pl. Erinyes, Furies), 603, 1075
Eteocles, 21–25, 55–57, 169–74, 194–97, 466–70, 899
Eurydice, 1180, 1291 n., 1292, 1300–1305, 1313, 1340–46
Gē (Earth), 338 n.
Hades, 361 n., 654, 911, 1284
Haemon, 572, 635–765, 1175, 1217, 1297, 1304, 1312, 1316,
    1340–46
Ismene, 1–99
Jocasta, 53–54, 898–99, 911
Kolonos, Appendixes A and B
Labdakidai, 593, 861
Laios (Laius), 165
Megareus = Menoeceus, 1303 n., 1312
Menoeceus (father of Creon), 211
Messenger, 1284–1316
Oedipus, 2, 49, 167, 193, 380, 758, 898, 911
Olympos, 758
Persephone (Persephassa), 894 n., 902
Pluto, see Hades
Polynices (Polyneices), 21–30, 43–47, 55–57, 71–73, 81, 110,

185

Selected Bibliography

Texts

CAMPBELL, LEWIS, ed. *Sophocles: The Plays and Fragments.* Vol. 1. 2d ed., rev. 1879. Reprint. Hildesheim: Georg Olms, 1969.

DAIN, A., ed., and Mazon, P., trans. *Sophocle.* Vol. 1. Paris: Les Belles Lettres, 1967.

JEBB, SIR RICHARD, ed. and trans. *Sophocles: The Plays and Fragments.* Part 3. *The Antigone.* 3d ed. Amsterdam: Servio Publishers, 1962.

MÜLLER, GERHARD. *Sophokles Antigone: Einleitung und Kommentar.* Heidelberg: Carl Winter, 1967.

PEARSON, A. C., ed. *Sophoclis Fabulae.* 1924. Reprint. Oxford: Clarendon Press, 1955.

SHUCKBURGH, E. S., ed. *The Antigone of Sophocles.* 11th ed. New York: Cambridge Univ. Press, 1971.

General Studies

ADAMS, S. M. *Sophocles the Playwright.* Toronto: Univ. of Toronto Press, 1957.

ADKINS, ARTHUR W. H. *Merit and Responsibility: A Study in Greek Values.* Oxford: Clarendon Press, 1960.

ALLEN, W. Sidney. *Vox Graeca.* Cambridge: Cambridge Univ. Press, 1968.

ALVAREZ, ALFRED. *The Savage God: A Study of Suicide.* New York: Random House, 1972.

BONNARD, ANDRÉ. *La tragédie et l'homme.* Neuchâtel and Paris: Baconnière, 1951.

———. *Greek Civilization.* Vol. 2, *From the Antigone to Socrates.* Translated by A. Lytton Sells. London: Allen and Unwin, 1959.

BOWRA, C. M. *Sophoclean Tragedy.* Oxford: Oxford Univ. Press, 1944.

BUTTERWORTH, E. A. S. *Some Traces of the Pre-Olympian World in Greek Literature and Myth.* Berlin: DeGruyer and Co., 1966.

CAMPBELL, LEWIS. *Paralipomena Sophoclea.* London: Rivingtons, 1907.
COOK, ALBERT. *Enactment: Greek Tragedy.* Chicago: Swallow Press, 1971.
CROSS, AMANDA. *The Theban Mysteries.* New York: Knopf, 1971.
DALE, A. M. *Lyrics Metres of Greek Drama.* London: Cambridge Univ. Press, 1968.
DAUBE, DAVID. *Civil Disobedience in Antiquity.* Edinburgh: Univ. Press, 1972.
DAWSON, CHRISTOPHER, trans. and comm. *The Seven Against Thebes.* Englewood Cliffs, N.J.: Prentice-Hall, 1970.
DENNISTON, J. O. *The Greek Particles.* Oxford: Clarendon Press, 1954.
DEROMILLY, JACQUELINE. *Time in Greek Tragedy.* Ithaca: Cornell Univ. Press, 1968.
———. *La loi dans la pensée grecque.* Paris: Les Belles Lettres, 1971.
DIELS, HERMANN. *Die Fragmente der Vorsokratiker.* Cambridge: Harvard Univ. Press, 1948.
DILLER, HANS, ed. *Sophokles.* Darmstadt: Wissenschaftliche Buchgesellschaft, 1967.
DODDS, E. R. *The Greeks and the Irrational.* Berkeley: Univ. of California Press, 1951.
———. ed. *Euripides' Bacchae.* 2d ed. Oxford: Clarendon Press, 1960.
EDMONDS, J. M. *Greek Elegy, Iambus, and Anacreontea.* Vol. 1. 1931. Reprint. Cambridge, Mass.: Harvard Univ. Press, 1968.
EHRENBERG, VICTOR. *The People of Aristophanes.* Oxford: Blackwell, 1951.
———. *Sophocles and Pericles.* Oxford: Blackwell, 1954.
———. *The Greek State.* Oxford: Blackwell, 1960.
ELIOT, T. S. *Collected Poems 1909–1935.* New York: Harcourt Brace, 1936.
———. *The Family Reunion.* New York: Harcourt Brace, 1939.
ELLENDT, F. *Lexicon Sophocleum.* 2d ed. Edited by H. Genthe. 1872. Reprint. Hildesheim: Georg Olms, 1958.
FERGUSON, JOHN. *A Companion to Greek Tragedy.* Austin: Univ. of Texas Press, 1972.
FINLEY, JOHN H. *Four Stages of Greek Thought.* Stanford: Stanford Univ. Press, 1965.
———. *Three Essays on Thucydides.* Cambridge: Harvard Univ. Press, 1967.

188

Selected Bibliography

GELLIE, G. H. *Sophocles: A Reading.* Carlton, Victoria: Melbourne Univ. Press, 1972.

GOHEEN, ROBERT F. *The Imagery of Sophocles' Antigone.* Princeton: Princeton Univ. Press, 1951.

GOMME, ARNOLD WYCOMBE. *More Essays in Greek History and Literature.* Edited by D. A. Campbell. Oxford: Blackwell, 1962.

GOODWIN, WILLIAM WATSON. *Greek Grammar.* New York: St. Martin's Press, 1965.

GOODWIN, WILLIAM WATSON, AND GULICK, CHARLES BURTON. *Greek Grammar.* New York: Blaisdell Publishing Co., 1965.

GUTHRIE, W. K. C. *The Sophists.* Cambridge: Cambridge Univ. Press, 1971.

HAMBURGER, KÄTE. *From Sophocles to Sartre.* Translated by H. Sebba. New York: Frederick Ungar, 1969.

HEGEL, GEORG WILHELM FRIEDRICH. *The Philosophy of Fine Art.* Vol. 1. Translated by F. P. B. Osmaston, London: G. Bell and Sons, 1920.

HEILBRUN, CAROLYN. *Toward a Recognition of Androgyny.* New York: Knopf, 1973.

JOHANSEN, HOLGER FRIIS. *General Reflection in Tragic Rhesis.* Copehhagen: Munksgaard, 1959.

KAGAN, DONALD. *The Outbreak of the Peloponnesian War.* Ithaca: Cornell Univ. Press, 1969.

KIRKWOOD, G. M. *A Study of Sophoclean Drama.* Cornell Studies in Classical Philology, vol. 31. Ithaca: Cornell Univ. Press, 1958.

KITTO, H. D. F. *Greek Tragedy.* Garden City, N.Y.: Doubleday and Co., 1954.

———. *Form and Meaning in Drama.* London: Methuen and Co., 1959.

KNOX, B. M. W. *The Heroic Temper: Studies in Sophoclean Tragedy.* Sather Series, vol. 35. Berkeley: Univ. of California Press, 1964.

KRANZ, W. *Stasimon.* Berlin; Weidmann, 1933.

LACEY, W. K. *The Family in Classical Greece.* Ithaca: Cornell Univ. Press, 1968.

LASSERRE, F. *La figure d'Eros dans la poésie greque.* Thése imprimèe à Lausanne, 1946.

LIDDELL, HENRY GEORGE; SCOTT, ROBERT; AND JONES, SIR HENRY STUART. *A Greek-English Lexicon.* 9th ed. Oxford: Clarendon Press, 1968.

LLOYD-JONES, HUGH. *The Justice of Zeus.* Sather Series, vol. 41. Berkeley: Univ. of California Press, 1971.

LONG, A. A. *Language and Thought in Sophocles.* London: Athlone Press, 1968.

LYNCH, WILLIAM F. *Images of Faith: An Exploration of the Ironic Imagination.* Notre Dame, Ind.: Notre Dame Univ. Press, 1973.

MACLEISH, ARCHIBALD. *A Continuing Journey.* Boston: Houghton Mifflin, 1968.

MÉAUTIS, GEORGES. *Sophocle: Essai sur le héros tragique.* Paris: Michel, 1957.

MUSURILLO, H. *The Light and the Darkness, Studies in the Dramatic Poetry of Sophocles.* Leiden: Brill, 1967.

PAGE, DENYS L. *Actors' Interpolations in Greek Tragedy.* Oxford: Clarendon Press, 1934.

PAGE, DENYS L. ed. *Euripides, Medea.* 1938. Reprint (with corrections). Oxford: Clarendon Press, 1961.

POHLSANDER, H. A. *Metrical Studies in the Lyrics of Sophocles.* Leiden: Brill, 1964.

RAVEN, DAVID S. *Greek Metre.* 2d ed. London: Faber, 1968.

REINHARDT, KARL. *Sophokles.* 3d ed. Frankfurt: Klostermann, 1947.

RICOEUR, PAUL. *The Symbolism of Evil.* New York: Harper and Row, 1967.

RONNET, GILBERTE. *Sophocle poète tragique.* Paris: Éditions E. De Boccard, 1969.

ROSENMEYER, THOMAS. *Aeschylus.* Edited by M. H. McCall. Englewood Cliffs, N.J.: Prentice-Hall, 1972.

SHEPPARD, JOHN T. *The Wisdom of Sophocles.* London: Allen and Unwin, 1947.

————. *Aeschylus and Sophocles: Their Work and Influence.* New York: Cooper Square Publishers, 1963.

SLATER, PHILIP E. *Glory of Hera: Greek Mythology and the Greek Family.* Boston: Beacon Press, 1968.

SMYTH, H. W. *Greek Grammar.* Edited by G. M. Messing. Rev. ed. Cambridge: Harvard Univ. Press, 1966.

SNELL, BRUNO. *The Discovery of the Mind.* Translated by T. G. Rosenmeyer. New York: Harper and Brothers, 1960.

————. *Poetry and Society.* Bloomington: Indiana Univ. Press, 1961.

STANFORD, W. B. *Sophocles Ajax.* London: Macmillan, 1963.

————. *The Sound of Greek.* Sather Series, vol. 38. Berkeley: Univ. of California Press, 1967.

THOMSON, GEORGE. *Greek Lyric Metre.* Cambridge: W. Heffer and Sons, 1961.

WALDOCK, A. J. A. *Sophocles the Dramatist.* Cambridge: Cambridge Univ. Press, 1966.

WEBSTER, T. B. L. *An Introduction to Sophocles.* Oxford: Clarendon Press, 1936.

————. *Greek Tragedy.* Oxford: Clarendon Press, 1971.

WEISS, ROBERT. *Loneliness: The Experience of Emotional and Social Isolation.* Cambridge: M.I.T. Press, 1973.

WEISSMAN, PHILIP. *Creativity in the Theater: A Psychoanalytic Study.* New York: Basic Books, 1965.

WHITMAN, C. H. *Sophocles, A Study of Heroic Humanism.* Cambridge: Harvard Univ. Press, 1951.

WOODARD, THOMAS. *Sophocles: A Collection of Critical Essays.* Englewood Cliffs, N.J.: Prentice Hall, 1966.

WOOLF, VIRGINIA. *The Common Reader.* New York: Harcourt Brace, 1925.

ARTICLES

AGARD, W. R. "*Antigone* 904–20." *Classical Philology* 32 (1937): 263–65.

ANOUILH, JEAN. "*Antigone.*" *Nouvelles pièces noires,* pp. 126–207. Paris: Les Éditions de la Table Ronde, 1961.

BRADSHAW VON, A. T. "The Watchman Scenes in the *Antigone.*" *Classical Quarterly,* n.s. 12 (1962): 200–211.

BULTMANN, RUDOLF. "Polis und Hades in der Antigone des Sophokles." In Hans Diller, *Sophokles,* pp. 311–24. Darmstadt: Wissenschaftliche Buchgesellschaft, 1967.

CALDER, WILLIAM M. "Was Antigone Murdered?" *Greek Roman and Byzantine Studies* 3 (1960): 31–35.

————. "Sophokles' Political Tragedy, *Antigone.*" *Greek Roman and Byzantine Studies* 9 (1968): 389–407.

DODDS, E. R. "On Misunderstanding the *Oedipus Rex*" *Greece and Rome* 13 (1966): 37–49.

FINLEY, JOHN H. "Politics and Early Attic Tragedy." *Harvard Studies in Classical Philology* 71 (1966): 1–13.

FRIEDLÄNDER, P. "Polla Ta Deina." *Hermes* 69 (1934): 56–63.

GARTON, C. "Characterization in Greek Tragedy." *Journal of Hellenic Studies* 77 (1957): 247–54.

HEIDEGGER, MARTIN. "The Ode on Man in Sophocles' *Antigone.*" In Thomas Woodard. *Sophocles,* pp. 86–100.

HERINGTON, C. J. "Classical Commentaries for Our Time: A Proposal." *Arion* 7 (1968): 558–68.

HOEY, THOMAS F. "Inversion in the *Antigone:* A Note." *Arion* 9 (1970): 337–45.

JOHANSEN, HOLGER FRISS. "Sophocles 1939–1959." *Lustrum* 7 (1962): 94–288.

KIRKWOOD, G. M. "The Dramatic Role of the Chorus in Sophocles." *Phoenix* 8 (1954): 1–22.

LINFORTH, I. M. "Antigone and Creon." *University of California Publications in Classical Philology* 15 (1961): 183–260.

MARGON, J. S. "The Second Burial of Polyneices." *Classical Journal* 68 (1972): 39–49.

McCALL, MARSH. "Divine and Human Action in Sophocles." *Yale Classical Studies* 22 (1972): 105–12.

MUSURILLO, H. "Fire-Walking in Sophocles' *Antigone* 618–19," *Transactions of the American Philological Association* 94 (1963): 167–75.

O'BRIEN, JOAN V. "Sophocles' Ode on Man and Paul's Hymn on Love: A Comparative Study." *Classical Journal* 71 (1975–76): 138–51.

PODLECKI, ANTHONY J. "Creon and Herodotus." *Transactions of the American Philological Association* 97 (1966): 359–71.

POMEROY, SARAH B. "Selected Bibliography on Women in Antiquity." *Arethusa* 6 (1973): 125–57.

RONNET, GILBERTE. "Sur le premier stasimon d' *Antigone.*" *Revue des études grecques* 80 (1957): 100–105.

SCHLESINGER, E. "Deinotes." *Philologus* 91 (1936–37): 59–66.

SEGAL, CHARLES PAUL. "Sophocles' Praise of Man and the Conflicts of the *Antigone.*" *Arion* 3 (1964): 46–66.

ZIOBRO, WILLIAM J. "Where Was Antigone? *Antigone,* 766–883." *American Journal of Philology* 92 (1971): 81–85.

Selected Bibliography

TRANSLATIONS

BANKS, THEODORE HOWARD, trans. *Sophocles: Three Theban Plays.* New York: Oxford Univ. Press, 1956.

BRAUN, RICHARD EMIL, trans. *Sophocles Antigone.* New York: Oxford Univ. Press, 1973.

FITTS, DUDLEY, and FITZGERALD, ROBERT, trans. *Sophocles, The Oedipus Cycle.* New York: Harcourt Brace, 1939.

KITTO, H. D. F., trans. *Sophocles: Three Tragedies.* New York: Oxford Univ. Press, 1962.

WATLING, E. F., trans. *Sophocles, the Theban Plays.* 1947. Reprint. Baltimore: Penguin, 1970.

WYCKOFF, ELIZABETH, trans. *"Antigone." The Complete Greek Tragedies.* Edited by David Grene and Richard Lattimore. Chicago: Chicago Univ. Press, 1954.

INDEX

I am indebted to Sandra Moffitt for the preparation of this index. The Greek words in parentheses are the Sophoclean equivalents for the English entries. The lines at which they occur can be found in the "Vocabulary," chapter 8. Commentary for those lines will discuss the word. Meanings of Greek entries will also be found in the "Vocabulary."—J.O'B.

Index

Bonnard, André, 174
Bowra, C. M., 59, 77, 182
Bradshaw von, A. T., 10
Braun, Richard Emil: on Athena reference, 119; commentary of, 171; on reunion after death, 172
Bribery: Cr.'s accusations of, 12, 46, 117
Bultmann, Rudolph, 58
Burial: Athenian laws concerning, 11, 14; as unwritten law, 12, 14, 34, 67, 68; in *Ajax*, 12, 34–35; woman's natural defense of, 14; of Persians at Marathon, 35; libations of, 40, 106; of Eteocles, 106
Burial of Polynices: Ism.'s refusal to collaborate in, 1–24 passim; as crime against *stratēgos*, 9; An.'s desire for recognition of, 9, 21; Cr.'s denial of, 11, 35; An.'s awareness of consequence of, 12, 18, 66, 109; double, 21; as *deina tolman*, 24, 108; proper, 40, 121; symbolic, 46, 65; divine and human action in double, 61, 71, 175; Hae.'s view of, 86; triple libation of, 106–7
Butterworth, E. A. S., 40

Cadmeans, 40
Calder, William M.: on view of Cr. as antagonist, 36, 37, 173, 179
Campbell, Lewis: on *deinos*, 52; on Cr.'s *nomos*, 68; on disputed passage, (904–20); on *dyskathartos*, 118; on Soph.'s style, 172; mentioned, 18, 60, 88, 110, 118, 123
Camus, 104
Catastrophe, 115–16
Character (*ēthos*), 86, 172
Character contrasts: through antithesis, 6, 8; An. and Ajax, 173, 176, 182. *See also Philia*
Choephoroi (Aeschylus' *Oresteia*), 48, 52, 53, 81, 176
Choral rhythms: iambic trimeter, 1, 51, 101, 119, 124, 181; dactyls, 50; *isonomia*, 50–51; quantitative

metrics, 50, 53; glyconics, 51; relationship between meter and thought, 51; Doric and Paeonic modes, 51; dochmaic, 51, 119; lyrics, 100, 124; anapaests, 124, 181; Aristotle on, 179; mentioned, 54, 56
Chorus of Elders: judgment of An., 18, 101, 110, 180; as inactive, 36; fear of Cr. in, 35, 42, 76, 83, 91; generalizations of, 47; as ironic persona, 47, 48, 176; in Ode on Man, 61; as intentional symbol, 62; on eternal themes, 70; Ode on Eros, 76–77; fatuity of in Sophoclean tragedy, 88; pious reflections of, 123; final "tag," 124; triple function theory, 176; mentioned, 22, 31, 33, 38, 177
Christ, 109
Chthonic realm: An. and, 15, 20, 89; Ism.'s neglect of, 17; and Cr.'s blasphemy, 42, 89, 91; use of *chthōn* and *gē*, 60; and Zeus, 68
Cimon, 167, 168
City-state. *See Polis*
Cleon, 34, 169
Clouds (Aristophanes), 83
Clytemnestra, 52
Cognition (*phronēma*), 48–49, 56, 57. *See also* Moral insight
Coldness (*psychron*): and hotness antithesis, 21, 182
Color imagery: in vocabulary of Hae., 86
Commentators: discussed, 171
Contest (*ăgon*), 73
Contrivance (*mēchanē*), 58. *See also* Resourcefulness of man
Cook, Albert: on disputed passage (904–20), 183; mentioned, 51, 55, 57
Corpse (*nekys*): Cr. as "breathing corpse" (*empsychon nekron*), 4, 109, 117–18; of Polynices, 7, 11, 12, 34; legal rights of, 35; Cr.'s defamation of, 35, 116; gods concern for, 42; Zeus' presence in, for An., 66; An.'s care for, 106, 107; of

Index

and use of *chthōn*, 60
Eckermann, 181
Edict. *See* Decree, edict
Ehrenberg, Victor, 69, 168, 177
Electra, 21, 23, 24, 83
Electra (Sophocles): women in, 11;
  monetary imagery in, 12;
  Chrysothemis and Ism. in, 13;
  Clytemnestra and Orestes in, 52;
  mentioned, 19, 36, 88, 109
Eliot, T. S., 116, 117
Elision, ix
Emptiness (*kenos*): and isolation
  (*erēmos*), 73–74; Cr.'s realization of
  his own, 74; writing tablet
  metaphor, 74, 87, 116, 117; in
  Euripides' *Hippolytus*, 87; Cr.'s, 88,
  123, 178; Hae.'s use of, 90; of Cr.'s
  judgments, 90–91; contrasted with
  An.'s wholeness, 115; and *philia*,
  117
Enemy (*echthros*): range of meanings,
  5–6; for Cr., 6; for An., 6, 10;
  Polynices as, 10; Homeric use of,
  21; Ism. as, 23; Odysseus and Ajax
  as, 34–35; natural (sea, earth,
  animal kingdom), 46; Greek
  outlook toward, 79; mentioned, 39,
  78, 90
Epigoni (sons of Argive Seven), 122
Erōs: as An.'s primary motivation, 20,
  22; Soph.'s use of, 22; mentioned,
  102, 123, 182
Eros: and Zeus, 69; in Ode on, 76;
  and eternal laws, 76; mentioned,
  51, 57, 67, 183
Eteocles: relationship to Polynices in
  Aeschylus' *Seven against Thebes*, 163,
  164; mentioned, 36, 106, 178
Eternity, 19–20, 70
Eumenides (Aeschylus): Athena and
  court of Areopagus, 82
Euripides: and daring, 62; divinity
  in, 122; death, 167; mentioned, 33,
  61, 79, 120, 184
Eurydice, 83, 110, 114, 119
Evil (*kakos*): An.'s use of, 10; *kakistos*,
  38; range of meanings, 89; utterly
  vile (*pankakistos*), 90; mentioned,

59, 70
Excess (*perissos*): in An., 3–4, 13, 17;
  in homeric heroes, 7; in *deinos*, 48
Exodus: disobedient midwives, 14

Fame (*kleos*), good fame (*eukleia*): in
  An.'s death, 7; Homeric, 7, 85; for
  An., 7, 86; for sons, 78, 87; and
  agalma, 86; for Cr., 86; for Pericles,
  86
Family. *See* Kinship
Family Reunion (T. S. Eliot), 117
Fate (*moros*): personification of, 69,
  124; ill-fated (*dystēnos*), 111; Cr.'s
  use of word, 122, 123
"Feminine": Ism. as, 6; virtue, 6;
  explanation of, 6; traditional traits,
  7; social sphere, 11; *kouphos*, 14, 54,
  55; traits in An., 40, 119, 181;
  neglected dimension in Ode on
  Man, 47; primitive instinct in
  Aeschylus' *Choephoroi*, 48, 53, 176;
  word association, 55, 56, 77, 114;
  weaving, 60; obedience as for Cr.,
  82; religious instinct as, 104, 115;
  in gynecandrism, 173, 178;
  elements in disputed passage
  (904–20), 194
Finley, J. H.: unwritten law and
  freedom, 69; on *koinon*, 172; on
  Creon-Archidamos parallels, 175
Fitts-Fitzgerald: on *hosia panourgēsās*,
  19; on *periphradēs*, 55; on *astynomos
  orgē*, 56
Folly: *dysboulia*, appearance of in An.,
  2; An.'s personification of and
  relation with, 23, 121; triple use of
  mōros/mōria, "fool/folly," 66, 70,
  71; as opposite of *euboulia*, 71, 79;
  and inversion of images, 125; Cr.
  as victim of his, 168
Foreigners. *See* Metic
Form and Meaning in Drama (Kitto),
  85, 119, 182
Freedom, 116, 180. *See also* Autonomy
Friedländer, P., 176
Friendship. *See* Philia
Frogs (Aristophanes), 167
Funeral Oration (Pericles): *polis* in,

Index

Index

121, 122, 123, 124; Hae.'s use of, 74

Seven against Thebes (Aeschylus): Eteocles and Polynices in, 11, 36, 163–64; *perissos* in, 18; spurious imitations of Soph. in, 18, 164; obedience in, 82; women in, 83; on Megareus, 120; dates, 163, 166

"Seven against Thebes: The Tragedy of War" (Rosenmeyer), 184

Sexual desire. *See Erōs*

Shakespeare, William, 37, 85, 89, 90

Shame. *See* Moral shame

Shield (Bacchylides), 183

Sicilian Expedition, 167

Sin (*hamartia*): two directions of, 110, 111; *autos hamartōn,* 111; mentioned, 4, 91, 121

Slater, Philip E., 83

Slave imagery, 41, 81, 91, 92

Smyth, H. W., 171

Snell, Bruno, 173

Social temper (*astynomous orgās*), 56, 116

Socrates, 3, 37, 167, 183

Solon, 64, 81

Solzhenitsyn, Alexander, 178

Sophism: and antithesis, 1, 2; and monetary imagery, 12; and depreciations of word meaning, 12, 52, 59; in disputed passage (904–20), 19, 71, 102, 103–4, 107, 108, 182; in *gnōmē,* 38; Protagoras, 47, 56, 176; and law, 65, 69; Cr.'s, 67, 74, 79, 116

Sophoclean style: reversals, 2; symbolism, 5; epic, 21, 40–41, 51; general clauses, 38; clausal relationships, 70; ironic imagination, 114, 117, 184; ambiguity, 115–16; structural technique, 117; "ethical" style, 172; G. H. Gellie on, 172

—diction: "key" words for essential themes, 4; intellectual vocabulary, 4, 24, 56; structured ordering of words, 7, 18, 24, 57, 172; use of *autos,* 15, 16; use of abstract noun for a concrete, 79; simplicity of

vocabulary, 172

—figures of speech: oxymora, 2–3, 8, 19, 20, 54, 57, 79; metaphor, 4, 12, 172; imagery and theme, 4, 124

—grammar: duals, 2–3, 8, 9, 10, 11, 16, 31, 163; first person pronoun, 9, 31–32, 39, 40; contemptuous neuter plural, 18, 53, 74, 79, 92; middle voice, 23, 56, 115; verb tenses in Ode on Man, 53, 58; repetition of grammatical form, 80, 89, 107

—sound technique: absence of caesura, 14; metrical variation, 18; alliteration, 53, 54; assonance, 54, 56; dramatic pause, 80; meaning through sound, 172

—stylistic devices: antithesis and balance, 1–8, 10, 21, 37, 75, 84, 89, 117–18; transferred modifiers, 11; asyndeton, 11, 88, 117, 122; anaphora, 19, 82, 106; ellipsis, 20, 88, 107; stichomythia, 88–89; pleonasm, 92. *See also* Choral rhythms; Irony

Sophocles, life of, 166–68

Sophocles and Pericles (Ehrenberg), 168, 175

"Sophokles Political Tragedy" (Calder), 36, 179

Sophos, 52, 59

Soul (*psychē*), 22, 24, 86

Sparta, 34, 166, 167, 168, 175

Spire (William Golding), 165

Stergein (to love), 22, 23

Stoning. *See* Death

Storm imagery, 8, 57, 82, 87

Stratēgos, 168. *See also* Military imagery

Suffering: for An., 7, 110; and wisdom, 124, 125

Suicide: An.'s, 16, 23, 102; Hae.'s, 74, 91, 106; Eurydice's, 106, 116, 119, 120, 121; in classical Athens, 183

Suppliants (Aeschylus), 77, 90, 177

Sumpathy (*to philanthrōpon*), 117

Symposium (Plato), 22

Tantalos, 180